Treatment Strategies for Refractory Depression

Compliments of
Sandoz Pharmaceuticals Corporation,
makers of

PAMELOR®
(nortriptyline HCl)

ROGRESS IN
SYCHIATRY

Number 25

David Spiegel, M.D.
Series Editor

Treatment Strategies
for Refractory Depression

Edited by
Steven P. Roose, M.D.
Alexander H. Glassman, M.D.

American Psychiatric Press, Inc.

Washington, DC
London, England

Note: The authors have worked to ensure that all information in this book concerning drug dosages, schedules, and routes of administration is accurate as of the time of publication and consistent with standards set by the U.S. Food and Drug Administration and the general medical community. As medical research and practice advance, however, therapeutic standards may change. For this reason and because human and mechanical errors sometimes occur, we recommend that readers follow the advice of a physician who is directly involved in their care or the care of a member of their family.

Books published by the American Psychiatric Press, Inc., represent the views and opinions of the individual authors and do not necessarily represent the policies and opinions of the Press or the American Psychiatric Association.

Copyright © 1990 American Psychiatric Press, Inc.
ALL RIGHTS RESERVED
Manufactured in the United States of America
First Edition   93 92 91   4 3 2

American Psychiatric Press, Inc.
1400 K Street, N.W., Washington, DC, 20005

The paper used in this publication meets the minimum requirements of the American National Standard for Information Sciences — Permanence of Paper for Printed Library Materials, ANSI Z39.48–1984.   ∞

Library of Congress Cataloging-in-Publication Data

Treatment strategies for refractory depression/edited by
Steven P. Roose, Alexander H. Glassman. — 1st ed.
    p.   cm. — (Progress in psychiatry : no. 25)
    Includes bibliographical references.
    ISBN 0-88048-184-6 (alk. paper)
    1. Depression, Mental—Treatment. 2. Depression,
Mental—Chemotherapy. 3. Depression, Mental—Relapse.
I. Roose, Steven P., 1948–   . II. Glassman, Alexander
H., 1934–   . III. Series.
    [DNLM: 1. Antidepressive Agents—therapeutic use.
2. Depressive Disorder—drug therapy. WM 171 T7848]
RC537.T747   1990
616.85′2706—dc20
DNLM/DLC
for Library of Congress   90-10
                                                                    CIP

British Cataloguing in Publication Data

A CIP record is available from the British Library.

Contents

Contributors

Richard Brown, M.D.
Research Psychiatrist, New York State Psychiatric Institute, Assistant Professor of Clinical Psychiatry, College of Physicians and Surgeons, Columbia University

Michael J. Devlin, M.D.
Postdoctoral Clinical Fellow in Psychiatry, New York State Psychiatric Institute, Instructor in Clinical Psychiatry, College of Physicians and Surgeons, Columbia University

Ellen Frank, Ph.D.
Associate Professor of Psychiatry and Psychology, Department of Psychiatry, University of Pittsburgh, School of Medicine, Western Psychiatric Institute and Clinic

Alexander H. Glassman, M.D.
Professor of Clinical Psychiatry, College of Physicians and Surgeons, Columbia University, Chief of Clinical Psychopharmacology, New York State Psychiatric Institute

Jack M. Gorman, M.D.
Associate Professor of Clinical Psychiatry, Department of Psychiatry, College of Physicians and Surgeons, Columbia University, Director, Department of Clinical Psychobiology, New York State Psychiatric Institute

Jeffrey K. Halpern, M.D.
Research Psychiatrist, New York State Psychiatric Institute, Instructor in Clinical Psychiatry, College of Physicians and Surgeons, Columbia University

Julie A. Hatterer, M.D.
Assistant in Clinical Psychiatry, Department of Psychiatry, College of Physicians and Surgeons, Columbia University

J. Sidney Jones, M.D.
Postdoctoral Clinical Fellow and Assistant in Clinical Psychiatry, Department of Psychiatry, College of Physicians and Surgeons, Columbia University, Division of Neuroscience, New York State Psychiatric Institute

David Kahn, M.D.
Assistant Professor of Clinical Psychiatry, College of Physicians and Surgeons, Columbia University, Director of Inpatient Psychiatry, Presbyterian Hospital, New York

James H. Kocsis, M.D.
Associate Professor of Psychiatry, Cornell University Medical College, Director of Affective Disorders Unit, Payne Whitney Psychiatric Clinic

David J. Kupfer, M.D.
Professor and Chairman, Department of Psychiatry, University of Pittsburgh, School of Medicine, Western Psychiatric Institute and Clinic

J. Craig Nelson, M.D.
Associate Professor of Psychiatry, Yale University School of Medicine, Director, Psychiatric Inpatient Services, Yale – New Haven Hospital

Joan Prudic, M.D.
Attending Psychiatrist, New York State Psychiatric Institute, Assistant Clinical Professor of Psychiatry, College of Physicians and Surgeons, Columbia University

Steven P. Roose, M.D.
Associate Professor of Clinical Psychiatry, College of Physicians and Surgeons, Columbia University, Research Psychiatrist, New York State Psychiatric Institute

Harold A. Sackeim, Ph.D.
Deputy Chief, Department of Biological Psychiatry, New York State Psychiatric Institute, Associate Professor of Clinical Psychiatry, College of Physicians and Surgeons, Columbia University

Michael Stanley, Ph.D.
Associate Professor, Departments of Psychiatry and Pharmacology, College of Physicians and Surgeons, Columbia University, Division of Neuroscience, New York State Psychiatric Institute

B. Timothy Walsh, M.D.
Associate Professor of Clinical Psychiatry, College of Physicians and Surgeons, Columbia University, Research Psychiatrist, New York State Psychiatric Institute.

Introduction to the
Progress in Psychiatry Series

The *Progress in Psychiatry* Series is designed to capture in print the excitement that comes from assembling a diverse group of experts from various locations to examine in detail the newest information about a developing aspect of psychiatry. This series emerged as a collaboration between the American Psychiatric Association's (APA) Scientific Program Committee and the American Psychiatric Press, Inc. Great interest is generated by a number of the symposia presented each year at the APA Annual Meeting, and we realized that much of the information presented there, carefully assembled by people who are deeply immersed in a given area, would unfortunately not appear together in print. The symposia sessions at the Annual Meetings provide an unusual opportunity for experts who otherwise might not meet on the same platform to share their diverse viewpoints for 3 hours. Some new themes are repeatedly reinforced and gain credence, while in other instances disagreements emerge, enabling the audience and now the reader to reach informed decisions about new directions in the field. The *Progress in Psychiatry* Series allows us to publish and capture some of the best of the symposia and thus provide an in-depth treatment of specific areas that might not otherwise be presented in broader review formats.

Psychiatry is by nature an interface discipline, combining the study of mind and brain, of individual and social environments, of the humane and the scientific. Therefore, progress in the field is rarely linear—it often comes from unexpected sources. Further, new developments emerge from an array of viewpoints that do not necessarily provide immediate agreement but rather expert examination of the issues. We intend to present innovative ideas and data that will enable you, the reader, to participate in this process.

We believe the *Progress in Psychiatry* Series will provide you with an opportunity to review timely new information in specific fields of interest as they are developing. We hope you find that the excitement of the presentations is captured in the written word and that this book proves to be informative and enjoyable reading.

David Spiegel, M.D.
Series Editor
Progress in Psychiatry Series

Progress in Psychiatry Series Titles

The Borderline: Current Empirical Research (#1)
Edited by Thomas H. McGlashan, M.D.

**Premenstrual Syndrome: Current Findings and Future
Directions (#2)**
Edited by Howard J. Osofsky, M.D., Ph.D., and Susan J.
Blumenthal, M.D.

Treatment of Affective Disorders in the Elderly (#3)
Edited by Charles A. Shamoian, M.D.

Post-Traumatic Stress Disorder in Children (#4)
Edited by Spencer Eth, M.D., and Robert S. Pynoos, M.D., M.P.H.

The Psychiatric Implications of Menstruation (#5)
Edited by Judith H. Gold, M.D., F.R.C.P. (C)

Can Schizophrenia Be Localized in the Brain? (#6)
Edited by Nancy C. Andreasen, M.D., Ph.D.

Medical Mimics of Psychiatric Disorders (#7)
Edited by Irl Extein, M.D., and Mark S. Gold, M.D.

Biopsychosocial Aspects of Bereavement (#8)
Edited by Sidney Zisook, M.D.

Psychiatric Pharmacosciences of Children and Adolescents (#9)
Edited by Charles Popper, M.D.

Psychobiology of Bulimia (#10)
Edited by James I. Hudson, M.D., and Harrison G. Pope, Jr., M.D.

Cerebral Hemisphere Function in Depression (#11)
Edited by Marcel Kinsbourne, M.D.

Eating Behavior in Eating Disorders (#12)
Edited by B. Timothy Walsh, M.D.

**Tardive Dyskinesia: Biological Mechanisms and Clinical
Aspects (#13)**
Edited by Marion E. Wolf, M.D., and Aron D. Mosnaim, Ph.D.

Current Approaches to the Prediction of Violence (#14)
Edited by David A. Brizer, M.D., and Martha L. Crowner, M.D.

Treatment of Tricyclic-Resistant Depression (#15)
Edited by Irl L. Extein, M.D.

Chapter 1

Methodological Issues in the Diagnosis, Treatment, and Study of Refractory Depression

Steven P. Roose, M.D.

Chapter 1

Methodological Issues in the Diagnosis, Treatment, and Study of Refractory Depression

The introduction of effective treatments for affective disorder necessarily defined a new group of patients, namely those who did not respond as expected. The label "nonresponder" and its synonyms "treatment-resistant" and "treatment-refractory" (all of which will be used interchangeably in this chapter) were first applied to patients who did not respond to electroconvulsive therapy. Subsequently, the use of these terms became more widespread, albeit less clear, with the introduction of pharmacological treatments for depression.

Over the years, there has been no dearth of symposia, no dearth of literature, and no dearth of suggestions on the diagnosis and treatment of refractory depression; there has been, and continues to be, a striking dearth of data. This paucity of data reflects the absence of an effective sustained research effort on this topic. The lack of research productivity can be traced to two problems: 1) the definition of a refractory patient used by investigators is so idiosyncratic that there has not developed a cumulative body of data on a reasonably homogeneous sample; and 2) investigators have not been able to conduct sustained research because despite the widespread clinical impression that these patients exist, they do not, in fact, exist in sufficient numbers to allow collection of large enough samples to conduct research protocols.

There are a number of substantial issues that have complicated the process of arriving at a definition of, and treatment recommendations for, treatment-resistant, depressed patients. My intention in this chapter is to clarify the most prominent of these methodological issues, and with a critical perspective based on an awareness of these methodological problems, consider the data that are currently available.

THE PROBLEM OF DIAGNOSIS

The concept of nonresponse intuitively implies that there is an established match between a diagnosis and a treatment. By analogy, one would not consider tuberculosis to be nonresponsive if the treatment given were penicillin; such a match would be immediately perceived as jarringly incongruent to any physician.

This is an important consideration to remember when reviewing studies (Boston Collaborative Drug Surveillance Program 1972; Medical Research Council 1965; Raskin et al. 1970; Wilson et al. 1967) on refractory depression before the development of more rigorous diagnostic criteria for affective disorder. In terms of modern diagnostic criteria (i.e., according to DSM-III-R (American Psychiatric Association 1987)), many of the patients in these studies who are "resistant" to tricyclic antidepressants or other pharmacological interventions would more likely meet criteria for schizoaffective disorder or borderline personality than major affective disorder.

Moreover, the issue of precision in diagnosis has gone beyond simply whether or not the patient has affective disorder, because there are subtypes of affective disorder for which there are specific treatments. For example, one would not consider a bipolar I patient refractory to treatment if he or she has only been treated with tricyclic antidepressants and not with lithium. In addition to lithium, there is a regimen of accepted pharmacological treatment for bipolar patients that is different from that for unipolar patients. Beyond the well-accepted bipolar and unipolar distinction, even with unipolar depression itself, there are two recognized subgroups for which specific treatments have been established. First, for delusionally depressed unipolar patients it is now recognized that tricyclic antidepressants, monoamine oxidase inhibitors (MAOIs), or antipsychotics alone are inadequate treatment, and patients should be treated with combination antidepressant/antipsychotics or electroconvulsive therapy (ECT) (Chan et al. 1987; Glassman and Roose 1981; Spiker et al. 1985). Second, for patients meeting criteria for atypical depression, a long-held clinical impression that MAOIs are superior to tricyclic antidepressants for this syndrome has finally been documented by well-conducted double-blind studies (Liebowitz et al. 1988; Quitkin et al. 1988).

Thus, in summary, the concept of a refractory patient assumes that a correct match between diagnosis and treatment has failed to produce the expected good response. Earlier studies of depression included patients who would not meet criteria for major affective disorder according to modern diagnostic criteria, and, thus, the correct match between diagnosis and treatment did not exist. Therefore, it would be premature to conclude that those patients have treatment-resistant depressions, much less that they are refractory to the appropriate treatment given their correct diagnosis. Moreover, within the group of patients who would meet modern diagnostic criteria for major affective disorder, there exist well-defined subgroups for which specific treatments have been determined to be most effective.

TREATMENT RESISTANCE VERSUS INADEQUATE TREATMENT

Just as the concept of treatment resistance intuitively implies that there is a correct match between diagnosis and treatment, it further implies that there is a definition of adequate treatment. The concept of adequate treatment has a number of dimensions: 1) that treatment is appropriate to diagnosis as discussed above, 2) that treatment is given in adequate amount, and 3) that it is given for sufficient duration. For example, in the treatment of a patient with major affective disorder, there would be universal agreement that a patient who has not responded to 25 mg of imipramine has not received an adequate dose of drug regardless of how long that drug has been given, and conversely a patient who has received 300 mg of imipramine daily but for only 3 days, would not, at that point, be considered a nonresponder because he or she has not been given treatment for an adequate duration.

Specifically, for the case of tricyclic antidepressants there is ample literature on what constitutes adequate dose or, more precisely, therapeutic plasma level for some of the tricyclics (American Psychiatric Association Task Force 1985). Although there are fewer specific data on what constitutes a sufficient duration of a drug's therapeutic plasma level, the available data are reviewed in this book in the chapter by Halpern and Glassman. Similarly, there are generally agreed-upon guidelines of adequate dose and duration or, more precisely, minimum dose and duration for treatment with MAOIs, as will be reviewed by Devlin and Walsh in another chapter. Even for ECT, which, until recently, had been considered the most straightforward in terms of dose if not duration, recent studies have demonstrated that it makes a difference as to what form and in what dose the current is delivered (Sackeim et al. 1987). In short, if we use a treatment, we must be sure that we are using it correctly before we consider a patient to be a nonresponder.

The concept of adequate treatment may seem self-evident and surely is one that no clinician or researcher would say is unimportant. In fact, it may so be self-evident that the reader may wonder why such a focus is made on this point. It is distressing that, in fact, a significant number of depressed patients receive clearly inadequate treatment. Striking documentation of this is offered by the National Institute of Mental Health, Clinical Research Branch Collaborative Program on the Psychobiology of Depression: Clinical Study (Keller et al. 1986). This study reports on the treatment received by 338 patients with nonbipolar major depressive disorder at five university medical centers. Only 50% of patients received 200 mg daily of imipramine or its equivalent for at least 4 weeks.

In actuality, most studies that have reported on treatments for allegedly treatment-resistant, depressed patients have included predominantly patients who have been inadequately treated. A case in point is the study of Davidson and associates (1978), who collected a sample of treatment-resistant, depressed patients and then treated half with MAOIs and half with ECT to determine the most efficacious treatment. However, the inclusion criterion for being considered a treatment-resistant patient was nonresponse to conventional psychotropic drugs in "clinically adequate doses," with neither "adequate dose" nor "conventional psychotropic" being further defined (Davidson et al. 1978, p. 640).

Only recently have some studies specifically defined criteria for adequate treatment that a patient must have failed before being declared a nonresponder. In a very informative study, Schatzberg and colleagues (1986) reported on 116 patients who were labeled as having "treatment-resistant depression." In fact, 17% of those patients had received no treatment and of the remaining patients, 58% had received less than 200 mg of imipramine for less than 2 weeks. Thus, only 35% of the patients diagnosed as treatment-resistant had received what the Schatzberg group considered to be adequate tricyclic treatment.

In the first study to incorporate data on therapeutic plasma levels and duration of treatment in the definition of adequate treatment, our group collected a series of unipolar nondelusional patients who did not respond to a therapeutic plasma level of imipramine or nortriptyline over a 4-week period (Roose et al. 1986). All tricyclic failures subsequently responded to MAOIs or ECT, but assignment to treatment after the tricyclic was not controlled, therefore limiting conclusions that can be drawn from these data. In a series of studies on lithium augmentation for tricyclic nonresponders, investigators at Yale have also clearly defined a minimum tricyclic dose necessary to be considered a treatment failure (Heninger et al. 1983; Price et al. 1986). These studies are exceptions in the literature because they define the adequate treatment that a patient must have failed before being considered treatment refractory. To date, most studies that have reported on treatment-resistant, depressed patients have, in reality, reported on patients who have been inadequately treated.

Even if a patient has been adequately treated with a specific drug (e.g., a tricyclic antidepressant) at a therapeutic plasma level for 4 weeks and the patient did not respond, it would be premature to conclude that the patient is treatment resistant. In fact, it would demonstrate only that the patient was a tricyclic nonresponder. This raises the question of what should be considered necessary treatments before concluding that a patient is a nonresponder. Obviously, this is to a degree arbitrary, but substantial data would suggest that if a patient has major affective disorder, the term treatment-resistant should be reserved for a patient who does not respond to the following:

- A therapeutic plasma level of tricyclic antidepressants for an adequate period of time (significant data would argue that the next step should be lithium augmentation of tricyclics)
- MAOIs
- Bilateral ECT

This list suggests the necessary treatments rather than the specific sequence of the treatments. Nonetheless, the sequence as outlined is a clinically cogent one.

With this somewhat arbitrary, but reasonable, definition of a treatment program for a patient with major affective disorder, it is now possible to understand why there are so few meaningful data available on the treatment of refractory depressions—namely, a patient sample is nearly impossible to collect. For example, let us consider that a researcher has a new treatment that he or she thinks will work where tricyclics fail. Assuming that delusional depressions are excluded, if one starts with a total sample size of 100 depressed patients and treats them with a therapeutic plasma level of tricyclics, approximately 75% to 80% will get better. Thus, at the end of studying 100 patients, the researcher may have 25 tricyclic nonresponders left. The most rigorous study design would be to split that sample of 25 patients and assign half to receive the new drug and half to continue the tricyclic treatment to control for the effect of time. Thus, after treating 100 patients, the researcher is left to compare two samples, each with 12 members, and obviously a sample of this size severely compromises the ability to find a meaningful difference between the two treatments. Even if such a meaningful difference exists, the chance of a type II error (i.e., to conclude falsely that there is no significant difference between the two treatments) is high because small sample sizes do not provide sufficient power to detect the difference. Thus, collecting a sample of tricyclic nonresponders, much less treatment-resistant patients, is a formidable task and necessarily limits research in this area.

When considering the chapters that follow in this book, the reader would do well to ask the following critical questions:

- Does the treatment fit the illness?
- Are the patients included refractory to treatment or simply inadequately treated, and if indeed they appear to be treatment resistant, resistant to what treatment?
- Is the methodology appropriately rigorous in studies assessing the effectiveness of alternative treatments in treatment-resistant depressions?

Obviously, most of the data presented in this book will be the result of open clinical trials and extensive clinical experience rather than carefully designed prospective studies. But given the difficulty in collecting an adequate sample size of refractory depressions to study, we have to rely on the experience and informed impressions of these investigators to guide us on what we might do with a treatment-resistant patient if, in fact, one ever comes along.

REFERENCES

American Psychiatric Association: Diagnostic and Statistical Manual of Mental Disorders, 3rd Edition, Revised. Washington, DC, American Psychiatric Association, 1987

American Psychiatric Association Task Force on the Use of Laboratory Tests in Psychiatry: Tricyclic antidepressants—blood level measurements and clinical outcome: an APA Task Force Report. Am J Psychiatry 142:155–162, 1985

Boston Collaborative Drug Surveillance Program: Adverse reactions to the tricyclic-antidepressant drugs. Lancet 1:529–531, 1972

Chan CH, Janicak PG, Davis JM, et al: Response of psychotic and non-psychotic depressed patients to tricyclic antidepressants. J Clin Psychiatry 48:197–200, 1987

Davidson J, McLeod M, Law-Yone B, et al: A comparison of electroconvulsive therapy and combined phenelzine-amitriptyline in refractory depression. Arch Gen Psychiatry 35:639–642, 1978

Glassman AH, Roose SP: Delusional depression: a distinct clinical entity? Arch Gen Psychiatry 38:424–427, 1981

Heninger GR, Charney DS, Sternberg DE: Lithium carbonate augmentation of antidepressant treatment: an effective prescription for treatment-refractory depression. Arch Gen Psychiatry 40:1335–1342, 1983

Keller MB, Lavori PW, Klerman GL, et al: Low levels and lack of predictors of somatotherapy and psychotherapy received by depressed patients. Arch Gen Psychiatry 43:458–466, 1986

Liebowitz MR, Quitkin FM, Stewart JW, et al: Antidepressant specificity in atypical depression. Arch Gen Psychiatry 45:129–137, 1988

Medical Research Council: Clinical trial of the treatment of depressive illness. Br Med J [Clin Res] 1:881–886, 1965

Price LH, Charney DS, Heninger GR: Variability of response to lithium augmentation in refractory depression. Am J Psychiatry 143:1387–1392, 1986

Quitkin FM, Stewart JW, McGrath PJ, et al: Phenelzine versus imipramine in the treatment of probable atypical depression: defining syndrome boundaries of selective MAOI responders. Am J Psychiatry 145:306–311, 1988

Raskin A, Schulterbrandt J, Reatig N: Differential response to chlorpromazine, imipramine, and placebo. Arch Gen Psychiatry 23:164–173, 1970

Roose SP, Glassman AH, Walsh BT, et al: Tricyclic nonresponders: phenomenology and treatment. Am J Psychiatry 143:345–348, 1986

Sackeim H, Decina P, Prohovnik I, et al: Seizure threshold in electroconvulsive therapy: effects of sex, age, electrode placement, and number of treatments. Arch Gen Psychiatry 44:355–360, 1987

Schatzberg AF, Cole JO, Elliott GR: Recent views on treatment-resistant depression, in Psychosocial Aspects of Nonresponse to Antidepressant Drugs. Edited by Halbreich U, Feinberg SS. Washington, DC, American Psychiatric Press, 1986, pp 93–109

Spiker DG, Weiss JC, Dealy RS, et al: The pharmacological treatment of delusional depression. Am J Psychiatry 142:430–436, 1985

Wilson IC, Rabon AM, Buffaloe WJ: Imipramine therapy in depressive syndromes: prediction of therapeutic outcome. Psychosomatics 8:203–207, 1967

Chapter 2

Adequate Tricyclic Treatment: Defining the Tricyclic Nonresponder

Jeffrey K. Halpern, M.D.
Alexander H. Glassman, M.D.

Chapter 2

Adequate Tricyclic Treatment: Defining the Tricyclic Nonresponder

Tricyclic antidepressants (TCAs), available for over 30 years and clearly beneficial in the treatment of patients with major affective disorders, are first-line drugs in the treatment of major depression. Unfortunately, not all depressed individuals respond to this treatment. The maxim has been two-thirds respond, one-third do not (Chan et al. 1987). Indeed, many investigations suggested that as many as 35% to 40% of depressed patients were TCA nonresponders. However, when studies are more rigorous in achieving adequate TCA treatment, about 15% to 20% of patients with endogenous depression are refractory to the TCAs (Glassman et al. 1977; Reisby et al. 1977). As experience grows in the use of antidepressant drugs, there is increasing interest in identifying those patients who will not respond to TCA treatment as an essential step in defining the concept of refractory depression. The depressed patient who does not respond to TCA treatment must be distinguished from the patient who has not been adequately treated. We need, therefore, to begin by defining adequate TCA treatment.

In this chapter, we will summarize and discuss the current thinking on what constitutes an adequate trial of a TCA and the chief difficulties in gathering and interpreting these data. There are three issues that are central to defining adequate TCA response: 1) diagnostic subtypes, 2) plasma levels, and 3) adequate length of treatment. We will also examine side effects, often cited as a cause of treatment failure, and their relation to plasma levels and to the concept of refractory depression.

DIAGNOSTIC CONSIDERATIONS AND TCA RESPONSE

Mood disorders are a heterogeneous diagnostic category and sub-

13

sume populations some of whom have markedly different responses to TCAs. Therefore, in defining TCA nonresponders, one must take diagnostic subsets into consideration. We will look at TCA response in melancholia, atypical depression, and depressions accompanied by panic disorder and anxiety, in addition to TCA response in depressions with varying severity and chronicity. We will also briefly review the distinct responses to TCAs of delusional depression and depression in bipolar disorder. We will not discuss here individuals who are medically ill and depressed (Muskin and Glassman 1983) or whose medical illness has been misdiagnosed as depression. In any depressed patient, and perhaps especially in the depressed patient not responsive to treatment, the possibility of an occult medical illness must be considered.

Melancholic Depression and Severity of Depression

Surprisingly, the term melancholic (or endogenous) type of major depressive episode, despite its widespread use in research and clinical practice, has not been validated as a distinct diagnostic category with reference to clinical course, family history, prior episodes, presence or absence of stressors, or biological markers. It has received some validation as a distinct symptom array from some statistical clustering techniques and the usually excellent response to TCAs in comparison with placebo. Diagnostic criteria for the melancholic type of major depressive episode were included in the DSM-III-R (American Psychiatric Association 1987) because of reports that melancholia predicts response to antidepressants.

Let us briefly review some of these reports. It is important that studies attempting to identify symptoms or biological markers predictive of a good response to antidepressants are prospective, are double-blind, use validated operational diagnostic criteria, relate individual symptoms to an assessment of global improvement, and include a placebo group. The data are confusing because few studies have met all these criteria. The Bielski and Friedel (1976) and Friedel (1983) reviews of the literature, limited by the markedly different methodologies of the studies, found predictors of positive response to TCAs were upper socioeconomic class, insidious onset, anorexia, weight loss, middle and late insomnia, and psychomotor disturbance. Predictors of poor response included neurotic, hysterical, and hypochondriacal traits; multiple prior episodes of depression; and delusions. Nelson and Charney (1981), also reviewing the literature, found that the best forecaster of antidepressant response is psychomotor change, particularly retardation. More recently, Nelson and colleagues (1988) in a prospective study of 83 consecutive inpatients with nondelusional unipolar major depression did not replicate his earlier retrospective analysis. Rather, they concluded that melancholic features, including psychomotor retardation, predicted only a poor response to hospitalization without drug treatment, but did not predict outcome with antidepressant (desmethylimipramine) treatment. They found that chronicity of depression, antecedent panic disorder, and low plasma drug concentrations portended poor drug response at 4 weeks.

In an attempt to find distinguishing characteristics of TCA non-responders within this group of unipolar, melancholic, nondelusional inpatients, Roose and co-workers (1986) retrospectively looked at patients who had failed to respond to TCAs but who had adequate plasma concentrations. Although these melancholic nonresponders tended to have higher anxiety scores and more prior episodes of depression when compared with the TCA responders, they were indistinguishable from the responders by other clinical or demographic data.

Although melancholia does not predict response to TCAs, the superiority of TCAs over placebo has been easiest to demonstrate in melancholic depression. There are a number of reasons for this, but the most important may be the lower placebo response in the severely depressed melancholic patients in comparison with the milder and nonmelancholic depressive patients.

Nonmelancholic and Milder Depressions

There has been a belief that milder nonendogenous depressions do not show the same clear response to TCAs as do more severe melancholic or endogenous depressions. Plasma level-response relationships have been easier to determine in the melancholic, more severely depressed patients than in the more heterogeneous, non-melancholic groups (American Psychiatric Association Task Force 1985; Reisby et al. 1977; Robinson et al. 1979). The explanation for this probably lies with the higher incidence of placebo response, spontaneous remission, and perhaps shorter duration of illness in the group with milder depressions. Another difficulty in determining response to TCAs is that the nonmelancholic patients are a more heterogeneous population, and hidden within this heterogeneity may be subsets that are insensitive to TCA treatment. Therefore, in order to establish a relationship between drug level and clinical outcome, it would be necessary in milder depressions to collect larger samples because the subsets will need to be stratified and a significant fraction of the sample will be "lost" to placebo.

Several investigators, aware of these methodological difficulties, have recently looked at mild depression and TCAs. Paykel and his co-workers (1988), in a study of 141 mild nonendogenous depressed patients, found amitriptyline to be superior to placebo in all but the mildest of depressive patients, that is, those who had Hamilton Rating Scale (Hamilton 1960) scores of less than 12. Similar results were obtained in an earlier study by Stewart and colleagues (1983) who found a marked desmethylimipramine-placebo difference in patients with Hamilton scores of 14 or above but not in patients with lower scores. They noted a significant drug-placebo difference even in patients with major depression without melancholia (Stewart et al. 1985).

Dysthymia and Double Depression: Chronicity

The diagnosis of dysthymic disorder, defined by DSM-III-R, requires that an individual have a predominantly depressed mood for at least 2 years without evidence of a major depression during that time. This differs from chronic major depression only in the estimate of severity and comparison with the individual's usual functioning. When dysthymic patients seek treatment at major psychiatric institutions, nearly all present with a superimposed major depression, often labeled a "double depression" (Kocsis 1988). In a naturalistic study where treatment varied and was not placebo controlled, Keller and Shapiro (1982) and the Keller group (1983) found that "double depression" had a significantly different course, cycle length, and worse outcome when compared with major depression alone. After 2 years, 61% of their patients with major depression superimposed on dysthymic disorder had not recovered from the chronic minor depression, a Research Diagnostic Criteria (RDC) (Spitzer et al. 1978) category that is similar to the DSM-III-R category of dysthymic disorder. Those patients who recovered from an episode of major depression but whose dysthymia persisted were at increased risk for relapse of the major depression. In contrast, Kocsis et al. (1988), in a prospective, placebo-controlled trial of imipramine in 86 outpatients with dysthymia (96% of whom on presentation had concomitant major depression), reported that 59% had "complete recovery" on imipramine as opposed to 13% on placebo. The investigator was unable to identify clinical or demographic characteristics predictive of response. The study by Kocsis suggests that after adequate treatment, the prognosis for chronic depression is not unlike that of major depression. Only 8% of the patients entering the study had received an adequate trial of an antidepressant (defined as equivalent to 150 mg or more of imipramine for 3 or more weeks), and a 33% had never received an antidepressant medication. That the patients in Kocsis's study received more consistent, adequate treatment may account for the dissimilar outcomes between the Kocsis and the Keller studies. It remains to be seen how these patients do on longer term follow-up.

It is also not clear how Kocsis's data on dysthymic patients fit with those of the Nelson group (1988) study mentioned earlier in which one of the predictors of poor TCA response to major depression was chronicity of depression. This needs further clarification.

Atypical Depression

Another subtype of depressed patients is described as "atypical" because, instead of the usual appetite loss, these patients complain of overeating; instead of insomnia, they complain of oversleeping; and instead of anhedonia, they are reactive despite their depressed mood. Since West and Dally (1959) originally called attention to this group, whom Klein (1980) called "hysteroid dysphorics," there have been a variety of definitions of the term "atypical" leading to confusion, especially whether anxiety, panic, and phobia are integral parts of this type of depression. The studies of Quitkin et al. (1988), Liebowitz et al. (1988), and Klein (1980) have been instrumental in honing the concept of an atypical subset of depressed patients. Defining atypically depressed patients as having a reactive mood and at least one of four associated symptoms (hyperphagia, hypersomnolence, leaden feeling, and sensitivity to rejection), they found phenelzine to be superior to imipramine and placebo (Quitkin et al. 1988).

Panic Disorder, Anxiety, and Depression

Between 15% and 30% of patients who present with a major depressive episode also have simultaneous panic attacks, and this appears to predict poor response to TCAs (Grunhaus 1988). Depressed patients with high levels of anxiety or panic attacks have been identified in several studies as less responsive to TCA treatment. It has been proposed, beginning over 30 years ago (West and Dally 1959), that these patients have better outcomes when treated with monoamine oxidase inhibitors (MAOIs) (Quitkin et al. 1979; Robinson et al. 1978; Sargant and Dally 1962). Grunhaus (1988) has reviewed the literature on treatment of patients with simultaneous panic disorder and major depression and, although noting that most of the studies to date suggest a superior response to MAOIs over TCAs, concludes that it is premature to recommend MAOIs as the first-line treatment for these patients.

Psychotic Depression

Patients with delusional depressions stand out in their poor response to TCA treatment. Since the initial report by Glassman and colleagues (1975) found that imipramine was significantly less effective in the treatment of patients with major depression and delusions or hallucinations than in nonpsychotic depressed patients, the treatment of delusional depression has been studied extensively. In a recent literature review of 1,054 psychotic and nonpsychotic depressed patients, Chan and his associates (1987) found that only 35% of the psychotic depressed patients responded to TCAs as compared with 67% of the nonpsychotic depressed patients. Although the response rate of delusionally depressed patients to TCAs alone is low, when TCAs are combined with an antipsychotic medication, studies have shown a response rate in delusional depressions comparable to that seen in patients with nondelusional depression treated with TCAs alone (Spiker et al. 1985).

Bipolar Disorder

Bipolar patients with depression are another group that do poorly when treated with TCAs alone. Although there is some disagreement (Lewis and Winokur 1987), most investigators concur that antidepressants can precipitate a manic episode in a significant number of bipolar patients and a small number of unipolar patients (Bunney 1978). Furthermore, in bipolar patients who are rapid cyclers, usually defined as individuals with four or more episodes of depression or mania a year, TCAs may speed the rate of cycling (Wehr and Goodwin 1979, 1987). However, in bipolar patients who do not have a history of rapid cycling, there is disagreement about whether TCAs increase the rate of cycling. In addition, there are questions about the protective effect of simultaneous treatment with lithium in each of the distinct but related situations just mentioned (Wehr and Goodwin 1979, 1987). Consequently, recommendations for treating acute bipolar depression vary and include using lithium alone (Extein et al. 1984), a TCA plus lithium as protection against mania, or lithium plus an antipsychotic without TCAs (Dunner and Clayton 1987).

In summary, there is strong evidence that TCA treatment can precipitate a manic episode in a depressed patient with bipolar disorder, and suggestive evidence that TCAs shorten intermorbid cycle length in some patients, particularly rapid cyclers. Therefore, TCAs alone are usually not appropriate treatment for depressed patients with bipolar disorder.

PLASMA LEVELS AND THEIR CLINICAL SIGNIFICANCE

Plasma levels are a crucial tool in discriminating the inadequately treated patient from the true TCA nonresponder. Studies have shown that when plasma levels are routinely measured, the proportion of patients whose depression responds to TCAs is between 80% and 85%, in striking contrast to the 60% to 65% response rates for TCAs in melancholic depression when TCA plasma levels were not used (Glassman et al. 1977; Reisby et al. 1977).

As it became possible to assay levels of certain TCAs in human plasma, it became clear that marked differences in steady-state drug levels exist between individuals taking the same dosage of TCA and that this could explain some of the variability in clinical response seen among patients. Of the approximately one dozen cyclic antidepressants on the market in the United States, imipramine, desmethylimipramine, and nortriptyline have been sufficiently studied in clinical trials to determine that interindividual variability in blood levels influences clinical response in a predictable manner. There are at least 16 studies of amitriptyline attempting to elucidate the relationship between the drug's plasma level and clinical outcome, but the data are equivocal. After 30 years of use, why is it that we do not know more about the relationship between clinical response and drug plasma levels?

It is interesting to look at these studies, which occurred primarily in the early 1970s. In all probability, the population samples collected in those days had a major influence on the findings. The successful studies almost all involved older inpatients with severe unipolar nondelusional melancholic depressions. In a study of plasma imipramine levels and response, Glassman and colleagues (1977) examined people, depressed for at least 1 month but less than a year, who had received less than 75 mg of imipramine or its equivalent. It is difficult now to collect a large sample of such patients because researchers simply do not now see recurrent, acutely ill, unipolar depressive patients who are untreated. In addition, investigators have increasingly turned to outpatient samples because of the cost of inpatient studies, and in outpatient samples, not only are the patients exposed to TCAs before entering the experimental trial, but they are inherently a more diverse group with milder depressions. As we have mentioned before, many studies show that the more moderately depressed the patient sample, the greater the placebo response, and such patients tend to obscure any relation between blood level of drug and clinical response. In addition, compliance is more difficult to ascertain in the outpatient, and observation of the patient is briefer and less accurate. All these factors militate against finding the relationship between blood level and outcome seen in the earlier acutely depressed, untreated inpatient studies. It is our impression that the difficulty in obtaining a sample of severely ill, unipolar depressive patients is the largest single reason that more recent attempts to demonstrate relationships between blood level and outcome have been so inconsistent.

Let us summarize the results of existing studies.

Imipramine

Two large independent studies by Glassman and colleagues (1977) and the Reisby group (1977) showed that as imipramine plasma levels increased, more patients responded to the drug, but that above levels of approximately 250 ng/ml, the response rate began to plateau. When the combined level of imipramine and its demethylated metabolite, desmethylimipramine, exceeded 200 ng/ml to 250 ng/ml, the percentage of patients who improved was over 80%. There are two smaller studies that have examined imipramine and are basically in agreement (Olivier-Martin 1975; Walter 1971). These findings in inpatients were reproduced in one small outpatient study (Matuzas et al. 1982). Higher plasma levels (> 250 ng/ml) produced more side effects but, in five of six studies, no further increases in clinical efficacy. A single study in children found that lower and higher blood levels were associated with poorer response, suggesting a curvilinear or inverted U-shaped relationship between plasma level and response (Preskorn et al. 1982). Overall, however, the studies describe a linear or, more accurately, a sigmoidal relationship between blood level and clinical outcome with a rapid rise in response rate between 180 ng/ml and 225 ng/ml of imipramine and its demethylated metabolite.

Desmethylimipramine (Desipramine)

Unfortunately, of the studies investigating the relationship between plasma desmethylimipramine concentration and clinical response, few were designed to screen out placebo responders or to administer the drug for more than 3 weeks. A notable exception is a well-designed study by Nelson and colleagues (1982) of 32 unipolar, melancholic, nondelusional patients in which plasma levels above 125 ng/ml proved to be more effective than lower plasma concentrations. This was confirmed in a second study of 18 patients by Nelson and colleagues (1985). There is one study (Friedel et al. 1979) that suggests that at plasma levels above 160 ng/ml, there is a decline in positive response, but this has not been replicated.

Nortriptyline

A curvilinear relationship, often called a therapeutic window, has been delineated between plasma levels of nortriptyline and therapeutic response. Above plasma levels of about 50 ng/ml but below 150 ng/ml, there is clinical improvement in patients with major depression. The reason for the upper limits of the so-called therapeutic window is not known, but it is not a result of toxicity (Kragh-Sorensen et al. 1976). Asberg (1981) observed that the recovery rate for patients at high blood levels of nortriptyline is lower than the rate for spontaneous remissions, suggesting that high levels of nortriptyline may maintain depression. The lower limit of 50 ng/ml for the nortriptyline therapeutic window is based on only five patients in one study plus a few additional patients from other studies.

Other Antidepressants

The relationship between amitriptyline plasma levels (and its demethylated metabolite, nortriptyline) and clinical response has remained veiled. There have been at least 16 different studies (see Guthrie et al. 1987) that have provided three different answers: 1) that the relationship is linear, 2) that it is curvilinear, or 3) that no relationship exists between plasma levels and response. The results have been similar whether the parent compound, its metabolite, or both have been measured. Clarification of the drug level/response relationship is difficult because analytic methods for reliably measuring amitriptyline were developed only in the late 1970s, many of the studies were done more recently, and the problems mentioned earlier exist in finding appropriate population samples.

Maprotiline, doxepin, protriptyline, mianserin, and clomipramine have been studied in a limited way but with inconclusive results.

Special Cases: Unusually High and Low Plasma Levels

Individuals are occasionally encountered in clinical practice who are taking standard doses of a TCA and yet their blood drug concentrations lie far outside the usual range. These outliers are infrequent—there are only case reports in the literature—and as a result our understanding of this phenomenon is limited. These uncommon clinical situations are discussed not so much for their bearing on defining adequate TCA treatment and the TCA nonresponder, but as an illustration that with TCA plasma levels, as with any test in medicine, there are exceptions to the usual rules, and that informed judgment is required to place the measurements within the clinical context.

A patient taking dosages of TCA within the usual range may develop TCA levels in the 1,000 ng/ml to 3,000 ng/ml range, understandably alarming the clinician, especially because plasma levels above 2,000 ng/ml regularly produce coma and death in individuals that have taken overdoses. Although the treating physician is wise to be concerned and to stop the drug in the presence of serious side effects or electrocardiographic abnormalities, there are patients with these high levels who have little in the way of side effects, have no cardiac abnormalities, and report relief of depressive symptoms (Garvey et al. 1984). If the dosage is cut and the plasma level drops to normal therapeutic levels, the patient's depression returns but improves again if the level is pushed to a range above that usually adequate for a therapeutic response. The reason for this is difficult to prove scientifically, but these individuals are extremely slow metabolizers of the parent compound resulting in the high levels while the drug's hydroxy metabolites are unusually low. These metabolites are active, ordinarily penetrate the central nervous system, and, although not usually measured, probably contribute to the biological effects seen from their parent drugs.

Several case reports have further complicated our understanding. There are reports of some patients who developed extraordinarily high drug plasma levels on usual dosages of TCA but only appeared to improve as their levels were reduced, the improvement reportedly not related to side effects (Appelbaum et al. 1979).

Inflammatory Disease and Plasma Levels

The greater than 30-fold differences in TCA plasma levels among individuals receiving the same dose of antidepressant is primarily due to genetic variation in the function of microsomal enzymes in the liver but may be influenced by certain disease states, concurrent use of some medications, and changes in plasma proteins. This last situation, involving changes in the amount of drug bound to plasma proteins, is relevant in clinical practice but less familiar to most clinicians than the other influences on drug levels. Acute phase reactants are a class of plasma proteins that derive their name because they rise in the presence of infections, malignancy, myocardial infarction, and other inflammatory processes. High levels of one of these proteins in particular can produce high measured TCA plasma levels without change in response to the drug or signs of toxicity (Jorgensen et al. 1980; Kragh-Sorensen and Larsen 1980). The particular acute phase reactant that has been implicated in rises in TCA blood levels is alpha-1-acid glycoprotein (Piafsky and Borga 1977; Piafsky et al. 1978). The greater portion of the TCA in the blood binds to plasma proteins and is inactive. It is the unbound drug that is pharmacologically active. Standard assays of TCA levels measure bound plus free drug. In patients with an inflammatory process, the percentage of free drug falls, whereas the bound fraction of the drug rises with rising acute phase reactants. Overall, one would expect no change in clinical efficacy because the absolute amount of free drug remains constant. However, the measured drug level can be much higher, leading to a disadvantageous reduction in antidepressant dosage by the unsuspecting physician.

Indications for Drug Plasma Levels

Having looked at some of the unusual complications and uses of TCA plasma levels, we will summarize the more common indications for plasma level measurements in clinical practice. A concise review of the use of TCA blood levels was done by the American Psychiatric Association Task Force (1985).

The available data delineating a relationship between the plasma concentration of a TCA and clinical response apply to levels of imipramine, nortriptyline, and desipramine and outcome in seriously depressed, unipolar inpatients with melancholia. The application of the above recommendations to other subtypes of depression is less clear. There are fewer data showing a relationship between plasma drug level and response for outpatients who often have milder or nonendogenous depressions, but preliminary evidence suggests that the same therapeutic ranges apply (Matuzas et al. 1982). There is also evidence that a plasma level-response relationship exists in panic disorder with agoraphobia but without depression (Mavissakalian and Perel 1989).

Plasma levels of these drugs are unequivocally useful for endogenously depressed patients who are not responding to usual doses or for high-risk individuals, such as patients with heart disease and the elderly, who should be on the lowest effective dose. We should emphasize that "therapeutic dosages" can result in a wide and unpredictable range of plasma levels. For example, in a study that highlighted interindividual plasma TCA level variability, when an average initial dose of 225 mg of imipramine was given, 40% of the patients failed to reach therapeutic concentrations (Glassman 1977). Plasma levels should also be obtained if a patient is concurrently on other medications that affect plasma TCA concentration or if clinical worsening is associated with changing to a different manufacturer of the same drug and a difference in bioavailability is suspected. Determining plasma concentration is occasionally useful when patients are disturbed by side effects (but see below), because in some instances, the dosage may be reduced while maintaining therapeutic levels.

The use of plasma levels early in treatment to confirm the presence of a therapeutic concentration eliminates one contribution to the delay in response and is valuable when prompt treatment is critical, as with the suicidal patient. Reducing response time is also an important consideration for inpatients because it reduces the cost of the hospital stay, reduces the time away from work and home when the patient is the principal wage earner or caregiver, and reduces suffering. This argument, of course, can be broadened to all patients or at least those treated with nortriptyline, imipramine, or desmethylimipramine and is a strong argument for preferring these drugs as first-line treatment.

When plasma levels for anticonvulsants became clinically feasible, one of the significant effects of their application was an increase in patient compliance in taking the medication. Plasma levels may be useful in determining patient compliance, as well as metabolic variability, when a patient is not responding to an antidepressant trial.

DURATION OF TREATMENT

We have so far addressed two of the issues that are critical in defining adequate TCA treatment: diagnosis and plasma levels. The third issue, duration of treatment, has been less carefully examined. How long should one continue treatment with a TCA before determining that there has been an inadequate response?

Four-week (Baldessarini 1980) and five-week (Klein 1980) periods have been recommended as adequate trials to determine whether a patient will respond. Quitkin and co-workers (1984), in an excellent review of the literature, noted that most antidepressant drug trials lasted 4 weeks or less, and there is little evidence about the possibility of delayed response to antidepressant drugs beyond 1 month. In addition, Quitkin and his colleagues reviewed their own drug trials in outpatients with mild to moderate, major, minor, or intermittent depression and concluded that a significant percentage of patients who showed no clear improvement at 4 weeks did improve by 6 weeks on drug but not on placebo.

There are two methodological concerns, both referred to by Quitkin, that need to be explicated. First, how broadly can one generalize this finding of a delayed response? In Quitkin's study, and a study he cites by Rowan and colleagues (1982) as one of the few that can be used to address the question about adequate duration of antidepressant treatment, the patients were mostly moderately depressed, about half with major depression and half intermittently depressed. They did not look at the more severely depressed or melancholic populations in whom one would anticipate a smaller placebo response and therefore a larger drug-placebo difference. In contrast to Quitkin's study in which there was no clear response to antidepressant by 4 weeks, Roose and colleagues (1986) examined more severely depressed, melancholic hospitalized patients and found marked differences in outcome by 4 weeks between patients with therapeutic and nontherapeutic drug blood levels, with over 80% of patients with satisfactory blood levels experiencing a good response.

The second methodological concern is the dosing schedule, that is, the time taken to arrive at a dosage that is likely to be therapeutic. In Quitkin's study, (Quitkin et al. 1984) imipramine dosage was increased gradually, and only by the third week were the patients on 200 mg of the medication. He acknowledged that the significant rise in responders between the fourth and sixth weeks could be the result of the schedule of dose increments but suggested that this has little clinical relevance because many patients cannot abide reaching full therapeutic doses within 1 week of the start of treatment. We disagree. In our inpatient studies with medically healthy depressed patients averaging about 60 years of age, we achieved doses above 200 mg of imipramine in 3 days with no significant untoward effects. Nelson et al. (1982), studying inpatients on desmethylimipramine, used a schedule of dose increases of one third of the target dose each day so that by the third day patients were on the full dose of 2.5 mg/kg per day without unusual problems. In another study of 25 elderly depressed patients between 60 and 80 years of age, Nelson et al. (1985) was able to treat all but two of the patients with full doses by the third day. Reisby and colleagues (1977) employed a standard dose of 225 mg per day of imipramine with 66 depressed inpatients, attaining that dose by the fourth day in all but five of the patients.

We think that the evidence justifies the practicality of more rapid dose increments than those advanced by Quitkin et al. (1984). It is not possible to state definitively whether Quitkin's findings of a delayed response are due to his population of depressive subtypes or the lengthy time taken to arrive at therapeutic doses. He found no difference at 4 weeks between drug and placebo but significant differences at 6 weeks. This is in sharp contrast to the major body of research that has found significant differences in response between drug and placebo by 4 weeks. It is our bias, although we cannot prove it from the existing literature, that arriving at therapeutic levels quickly should speed recovery. Needlessly slow escalation of dosage over weeks instead of days prolongs the patient's suffering.

SIDE EFFECTS IN RELATION TO DRUG PLASMA LEVELS AND TREATMENT FAILURE

Side effects are cited by some clinicians as a reason for not increasing the dosage of TCA, and, as a result, adequate plasma levels are often not achieved and treatment fails. It is important to know, however, that intolerable side effects are often difficult to distinguish from symptoms of depression and that some adverse effects of TCAs cannot be ameliorated by lowering the dose.

The difficulty in distinguishing between symptoms of depression and intolerance to the antidepressant was shown in a survey by Schatzberg and his colleagues (1983). They found that intolerance occurred in 47% of patients receiving inadequate dosages of an antidepressant as opposed to 6% of patients who received adequate dosages. A study by Nelson and associates (1984) found that subjective complaints during desmethylimipramine treatment correlated with pretreatment symptoms and current level of depression but not with drug plasma level. Only tremors and light-headedness showed a relationship with blood concentration of desmethylimipramine.

Some clinicians tend to adjust the dosage of TCA in response to the patient's complaints of side effects. The Preskorn group (1983) looked at common symptoms of depression or side effects of antidepressant medications among depressed children and found no correlation between the symptoms and drug plasma levels. This lack of relationship between plasma levels and most so-called side effects suggests that adjusting the dose based on side effects is not a reliable way of reaching a therapeutic level.

Some adverse symptoms reach maximal effect at low concentrations, below levels necessary for an antidepressant effect. This means that lowering the dose of drug will not be useful. Saliva secretion, for example, diminishes at subtherapeutic to low therapeutic plasma levels of both nortriptyline and desmethylimipramine, thus making a dry mouth an unavoidable side effect (Bertram et al. 1979; Rudorfer and Young 1980). Orthostatic hypotension, the most potentially serious common side effect, has been well documented to occur at very low plasma levels of imipramine and does not worsen with increased drug levels, so that if the patient is tolerating the postural blood pressure changes, one can safely raise the dose if necessary (Glassman et al. 1979). If the patient is intolerant of the blood pressure drops, lowering the dose will not alleviate the problem without losing antidepressant efficacy. Such a patient should be considered intolerant of TCA treatment but not necessarily refractory. Intolerance to side effects as a cause of nonresponse needs to be distinguished from refractoriness to an adequate trial of an antidepressant.

SUMMARY

In order to identify depression that is refractory to standard TCA treatment, it is essential to define adequate TCA treatment. Only then can we distinguish the true tricyclic nonresponder from the inadequately treated nonresponder. Adequate TCA treatment needs to be defined in terms of the diagnosis of the patient who is being treated, the achievement of therapeutic plasma levels, and treatment for a sufficient duration of time.

Disorders of mood comprise a heterogeneous group differing in response to TCAs: delusional depressions and bipolar depressions respond poorly to TCAs alone; depressions associated with panic disorder or high levels of anxiety may respond preferentially to MAOIs, as may atypical depressions. In addition, some subtypes of depression vary in their rate of spontaneous recovery. Other subtypes of depression may need to be further differentiated in order to define treatment sensitivity and resistance.

Both as an investigational and as a clinical tool, plasma TCA levels have been crucial in defining adequate TCA treatment, and their use increases the number of patients who recover. Where possible, plasma drug levels, not dosages, should be used to determine the TCA nonresponder and to unmask the pseudorefractory patient who has inadequate TCA plasma levels on apparently adequate dosages of medication.

In addition to achieving therapeutic drug levels, a patient must be at the level for some period of time for a response to be seen, although establishing an adequate duration of treatment requires further study. The early achievement of the therapeutic dosages may shorten one constituent of the initial "lag period" in treatment.

Finally, it is important to distinguish intolerance to adverse effects from refractoriness to an adequate trial of a TCA and to realize that some drug side effects are, in fact, symptoms of depression that respond to TCA treatment.

REFERENCES

American Psychiatric Association: Diagnostic and Statistical Manual of Mental Disorders, 3rd Edition, Revised. Washington, DC, American Psychiatric Association, 1987

American Psychiatric Association Task Force: Tricyclic antidepressants—blood level measurements and clinical outcome: an APA task force report. Am J Psychiatry 142:155–162, 1985

Appelbaum PS, Vasile RG, Orsulak PJ, et al: Clinical utility of tricyclic antidepressant blood levels: a case report. Am J Psychiatry 136:339–341, 1979

Asberg M: On the clinical importance of plasma concentrations of tricyclic antidepressant drugs: a review of the evidence, in Clinical Pharmacology in Psychiatry. Edited by Usdin E. New York, Elsevier, 1981, pp 301–309

Baldessarini RJ: Drugs and the treatment of psychiatric disorders, in The Pharmacological Basis of Therapeutics, 7th Edition. Edited by Gilman AG, Goodman LS. New York, Macmillan, 1985, pp 387–445

Bertram U, Kragh-Sorensen P, Rafaelsen OJ, et al: Saliva secretion following long-term antidepressant treatment with nortriptyline controlled by plasma levels. Scand J Dent Res 87:58–64, 1979

Bielski RJ, Friedel RO: Prediction of tricyclic antidepressant response. Arch Gen Psychiatry 33:1479–1489, 1976

Bunney WE Jr: Psychopharmacology of the switch process in affective illness, in Psychopharmacology: A Generation of Progress. Edited by Lipton MA, DiMascio A, Killam KF. New York, Raven Press, 1978, pp 1249–1259

Chan CH, Janicak PG, Davis JM, et al: Response of psychotic and non-psychotic depressed patients to tricyclic antidepressants. J Clin Psychiatry 48:197–200, 1987

Dunner DL, Clayton PJ: Drug treatment of bipolar disorder, in Psychopharmacology: The Third Generation of Progress. Edited by Meltzer HY. New York, Raven Press, 1987, pp 1077–1083

Extein I, Gold MS, Pottash ALC: Psychopharmacologic treatment of depression. Psychiatr Clin North Am 7:503–517, 1984

Friedel RO: Clinical predictors of treatment response: an update, in The Affective Disorders. Edited by Davis JM, Maas JW. Washington, DC, American Psychiatric Press, 1983, pp 379–384

Friedel RO, Veith RC, Bloom V, et al: Desipramine plasma levels and clinical response in depressed outpatients. Communications in Psychopharmacology 3:81–87, 1979

Garvey MJ, Tuason VB, Johnson RA, et al: Elevated plasma tricyclic levels with therapeutic doses of imipramine. Am J Psychiatry 141:853–856, 1984

Glassman AH, Kantor SJ, Shostak M: Depression, delusions and drug response. Am J Psychiatry 132:716–719, 1975

Glassman AH, Perel JM, Shostak M, et al: Clinical implications of imipramine plasma levels for depressive illness. Arch Gen Psychiatry 34:197–204, 1977

Glassman AH, Bigger JT Jr, Giardina EV, et al: Clinical characteristics of imipramine-induced orthostatic hypotension. Lancet 1:468–472, 1979

Grunhaus L: Clinical and psychobiological characteristics of simultaneous panic disorder and major depression. Am J Psychiatry 145:1214–1221, 1988

Guthrie S, Lane EA, Linnoila M: Monitoring of plasma drug concentrations in clinical psychopharmacology, in Psychopharmacology: The Third Generation of Progress. Edited by Meltzer HY. New York, Raven Press, 1987, pp 1323–1338

Hamilton M: A rating scale for depression. J Neurol Neurosurg Psychiatr 23:56–62, 1960

Jorgensen OS, Lober M, Christiansen J, et al: Plasma concentration and clinical effect in imipramine treatment of childhood enuresis. Clin Pharmacokinet 5:386–393, 1980

Keller MB, Shapiro RW: "Double depression": superimposition of acute depressive episodes on chronic disorders. Am J Psychiatry 139:438–442, 1982

Keller MB, Lavori PW, Endicott J, et al: "Double depression": two year follow-up. Am J Psychiatry 140:689–694, 1983

Klein DF: Diagnosis and Drug Treatment of Psychiatric Disorders: Adults and Children, 2nd Edition. Baltimore, MD, Williams & Wilkins, 1980

Kocsis JH, Frances AJ, Voss C, et al: Imipramine treatment for chronic depression. Arch Gen Psychiatry 45:253–257, 1988

Kragh-Sorensen P, Hansen CE, Baastrup PC, et al: Self-inhibiting action of nortriptyline's antidepressive effect at high plasma levels. Psychopharmacologia 45:305–312, 1976

Kragh-Sorensen P, Larsen NE: Factors influencing nortriptyline steady-state kinetics: plasma and saliva levels. Clin Pharmacol Ther 28:796–803, 1980

Lewis JL, Winokur G: The induction of mania: a natural history study with controls. Psychopharmacol Bull 23:74–78, 1987

Liebowitz MR, Quitkin FM, Stewart JW, et al: Antidepressant specificity in atypical depression. Arch Gen Psychiatry 45:129–137, 1988

Matuzas W, Javaid IJ, Glass R, et al: Plasma concentrations of imipramine and clinical response among depressed outpatients. J Clin Psychopharmacol 2:140–142, 1982

Mavissakalian MR, Perel JM: Imipramine dose-response relationship in panic disorder with agoraphobia. Arch Gen Psychiatry 46:127–131, 1989

Muskin PR, Glassman AH: The use of tricyclic antidepressants in a medical setting, in Consultation-Liaison Psychiatry: Current Trends and New

Perspectives. Edited by Finkel JB. New York, Grune & Stratton, 1983, pp 137–158

Nelson JC, Charney DS: The symptoms of major depressive illness. Am J Psychiatry 138:1–13, 1981

Nelson JC, Jatlow P, Quinlan DM, et al: Desipramine plasma concentration and antidepressant response. Arch Gen Psychiatry 39:1419–1422, 1982

Nelson JC, Jatlow PI, Quinlan DM: Subjective complaints during desipramine treatment. Arch Gen Psychiatry 41:55–59, 1984

Nelson JC, Jatlow PI, Mazure C: Desipramine plasma levels and response in elderly melancholic patients. J Clin Psychopharmacol 5:217–220, 1985

Nelson JC, Mazure C, Jatlow PI, et al: Predictors of response in major depression, in Proceedings, Annual Meeting of the American College of Neuropsychopharmacology. San Juan, PR, 1988

Olivier-Martin R, Marzin D, Buschsenschutz E, et al: Concentrations plasmatiques de l'imipramine et de la desmethylimipramine et effet antidepresseur au cours d'un traitement controle. Psychopharmacologia 41:187–195, 1975

Paykel ES, Freeling P, Hollyman JA: Are tricyclic antidepressants useful for mild depression? A placebo controlled trial. Pharmacopsychiatry 21:15–18, 1988

Piafsky KM, Borga O: Plasma protein binding of basic drugs, II: importance of alpha-1-acid glycoprotein for interindividual variation. Clin Pharmacol Ther 22:545–549, 1977

Piafsky KM, Borga O, Odar-Cederlof I, et al: Increased plasma protein binding of propranolol and chlorpromazine mediated by disease-induced elevations of plasma alpha-1-acid glycoprotein. N Engl J Med 229:1435–1439, 1978

Preskorn SH, Weller EB, Weller RA: Depression in children: relationship between plasma imipramine levels and response. J Clin Psychiatry 43:450–453, 1982

Preskorn SH, Weller EB, Weller RA, et al: Plasma levels of imipramine and adverse effects in children. Am J Psychiatry 140:1332–1335, 1983

Quitkin F, Rifkin A, Klein DF: Monoamine oxidase inhibitors. Arch Gen Psychiatry 36:749–764, 1979

Quitkin FM, Rabkin JG, Ross D, et al: Duration of antidepressant drug treatment: what is an adequate trial? Arch Gen Psychiatry 41:238–245, 1984

Quitkin FM, Stewart JW, McGrath PJ, et al: Phenelzine versus imipramine in the treatment of probable atypical depression: defining syndrome boundaries of selective MAOI responders. Am J Psychiatry 145:306–311, 1988

Reisby N, Gram LF, Bech P, et al: Imipramine: clinical effects and pharmacokinetic variability. Psychopharmacology (Berlin) 54:263–272, 1977

Robinson DS, Nies A, Ravaris CL, et al: Clinical pharmacology of phenelzine. Arch Gen Psychiatry 35:629–635, 1978

Robinson DS, Cooper TB, Ravaris CL, et al: Plasma tricyclic drug levels in amitriptyline-treated depressed patients. Psychopharmacology (Berlin) 63:223–231, 1979

Roose SP, Glassman AH, Walsh BT, et al: Tricyclic nonresponders: phenomenology and treatment. Am J Psychiatry 143:345–348, 1986

Rowan PR, Paykel ES, Parker RR: Phenelzine and amitriptyline: effects on symptoms of neurotic depression. Br J Psychiatry 140:475–483, 1982

Rudorfer MV, Young RC: Anticholinergic effects and plasma desipramine levels. Clin Pharmacol Ther 28:703–706, 1980

Sargant W, Dally P: Treatment of anxiety states by antidepressant drugs. Br Med J 1:6–9, 1962

Schatzberg AF, Cole JO, Cohen BM, et al: Survey of depressed patients who have failed to respond to treatment, in The Affective Disorders. Edited by Davis JM, Maas JW. Washington, DC, American Psychiatric Press, 1983, pp 73–85

Spiker DG, Weiss JC, Dealy RS, et al: The pharmacological treatment of delusional depression. Am J Psychiatry 142:430–436, 1985

Spitzer RL, Endicott J, Robins E: Research Diagnostic Criteria (RDC) for a selected group of functional disorders, 3rd Edition. New York, 1978

Stewart JW, Quitkin FM, Liebowitz MR, et al: Efficacy of desipramine in depressed outpatients: response according to Research Diagnostic Criteria and severity of illness. Arch Gen Psychiatry 40:202–207, 1983

Stewart JW, McGrath PJ, Liebowitz MR, et al: Treatment outcome validation of DSM-III depressive subtypes: clinical usefulness in outpatients with mild to moderate depression. Arch Gen Psychiatry 42:1148–1153, 1985

Walter CJS: Clinical significance of plasma imipramine levels. Proc R Soc Med 64:282–285, 1971

Wehr TA, Goodwin FK: Rapid cycling in manic-depressives induced by tricyclic antidepressants. Arch Gen Psychiatry 36:555–559, 1979

Wehr TA, Goodwin FK: Do antidepressants cause mania? Psychopharmacol Bull 23:61–65, 1987

West ED, Dally PJ: Effects of iproniazid in depressive syndromes. Br Med J 1:1491–1494, 1959

Chapter 3

Lithium Augmentation in Refractory Depression

J. Craig Nelson, M.D.

Chapter 3

Lithium Augmentation in Refractory Depression

Although antidepressant drugs are effective for most depressed patients, 15% to 30% of those treated will fail to respond. Treatment of refractory depression remains a challenge and as a result, the development of strategies and alternatives for the pharmacologic treatment of refractory depression is an important goal in psychiatry. Lithium augmentation is one of the promising alternatives.

Unlike most important advances in psychopharmacology, which were discovered by chance observation, lithium augmentation was proposed and tested on the basis of a neurochemical rationale. Having demonstrated in prior animal studies that chronic antidepressant treatment increased postsynaptic serotonin receptor sensitivity (de-Montigny and Aghajanian 1978), deMontigny and co-workers (1981) suggested that the addition of lithium to ongoing antidepressant treatment might augment the effects of the antidepressant. They administered lithium at 300 mg tid to eight depressed patients who had improved less than 40% after a minimum of 21 days of treatment with a variety of antidepressant drugs. Within 48 hours, all of the patients improved, and six of the eight recovered (had a Hamilton Rating Scale score <7) (Hamilton 1960).

Subsequently, rapid response following lithium augmentation was observed when lithium was added to a variety of antidepressant drugs. We described rapid response after the addition of lithium in three cases who had been unresponsive to treatment with high doses of phenelzine (Nelson and Byck 1982). Birkhimer and colleagues (1983) noted the successful augmentation of trazodone. De-Montigny and associates (1985) observed a positive effect of lithium augmentation when used with iprindole in seven patients. This observation was of interest because iprindole does not block monoamine reuptake. Other reports described successful augmentation of dothiepin and mianserin (Joyce et al. 1983), amoxapine (Louie and Meltzer 1984), clomipramine (Schrader and Levien 1985),

35

zimelidine (Joyce 1985), maprotiline (Kushnir 1986), tranyl-cypromine (Tariot et al. 1986), fluvoxamine (Delgado et al. 1988), and fluoxetine (Pope et al. 1988).

The case report literature also notes the value of lithium augmentation in very refractory patients. Joyce and co-workers (1983) described successful treatment with lithium augmentation in two very refractory cases who had both failed to respond to antidepressants and electroconvulsive therapy (ECT). Schrader and Levien (1985) described a positive response to lithium augmentation of clomipramine in a patient refractory to neuroleptics, a tricyclic, a monoamine oxidase inhibitor (MAOI), and ECT. Rapid response to the addition of lithium was noted by Roy and Pickar (1985) in three carefully monitored patients who remained depressed after 4 weeks off medication and after 1 month of imipramine at 350 mg a day or more. Improvement within 12 hours of the addition of lithium to tranylcypromine was noted by Tariot and associates (1986) in a patient who had been continuously depressed for 17 weeks of hospitalization during which trials of placebo, deprenyl, and tranyl-cypromine alone had failed.

Lithium augmentation has been demonstrated to be of value in a variety of clinical situations in which conventional treatment may be problematic. We reported that lithium augmentation was effective in some patients with psychotic depression, a severe syndrome that can be resistant to drug treatment and often requires ECT (Nelson and Mazure 1986). This observation has been supported by the case report literature in which several of the lithium augmentation responders were noted to have psychotic features (Delgado et al. 1988; deMontigny et al. 1985; Joyce 1985; Joyce et al. 1983; Louie and Meltzer 1984; Schrader and Levien 1985; Pope et al. 1988).

Lithium augmentation has also been noted to be of value in medically ill geriatric patients. Kushnir (1986) described five such cases in whom conventional antidepressant treatment had been difficult because of side effects. He suggested that the addition of low-dose lithium allowed the use of lower doses of antidepressants, which helped to avoid side effects.

Lithium augmentation has also been found to be efficacious in patients unresponsive to T3 augmentation. Garbutt and colleagues (1986) described four patients who had failed to respond to tricyclic antidepressants alone and were unresponsive to potentiation of the tricyclic with T3. The authors suggested that both augmentation strategies might be employed before concluding the original antidepressant was ineffective. They noted that they were unable to predict which treatment would be effective.

The case report literature documents rapid response to the addition of lithium but also notes a greater variability in the timing of response than was originally reported. Although several descriptions of lithium augmentation mention improvement within 1 or 2 days (deMontigny et al. 1985; Joyce 1985; Joyce et al. 1983; Louie and Meltzer 1984; Nelson and Byck 1982; Price et al. 1983; Tariot et al. 1986), response may require 2 or 3 weeks of lithium augmentation (Garbutt et al. 1986; Kushnir 1986; Louie and Meltzer 1984; Price et al. 1983; Roy and Pickar 1985).

In addition, although the initial report and subsequent individual case studies presented only positive cases, a small series of cases noted greater variability in the rate and nature of response. We noted good response to lithium augmentation in three of six psychotic depressive patients, partial improvement in two, and no response in one patient (Price et al. 1983). Louie and Meltzer (1984) noted a range of response in a series of nine cases; two patients had a good response to lithium augmentation, but in two others the response was transient. They also described the development of mania in two patients, an observation subsequently noted by two other investigators (Joyce 1985; Price et al. 1984). This observation was of particular interest because the development of mania following the addition of lithium is consistent with the augmentation hypothesis, that is, that the effect of lithium addition appears to be the enhancement of the primary antidepressant drug, which is known to trigger mania, rather than a primary effect of lithium, which would not be expected to produce mania.

Nevertheless, it is the nature of case reports to describe positive outcomes, and these reports do confirm the observation of rapid improvement after the addition of lithium to ongoing antidepressant treatment. These reports suggest lithium is effective in augmenting all types of antidepressant agents, and they illustrate the value of lithium augmentation in a variety of clinical circumstances. The reports describing the value of lithium augmentation in patients who have been refractory to a variety of treatments including ECT provide persuasive support for the potential value of lithium augmentation in refractory depression. Although the possibility of spontaneous change or placebo response cannot be excluded in these uncontrolled cases, the history of poor response to a variety of prior treatments makes these possibilities remote.

PLACEBO-CONTROLLED STUDIES

The literature on placebo-controlled lithium augmentation is limited to six studies. The first study to use a design in which lithium or placebo was added to ongoing antidepressant treatment was reported by the Heninger group (1983). Fifteen patients who were treated with either desipramine, amitriptyline, or mianserin and had improved less than 50% on the Hamilton Rating Scale were studied. Lithium was added to the antidepressant in half of the sample; placebo was added in the other patients. At 12 days, the placebo group was crossed over to lithium. Lithium and placebo were administered double blind, but patients were not randomly assigned. Statistically significant improvement with lithium was noted on a nurse-rated depression scale after 1 and 2 days, but the magnitude of the change was slight. More meaningful differences occurred during the second week of lithium treatment. Hamilton scores available on 11 patients improved 57% on lithium and 15% on placebo. The clinician, who was blind to the drug treatment received, rated 12 of the 15 patients as responders during lithium administration.

The second study that used a lithium versus placebo design was reported by Cournoyer and associates in 1984. In 12 patients who failed to respond to antidepressant drugs, lithium or placebo was added for 2 days. After an interval of a week, the alternative treatment was administered. Significant improvement occurred with lithium, but not placebo. This brief report did not directly compare improvement with lithium and placebo. In addition, it was unclear in this crossover design how changes during the first treatment affected change during the second treatment.

Kantor and colleagues (1986) reported a small placebo-controlled study using a similar design; lithium or placebo was added to ongoing antidepressant treatment that had been given for at least 21 days with less than 40% improvement in the depression. Four patients received lithium and three patients were given placebo. After 48 hours, one of the lithium patients responded (the Hamilton score dropped from 24 to 7), but none of the placebo patients improved. The authors concluded that their study suggested no difference between lithium and placebo but acknowledged that their sample was small. This study is at variance with response rates described by deMontigny and co-workers (1981, 1985); however, a 1-in-4 *remission* rate within 48 hours is of clinical consequence and is not inconsistent with the literature overall for rates of remission at 48 hours.

A larger placebo-controlled trial reported by Zusky and colleagues (1988) failed to find a difference between lithium and placebo. Depressed outpatients in this study appeared to be a relatively more refractory group having received prior antidepressant treatment for an average of 9 months. They were then placed on lithium or placebo (for a minimum of 14 days. Lithium 300 mg was administered for the first week. This dose was increased in the second week. Three of eight patients receiving lithium responded whereas two of eight patients receiving placebo responded. The difference between the groups was not significant. The response rate in the lithium-treated group is similar to that found in other studies of refractory patients, but was not superior to placebo. It is likely that demonstration of drug-placebo differences may prove to be more difficult in more refractory patients. While the authors note that the low lithium dose and low levels during the first week should be sufficient to enhance pre-synaptic serotonin transmission, nevertheless, this dose was lower than that used in any other study.

The largest placebo-controlled study was recently reported by Schopf and associates (1989). Twenty-seven inpatients with endogenous depression who had failed to respond to a month of conventional antidepressant treatment were randomly and blindly assigned to either 800 mg of lithium carbonate given for 2 weeks or placebo given for 1 week followed by 2 weeks of lithium. The placebo-treated patients experienced almost no change in mean Hamilton scores during the first week. However, Hamilton scores in the lithium-treated group improved nearly 50% during this period. Improvement with lithium and placebo differed significantly. The 27 patients all received lithium for 2 weeks during some phase of the study, 9 (33%) improved by 50% at 1 week; 13 (48%) of 27 experienced 50% improvement in 2 weeks.

Another recent study (Kramlinger and Post 1989), while not a parallel comparison, employed a lithium-for-placebo substitution design. Fifteen patients, 13 of whom were bipolar and all of whom were unresponsive to carbamazepine, received lithium which was substituted for placebo and added to carbamazepine. Both patients and raters were blind to the timing of the substitution of lithium for placebo. The mean lithium dose was 890 mg per day. Eight of the 15 patients significantly improved; 7 showed little change. In the responders, substantial improvement was noted in 4 days, although improvement continued over the 21 days of the lithium augmentation trial.

DeMontigny and associates (1983) described a placebo-controlled study designed to test the importance of pretreatment with an antidepressant before addition of lithium. In this study, five patients were pretreated with amitriptyline and five with placebo for 21 days. Then lithium was added in all patients. After 48 hours, all of the patients pretreated with amitriptyline responded, whereas only one of the five pretreated with placebo responded to the addition of lithium. This study indicates the importance of pretreatment with an antidepressant and suggests that augmentation effects at 48 hours are not a direct effect of lithium.

In summary, six placebo-controlled studies have been conducted. One of these demonstrated that pretreatment with antidepressant rather than placebo was necessary for lithium augmentation effect. In the five studies comparing the addition of placebo or lithium to ongoing antidepressant treatment, three were positive. In one of the negative studies, the sample was too small to be informative (Kantor et al. 1986). In the other negative study (Zusky et al. 1988) the use of a low initial lithium dose and relatively refractory patients may have reduced the chances of demonstrating differences between lithium and placebo. The three positive studies cited provide moderate confirmation for the lithium augmentation effect. Larger placebo-controlled studies in truly refractory outpatients would be helpful because these are the patients in whom this treatment would be indicated. In anticipation of a lower response rate in refactory patients, however, groups would need to be of sufficient size so that true differences could be detected.

HOW EFFECTIVE IS LITHIUM AUGMENTATION IN REFRACTORY DEPRESSION?

Although placebo-controlled studies help to confirm that augmentation occurs, they do not necessarily address the important clinical questions of its degree of effectiveness in truly refractory patients or its effectiveness in comparison with alternative treatments. Four studies using larger samples provide some information regarding the clinical efficacy of lithium augmentation.

DeMontigny and colleagues (1983) examined frequency of response to lithium augmentation in 34 unipolar patients who had failed to respond to a variety of antidepressants for a minimal 3-week period. Eight patients received two completed trials for a total of 42 observations. Thirty-one of the 42 (75%) treatment trials resulted in a greater than 50% improvement in Hamilton depression ratings within 48 hours. This is the highest rate of response reported in a larger sample; however, patients with a history of antidepressant failure prior to the current antidepressant trial were excluded.

Nelson and Mazure (1986) described lithium augmentation in 21 patients with psychotic depression who had been treated with desipramine and either perphenazine or haloperidol for 3 to 5 weeks and had failed to respond. Lithium was then added to this regimen for a 2-week period. Eleven of the 21 patients were retrospectively judged to be responders. Response occurred during days 6 through 14 and was significantly more frequent in bipolar patients. Eight of 9 bipolar patients but only 3 of 12 unipolar patients responded. Response to lithium augmentation was also compared with ECT response in a group of 15 unipolar psychotic depressives who were diagnostically similar and had been unresponsive to similar combined desipramine-antipsychotic treatment. Patients were not randomly assigned to ECT or lithium; most patients received lithium first. ECT was effective in 9 of 15 patients and appeared to be a more effective treatment than lithium augmentation in unipolar patients. However, the rate of response for lithium augmentation in the bipolar patients was comparable to, if not better than, that for ECT. When lithium augmentation was successful, the timing of response was as rapid as that seen with ECT.

The largest study to examine the effectiveness of lithium augmentation was reported by Price and colleagues (1986). They studied 84 patients with major depressive disorder, including unipolar and bipolar patients. Of the 84 patients, 26 (30%) exhibited a marked response, and 47 (56%) showed at least partial response. Different from previous reports, duration of the lithium augmentation was 24 days, and 15 of the 26 patients with marked response reached this criterion in the last week of the augmentation. Only 3 of the 84 patients had a marked response during the first 6 days.

Other data bearing on the clinical value of lithium augmentation were provided by the Delgado group (1988) who described the use of lithium combined with fluvoxamine. This study was unusual in documenting prior treatment failure; the sample had an average of four prior antidepressant trials that were unsuccessful. Twenty-eight patients completed a 2-week placebo trial followed by 4 to 6 weeks of fluvoxamine. Eight were judged responders to fluvoxamine. Of the 20 patients failing to respond, 18 underwent augmentation with lithium or, in the case of psychotic patients, lithium plus perphenazine. Five of the 18 (28%) patients were judged to have a marked response to lithium (the Hamilton score decreased 50% and was less than 15), and five others were partial responders (were able to be discharged but did not meet the Hamilton criteria). This study demonstrated that lithium augments fluvoxamine and that, in a group of clearly refractory patients, lithium augmentation reduced the number of nonresponding patients substantially.

A recent report provides further information about lithium efficacy. Thase and associates (1989) reported a 65% response rate to a 6 week trial of lithium augmentation in 20 patients who had failed to respond to 12 or more weeks of treatment with imipramine and psychotherapy. Although this was not a blind trial, response was significantly greater than the 25% rate observed in a matched historical group who continued on imipramine and psychotherapy but without lithium. The authors noted only 1 patient responded to lithium during the first week. Most responses occurred in the second week, but the number responding increased through week 6. The criteria for response were equivalent to marked response in the preceding reports but the higher rate (65%) may reflect a less refractory sample.

In summary, efficacy studies in larger samples indicate that response rates to lithium augmentation vary. In patients with no history of drug failure prior to the current trial, 75% were responsive to augmentation (deMontigny et al. 1983). In more severely ill psychotic patients or patients refractory to multiple drug trials, rates vary between 30% and 50% (Delgado et al. 1988; Nelson and Mazure 1986; Price et al. 1986). If the clinician is using marked response as the endpoint, a 30% rate of response might be expected in patients refractory to prior drug trials. Although this rate of response might seem low, one should expect lower rates in refractory patients than those seen in pharmacologically naive patients.

THE CLINICAL USE OF LITHIUM

From a practical perspective, lithium augmentation is an attractive alternative in a nonresponding depressed patient; the effect can be rapid and the problems associated with withdrawing one antidepressant and starting a new drug may be avoided. The usual dosage of lithium during augmentation is 300 mg tid. Although some studies have adjusted dosage, none have employed high dosage. Lithium levels achieved have been in the range of 0.4 to 1.0 mEq/L, and within this range, response appears to be unrelated to lithium levels (deMontigny et al. 1983; Nelson and Mazure 1986; Price et al. 1986).

There is no accepted rule for how long to continue a lithium augmentation trial. Response can occur in 48 hours, but most studies have administered lithium over at least 2 weeks. The study by Price and associates (1986), which continued the lithium augmentation phase for 24 days, suggests that response to lithium addition can occur during the third week of administration. Thase and associates (1989) noted an increase in the number responding over a 6-week period. The clinician must weigh the relative merits of a prolonged lithium augmentation trial against a new drug trial. In most patients, a 2-week period of augmentation should be adequate. However, in patients who have been refractory to several prior antidepressant trials, a longer trial of combined lithium augmentation might be warranted to allow for the possibility of a late response.

Lithium augmentation has been observed with all the known

antidepressant drug classes, but it is reasonable to question whether certain antidepressants would show a more robust response to the addition of lithium than others. DeMontigny and colleagues (1983) reported that the rate of response to lithium augmentation was comparable in the various tricyclic antidepressants that they gave. Comparing drugs of different classes, Price and associates (1986) found lower rates of response with lithium augmentation for trazodone and adinazolam.

Studies examining lithium augmentation have reported few side effects associated with the addition of lithium, although bipolar patients may be at greater risk for lithium-induced mania (Louie and Meltzer 1984). The low frequency of side effects may be in part the result of the lower levels of lithium achieved during augmentation. As noted above, one report (Kushnir 1986) suggested lithium augmentation might help to avoid side effects in geriatric and medically ill patients because this combination might allow lower doses of both lithium and the antidepressant. This is an interesting possibility, but it has not been established that lithium augmentation is effective if the dose or blood level of the antidepressant is subtherapeutic.

It is not clear at this point which patients are most likely to respond to lithium augmentation. We found a much higher response rate in bipolar psychotic depressives than in unipolar psychotic depressives (Nelson and Mazure 1986); this might be consistent with the effectiveness of lithium as a primary antidepressant in bipolar but not unipolar patients (Goodwin et al. 1972). Price and co-workers (1986) subsequently found no difference in effectiveness of lithium augmentation in bipolar and unipolar patients but noted that their bipolar depressive patients, although frequently psychotic, were not receiving antipsychotic-antidepressant combinations as had been the case in our study. Although lithium augmentation does not require the concomitant administration of neuroleptic drugs in psychotic depression (deMontigny et al. 1981, 1985; Schrader and Levien 1985), in most reports using lithium augmentation in delusionally depressed patients, neuroleptic drugs were also employed (Delgado et al. 1988; Joyce et al. 1983; Louie and Meltzer 1984; Nelson and Mazure 1986; Pope et al. 1988; Price et al. 1983; Roy and Pickar 1985).

If lithium augmentation is effective, the clinician is faced with the question of how long to continue the lithium. There are few data bearing on this question. DeMontigny and co-workers (1983) examined the effects of lithium withdrawal by discontinuing lithium in nine patients who had been responsive to augmentation. Five of the patients relapsed, but the other four continued to do well. The finding suggests that because there is a good chance improvement will be maintained, termination of the lithium might be warranted and will identify those patients in whom continued treatment with lithium is unnecessary. Of course, the clinician should remain alert to the possibility of relapse and the need to reinstitute lithium.

THE MECHANISM OF LITHIUM AUGMENTATION

At a clinical pharmacologic level, there are three possible explanations for the effects of lithium augmentation. As initially proposed, the effect may be a true "augmentation" of the underlying effect of the antecedent antidepressant. Alternatively, the chronic administration of lithium combined with an antidepressant may have a synergistic effect. Finally, it is possible lithium may have a primary antidepressant effect.

The last possibility is supported by studies of the effectiveness of lithium when used alone as a primary antidepressant. Comprehensive reviews of these studies have been previously published (Mendels 1976; Noyes and Dempsey 1974). The results suggest that lithium is an effective antidepressant in bipolar depressed patients, but its efficacy in unipolar patients is questionable. Our finding of more frequent response to lithium augmentation in bipolar patients is consistent with this possibility (Nelson and Mazure 1986). The increased number of responders during the third week of lithium augmentation noted in another study (Price et al. 1986) is also consistent with the timing of lithium action when used as a primary antidepressant (Noyes and Dempsey 1974). However, the rapid effects of lithium augmentation sometimes observed during the first week, the observation of mania following addition of lithium, and the lack of any correlation between lithium levels and response are not consistent with the hypothesis that lithium is acting as a primary antidepressant.

A second hypothesis is that the combination of lithium and an antidepressant is synergistic, but the effects are not the result of augmentation of the antidepressant and do not depend on the sequence of antidepressant followed by lithium described by the deMontigny group (1981). Several retrospective or naturalistic reports describe the value of combining lithium with an MAOI from the initiation of treatment. Zall (1971) noted the value of lithium combined with isocarboxazid in three patients with difficult, recurrent depressions. Himmelhoch and colleagues (1972) found the lithium-tranylcypromine combination particularly effective in refractory outpatients and suggested that hypersomnia might predict response. Price and associates (1985) recently reported that lithium combined with tranylcypromine was effective in 11 of 12 inpatients with major depression who had failed to respond to at least two prior antidepressant trials. Only one prospective placebo-controlled study, however, has investigated this question. Lingjaerde and associates (1974) conducted a multisite study in which an antidepressant was combined with lithium or placebo. Patients at the largest single site did have a better response when lithium was combined with the antidepressant; however, the combined data from all sites did not show the combination with lithium to be superior. The distinction between the chronic administration of this combination and the acute effect of lithium augmentation might seem minor. The two types of effects are not mutually exclusive, both may occur, and in either case the effect of the lithium-antidepressant combination may be mediated by changes in the serotonin system. Essentially, the question is whether there is any advantage to administering lithium at the start of antidepressant treatment rather than during the fourth week. This has not been tested.

The mechanism of lithium augmentation has also been addressed at the neurochemical level. The original hypothesis suggested that chronic treatment of 2 to 3 weeks with antidepressant drugs increased postsynaptic serotonin receptor sensitivity (deMontigny and Aghajanian 1978). Once receptor sensitivity developed, the addition of lithium would facilitate serotonin transmission by rapidly increasing serotonin turnover (Grahame-Smith and Green 1974). The observation that lithium augmented iprindole (deMontigny et al. 1985), an antidepressant that does not block amine reuptake but does sensitize serotonin receptors, supported the hypothesis and suggested the interaction was not related to reuptake mechanisms.

The observation that lithium augmentation occurred with essentially all the known antidepressant drugs suggested a common mechanism. However, MAOIs and selective serotonin reuptake blockers do not increase postsynaptic serotonin receptor sensitivity. It has been suggested that chronic administration of both MAOIs (Blier et al. 1986) and selective reuptake blockers (Blier et al. 1984) results in a desensitization of presynaptic serotonergic autoreceptors that reduces their inhibitory effects and facilitates serotonin transmission. Augmentation of these drugs with lithium further enhances these effects. A more detailed discussion of the current hypotheses about the actions of antidepressant drugs on the serotonin system and the action of lithium during augmentation has been presented elsewhere (Blier et al. 1987).

CONCLUSION

Lithium augmentation appears to be a promising treatment for refractory depression. Its clinical value has been documented in a sizable case report literature. It is useful in a variety of clinical circumstances, including in patients with severe or psychotic depression and in patients who have failed to respond to ECT. Placebo-controlled evidence supporting lithium augmentation is provided by three studies. The rate of response to lithium augmentation appears to vary in relation to prior drug failure. In patients who have been refractory to prior drug trials, 30% might be expected to have marked improvement. This rate may seem low in relation to response rates in untreated depressed patients but is not inconsequential for truly refractory patients. Future studies are needed to determine which patients are most likely to benefit from lithium augmentation and which antidepressants are most responsive to augmentation. Answers to these questions might help the clinician decide when to add lithium and when to switch to a different antidepressant.

REFERENCES

Birkhimer LJ, Alderman AA, Schmitt CE, et al: Combined trazodone-lithium therapy for refractory depression. Am J Psychiatry 140:1382–1383, 1983

Blier P, deMontigny C, Tardif D: Effects of the two antidepressant drugs mianserin and indalpine on the serotonergic system: single cell studies in the rat. Psychopharmacology (Berlin) 84:242–249, 1984

Blier P, deMontigny C, Azzaro AJ: Modification of serotonergic and noradrenergic neurotransmission by repeated administration of monoamine oxidase inhibitors: electrophysiological studies in the rat central nervous system. J Pharmacol Exp Ther 237:987–994, 1986

Blier P, deMontigny C, Chaput Y: Modifications of the serotonin system by antidepressant treatments: implications for the therapeutic response in major depression. J Clin Psychopharmacol 7:24S–35S, 1987

Cournoyer G, deMontigny C, Ouellette J, et al: Lithium addition in tricyclic-resistant unipolar depression: a placebo-controlled study. Coll Int Neuro-Psychopharmacol 14:F-177:179, 1984

Delgado PL, Price LH, Charney DS, et al: Efficacy of fluvoxamine in treatment-refractory depression. J Affective Disord 15:55–60, 1988

deMontigny C, Aghajanian GK: Tricyclic antidepressants: long-term treatment increases responsitivity of rat forebrain neurons to serotonin. Science 202:1303–1306, 1978

deMontigny C, Grunberg F, Mayre A, et al: Lithium induces rapid relief of depression in tricyclic antidepressant drug non-responders. Br J Psychiatry 138:252–256, 1981 deMontigny C, Cournoyer G, Morissette R, et al: Lithium carbonate addition in tricyclic antidepressant-resistant unipolar depression. Arch Gen Psychiatry 40:1327–1334, 1983

deMontigny C, Elie R, Caille G: Rapid response to the addition of lithium in iprindole-resistant unipolar depression. Am J Psychiatry 142:220–223, 1985

Garbutt JC, Mayo JP, Gillette GM, et al: Lithium potentiation of tricyclic antidepressants following lack of T3 potentiation. Am J Psychiatry 143:1038–1039, 1986

Goodwin FK, Murphy DL, Dunner DL, et al: Lithium response in unipolar versus bipolar depression. Am J Psychiatry 129:44–47, 1972

Grahame-Smith DG, Green AR: The role of brain 5-hydroxy-tryptamine in the hyperactivity produced in rats by lithium and monoamine oxidase inhibition. Br J Pharmacol 52:19–26, 1974

Heninger G, Charney DS, Sternberg DE: Lithium carbonate augmentation of antidepressant treatment. Arch Gen Psychiatry 40:1335–1342, 1983

Himmelhoch JM, Detre T, Kupfer DJ, et al: Treatment of previously intractable depressions with tranylcypromine and lithium. J Nerv Ment Dis 155:216–220, 1972

Joyce PR: Mood response to methylphenidate and the dexamethasone suppression test as predictors of treatment response to zimelidine and lithium in major depression. Biol Psychiatry 20:598–604, 1985

Joyce PR, Hewland HR, Jones AV: Rapid response to lithium in treatment resistant depression. Br J Psychiatry 142:204–214, 1983

Kantor D, McNevin S, Leichner P, et al: The benefit of lithium carbonate adjunct in refractory depression—fact or fiction? Can J Psychiatry 31:416–418, 1986

Kramlinger K, Post R: The addition of lithium to carbamazepine. Arch Gen Psychiatry 46:794–800, 1989

Kushnir SL: Lithium-antidepressant combinations in the treatment of depressed, physically ill geriatric patients. Am J Psychiatry 143:378–379, 1986

Lingjaerde O, Edlund AH, Gormsen CA, et al: The effect of lithium carbonate in combination with tricyclic antidepressants in endogenous depression. Acta Psychiatr Scand 50:233–242, 1974

Louie AK, Meltzer HY: Lithium potentiation of antidepressant treatment. J Clin Psychopharmacol 4:316–321, 1984

Mendels J: Lithium in the treatment of depression. Am J Psychiatry 133:373–378, 1976

Nelson JC, Byck R: Rapid response to lithium in phenelzine non-responders. Br J Psychiatry 141:85–86, 1982

Nelson JC, Mazure CM: Lithium augmentation in psychotic depression refractory to combined drug treatment. Am J Psychiatry 143:363–366, 1986

Noyes R Jr, Dempsey GM: Lithium treatment of depression. Diseases of the Nervous System 35:573–576, 1974

Pope HG, McElroy SL, Nixon RA: Possible synergism between fluoxetine and lithium in refractory depression. Am J Psychiatry 145:1292–1294, 1988

Price LH, Conwell Y, Nelson JC: Lithium augmentation of combined neuroleptic-tricyclic treatment in delusional depression. Am J Psychiatry 140:318–322, 1983

Price LH, Charney DS, Heninger GR: Efficacy of lithium-tranylcypromine treatment in refractory depression. Am J Psychiatry 142:619–623, 1985

Price LH, Charney DS, Heninger GR: Manic symptoms following addition of lithium to antidepressant treatment. J Clin Psychopharmacol 4:361–362, 1984

Price LH, Charney DS, Heninger GR: Variability of response to lithium augmentation in refractory depression. Am J Psychiatry 143:1387–1392, 1986

Roy A, Pickar D: Lithium potentiation of imipramine in treatment resistant depression. Br J Psychiatry 147:582–583, 1985

Schopf J, Baumann P, et al: Treatment of endogenous depressions resistant to tricyclic antidepressants or related drugs by lithium addition: results of a placebo-controlled double-blind study. Pharmacopsychiat 22:183–187, 1989

Schrader GD, Levien HE: Response to sequential administration of clomipramine and lithium carbonate in treatment-resistant depression. Br J Psychiatry 147:573–575, 1985

Tariot PN, Murphy DL, Sunderland T, et al: Rapid antidepressant effect of addition of lithium to tranylcypromine. J Clin Psychopharmacol 6:165–167, 1986

Thase ME, Kupfer DJ, Frank E, et al: Treatment of imipramine-resistant recurrent depression, II: an open clinical trial of lithium augmentation. J Clin Psychiatry 50:413–417, 1989

Zusky PM, Biederman J, Rosenbaum J, et al: Adjunct low dose lithium carbonate in treatment-resistant depression: a placebo-controlled study. J Clin Psychopharmacol 8:120–124, 1988

Zall H: Lithium carbonate and isocarboxazid—an effective drug approach in severe depression. Am J Psychiatry 127:1400–1403, 1971

Chapter 4

The Use of Monoamine Oxidase Inhibitors in Refractory Depression

Michael J. Devlin, M.D.
B. Timothy Walsh, M.D.

Chapter 4

The Use of Monoamine Oxidase Inhibitors in Refractory Depression

In one of the earliest articles to deal with the use of monoamine oxidase inhibitors (MAOIs) in depressive states, West and Dally (1959) made the following statement concerning iproniazid, an early MAOI no longer in use:

> We have now used iproniazid in over 500 patients in the past two years, and, as a result, we have started to recognize a group of patients showing somewhat atypical depressive states . . . who seem to be specifically and almost completely relieved of their disabling symptoms by iproniazid after the failure of all other forms of treatment. (pp 1491–1492)

These initial open studies, in addition to providing preliminary support for the efficacy of MAOIs in treating depression, took the important further step of attempting to define the characteristics of MAOI responders and nonresponders (see Table 4-1). Much of the work on MAOIs since that time has attempted to validate these clinical impressions by answering the following questions: Is there a group of patients with an atypical form of depression who are especially responsive to MAOIs, and are MAOIs useful in the treatment of depression when other drugs have failed? In this chapter, we will first review the definition of refractory depression and discuss specifically how it might be applied to an "ideal" study of MAOIs in refractory depression. We will proceed to summarize the evidence indicating that there is a subgroup of patients who do particularly well on MAOIs. Such evidence logically implies, although it does not directly demonstrate, that these patients, if refractory to tricyclic antidepressants, respond to MAOIs. We will then review some of the few studies that have attempted to examine directly the response to MAOIs of patients who have failed standard treatment. Finally, we will discuss the use of MAOIs in combination with tricyclic antidepressants in treating refractory depression.

The criteria for refractory depression, specifically the requirement for failure to respond to treatments of adequate dose and adequate duration, have been discussed in previous chapters. Ideally, we would wish to review in this chapter data from patients who met these criteria and were randomized to receive MAOIs or some control treatment. Unfortunately, there are no such data. Several studies of refractory depression employ heterogeneous groups of patients, some of whom might not be considered to have a major depressive disorder by current standards. Many of the studies, in defining treatment failures, do not apply stringent criteria for adequacy of treatment; few, for example, have explicitly used plasma tricyclic antidepressant levels as a criterion for adequacy of dose. Therefore, we must forego at the outset our desire to review "ideal" studies of MAOIs in refractory depression. Instead, we will review some of the circumstantial evidence and some less than perfect but nonetheless persuasive studies concerning MAOIs in refractory depressed patients.

Table 4-1. Characteristics of iproniazid responders and nonresponders

	Percent responders ($n = 58$)	Percent nonresponders ($n = 43$)	Significance[a] level
Self-reproach	17.2	44.2	$P < .05$
Worse in A.M.	20.7	48.8	$P < .05$
Worse in P.M.	20.7	2.3	$P < .05$
Initial insomnia	72.4	60.4	NS
Early morning awakening	17.2	48.8	$P < .05$
Hypochondriasis	37.9	37.2	NS
Retardation	22.4	23.2	NS
Bewilderment	31.0	23.2	NS
Phobias	44.8	23.2	$P < .05$
Hysterical conversions	7.2	0.0	$P < .05$
Tremor	29.3	7.0	$P < .05$
Cardiovascular symptoms	77.6	41.8	NS
Gastrointestinal symptoms	44.8	27.9	NS
Other somatic	79.3	72.0	NS
% ECT cases made worse by ECT	22.2	8.1	$P < .05$

Note.   ECT = electroconvulsive therapy.
[a]By χ^2-test.
Source.   Adapted from West and Dally 1959.

STUDIES OF MAOIs IN ATYPICAL DEPRESSION

The evidence that there exists a subgroup of depressed patients who respond especially well to MAOIs is related to the treatment of refractory depression insofar as it implies that such patients, when refractory to tricyclics, might respond preferentially to MAOIs. The studies that provide evidence of such a depressed subgroup are outlined in Table 4-2.

Documentation for the concept of a group of patients who are particularly responsive to MAOIs began to grow from the studies of Robinson, Ravaris, Nies, and colleagues in the 1970s and early 1980s. In two early studies (Ravaris et al. 1976; Robinson et al. 1973) which played an important role in securing a place for MAOIs in this country, these investigators conclusively demonstrated that phenelzine was superior to placebo in the treatment of a group of outpatients with moderate to severe depressive and anxiety symptoms. In addition to proving phenelzine's efficacy compared to placebo, they obtained evidence that suggested that, in this group of patients, the less endogenously and more atypically depressed patients obtained the greatest benefit from phenelzine (Nies et al. 1975). The investigators interpreted this finding to be in accord with West and Dally's (1959) notion that patients with atypical forms of depression are particularly likely to respond to MAOIs. Features considered atypical in this series of studies included anxiety, reverse vegetative signs, and mood reactivity. These were patients who, according to the traditional clinical wisdom, would be thought less likely to respond to standard tricyclic antidepressant treatment.

In a later study, Ravaris and colleagues (1980) compared phenelzine at 60 mg daily to a modest dose (150 mg) of amitriptyline. Once again, the population treated was made up of depressive outpatients, some with more endogenous features and some with less. Their expectation was that the more atypically (less endogenously) depressed patients would respond better to phenelzine and that the more endogenously depressed patients would do better on amitriptyline. They found that phenelzine and amitriptyline, overall, were about equal in efficacy. However, they found that phenelzine produced a greater reduction in anxiety than did amitriptyline. Later analyses (Nies 1984) revealed that higher pretreatment anxiety predicted a better response to phenelzine than to amitriptyline and that patients with panic attack might be especially likely to respond (see Table 4-3). In the most recent compilation of data from this study (Robinson et al. 1985), the investigators reported that patients with panic attacks responded at higher rates to phenelzine than to amitriptyline; however, atypical depression (defined according to Liebowitz

Table 4-2. Studies supporting efficacy of MAOIs in depressive subgroups

Study	Sample	Design	Treatment[a]	Result
Robinson et al. 1973	87 outpatients with depression	Double-blind 6 weeks	Phenelzine (59 mg) vs. placebo	Most marked improvement in anxiety, fatigue, phobic symptoms
Ravaris et al. 1976	62 outpatients with depression and anxiety	Double-blind 6 weeks	Phenelzine (60 mg) vs. phenelzine (30 mg) vs. placebo	Phenelzine 60 mg > phenelzine 30 mg = placebo
Ravaris et al. 1980	105 outpatients with depression and anxiety	Double-blind 6 weeks	Phenelzine (60 mg) vs. amitriptyline (150 mg)	Overall phenelzine = amitriptyline; suggests nonendogenous patients respond better to MAOI
Nies 1984	Further analyses of above data	—	—	Anxiety symptoms predict better response to phenelzine
Robinson et al. 1985	169 outpatients with various depressive syndromes (including 105 reported in Ravaris et al. 1980)	Double-blind 6 weeks	Phenelzine (60 mg) vs. amitriptyline (150 mg)	Overall comparable efficacy; better MAOI response in patients with panic

Paykel et al. 1979	64 in-, out-, and day-patients with depression	Open 4 weeks	Phenelzine (45–60 mg)	Better response in outpatients and in atypical, less severe, anxious, and hostile patients
Paykel et al. 1982	131 outpatients with depression, variably anxious	Double-blind 6 weeks	Phenelzine (1 mg/kg) vs. amitriptyline (2.5 mg/kg) vs. placebo	Weak tendency for better response to phenelzine in more anxious patients
Rowan et al. 1982	As above	As above	As above	As above
Liebowitz et al. 1988	119 outpatients with atypical depression	Double-blind 6–12 weeks	Phenelzine (73 mg) vs. imipramine (265 mg) vs. placebo	Phenelzine better than imipramine, especially in panic and hysteroid dysphoric patients

[a]Dosage refers to mean prescribed dosage, where provided, or to dosage range.
Source. Reprinted from Devlin and Walsh 1990, pp. 79–80, with permission from American Psychiatric Press, Inc.

and colleagues as outlined below) did not predict a preferential response to phenelzine.

In a similarly designed series of studies, Paykel and colleagues (1979) initially studied a mixed group of depressed inpatients and outpatients in order to identify clinical predictors of response to a 4-week trial of phenelzine. The strongest predictors of response to phenelzine were outpatient status; greater degree of atypicality using the criteria of Robinson, Nies, and others outlined above; milder depression; and presence of anxiety, hostility, and agitation. These investigators (Paykel et al. 1982; Rowan et al. 1982) went on to

Table 4-3. Predictors of phenelzine vs. amitriptyline response

Predictor subgroup	Phenelzine	Amitriptyline	Significance level
	Percent improvement in score		
Patients with high somatic anxiety[a]	$(N = 37)$	$(N = 28)$	
17-item HAM-D	52 ± 4	49 ± 5	NS
SDI total anxiety	60 ± 5	44 ± 2	.02
SDI total depression	69 ± 5	58 ± 5	.04
Patients with low somatic anxiety[b]	$(N = 49)$	$(N = 55)$	
17-item HAM-D	40 ± 4	52 ± 3	.04
SDI total anxiety	51 ± 4	48 ± 4	NS
SDI total depression	60 ± 5	58 ± 5	NS
Patients with panic episodes[c]	$(N = 24)$	$(N = 22)$	
Total symptoms	64 ± 4	41 ± 7	.06
Depression	68 ± 5	49 ± 7	.05
Anxiety	69 ± 5	45 ± 6	.007
	Proportion of patients improved		
Patients with high hysteroid dysphoria[d]			
Global improvement	9/9 = 100%	3/5 = 60%	.05
Patients with low hysteroid dysphoria[e]			
Global improvement	11/14 = 80%	15/19 = 80%	NS

Notes. HAM-D is the Hamilton Rating Scale for Depression (Hamilton 1960). SDI is the Structured Depression Interview of these authors (Nies et al. 1975). SCL-90 is the 90-item Symptom Check List (Derogatis et al. 1973).
[a]SDI ≥ 12. [b]SDI < 12. [c]According to SCL-90. [d]Hysteroid Dysphoria Scale (Liebowitz) ≥ 13. [e]Hysteroid Dysphoria Scale (Liebowitz) < 13.
Source. Adapted from Nies 1984.

compare responses to phenelzine versus amitriptyline in a heterogeneous collection of outpatients with depression. They found that phenelzine and amitriptyline were quite similar, and both were superior to placebo in relieving depression in this group. Anxiety symptoms seemed to respond preferentially to phenelzine compared to amitriptyline, suggesting that the presence of anxiety might predict a favorable MAOI response. However, these differences were relatively slight, and the investigators concluded "that the two classes of antidepressants affect similar clinical subgroups within the outpatient depressive spectrum with only relatively weak differences" (Paykel et al. 1982, p. 1041). In sum, the comparative studies of the Robinson and Paykel groups, although hinting at a subgroup of patients who might respond preferentially to MAOIs compared to tricyclic antidepressants, were less effective in documenting the existence of such a subgroup than the investigators may have imagined when the studies were initiated.

Most recently, Georgotas and colleagues (1987a, 1987b) reported on a series of elderly patients with Research Diagnostic Criteria (RDC) (Spitzer et al. 1978) major depression who received nortriptyline, phenelzine, or placebo in a double-blind fashion. Although, as expected, both active medications were superior to placebo, the authors were unable to identify particular symptoms or subtypes of depression that responded preferentially to phenelzine.

The existence of a subgroup of patients particularly responsive to MAOIs was also addressed with a fundamentally different strategy by Liebowitz and colleagues (1988). Rather than administering antidepressants to a heterogeneous collection of depressed patients and measuring response in various subgroups, these investigators selected for their study only patients who met criteria for atypical depression. These criteria included the presence of RDC major, minor, or intermittent depression; mood reactivity; and at least two of the following four symptoms: 1) increased appetite, 2) oversleeping, 3) severe fatigue, and 4) rejection sensitivity. Thus, the study focused on one particular type of depression and then compared the effect of an MAOI (phenelzine) to that of a tricyclic antidepressant (imipramine) and to placebo. The recently published results in a group of 119 atypically depressed patients are summarized in Figure 4-1.

This figure depicts the degree of global improvement in the three groups. In general, the phenelzine-treated patients showed a greater degree of improvement than the imipramine-treated patients. However, the imipramine-treated patients showed a greater response on many measures than the placebo group. An unexpected finding in this study was that the differential response to phenelzine was largely accounted for by patients with a history of spontaneous panic attacks and those who were thought to show hysteroid dysphoric features. An additional study by this group (Quitkin et al. 1988) found that patients with a partial atypical syndrome (those with mood reactivity and at least one of the associated symptoms outlined above) showed a comparable response pattern to those with the full atypical syndrome. This study was unable to replicate the finding that the superiority of phenelzine to imipramine was most marked in patients with a history of panic disorder. Nonetheless, these data are among the most convincing in demonstrating that a subgroup of patients with features like those originally described by West and Dally may be especially responsive to MAOIs. This, in turn, suggests that some such patients who may not respond to tricyclic antidepressants should

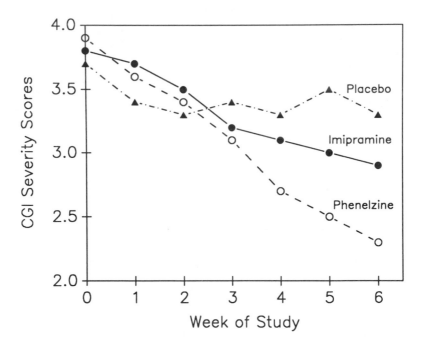

Figure 4-1. Responses of atypical depressive patients to phenelzine vs. imipramine vs. placebo. CGI = Clinical Global Impression. Reprinted from Liebowitz MR, Quitkin FM, Stewart JW, et al: Antidepressant specificity in atypical depression. Arch Gen Psychiatry 45:129–137, 1988. Reprinted with permission from the American Medical Association.

respond to MAOIs and, in this way, provides indirect evidence in support of the efficacy of MAOIs in at least a subgroup of tricyclic nonresponders.

STUDIES OF MAOIs IN TREATMENT NONRESPONDERS

The evidence that MAOIs are particularly effective in treating atypical depression, and the suggestion that some atypically depressed patients who fail standard treatment may respond to an MAOI, should not be taken to imply that the usefulness of MAOIs is limited to atypically depressed patients. In fact, more typically depressed patients, even those meeting criteria for melancholia, have been shown to respond to MAOI treatment (McGrath et al. 1984, 1986). Given the evidence that both atypical depression and melancholia may be amenable to MAOI treatment, an important clinical question concerns the likelihood that depressed patients of other types who have been unresponsive to previous treatments will improve with MAOIs. Several studies have attempted to evaluate more directly the response to treatment with MAOIs of depressed patients refractory to standard treatment. These studies are summarized in Table 4-4.

Although several of these studies suggest that MAOIs can be useful in the treatment of such patients, there are major flaws in most. Thus, some degree of caution is required in their interpretation. An early study by Himmelhoch and colleagues (1972) illustrates some of these problems. Their sample of 21 depressed patients with "bipolar characteristics" consisted of a mixed group of 13 bipolar and 8 unipolar depressive patients, all of whom had failed recent or past tricyclic antidepressant treatment. The study was conducted in an open fashion and was uncontrolled. All but one of the patients were already receiving lithium when tranylcypromine was added. Although 16 of 21 patients showed marked improvement on tranylcypromine, the methodologic flaws in this study render its interpretation difficult. An additional study (Price et al. 1985) in which an MAOI was added to the treatment regimen (in this case, tranylcypromine added to a preexisting regimen of lithium) reported 8 of 12 patients much improved. However, this study was limited by its uncontrolled design and by the heterogeneity of its refractory patients. Two of the 12 depressed subjects were bipolar and 6 were psychotic. The subject pool included patients who had been unresponsive to desipramine, bupropion, or adinazolam, the latter two groups also having previously been refractory to an unspecified tricyclic treatment.

Further open studies have examined the response of refractory

Table 4-4. Studies of MAOIs in refractory depression

Study	Sample	Design	Refractory to:[a]	Treatment[a]	Response
Himmelhoch et al. 1972	21 Depressed patients (13 bipolar, 11 unipolar)	Open; ? duration	Recent (11) or past (8) trials of TCA	Tranylcypromine (30 mg) and lithium	16/21 Markedly improved
Price et al. 1985	12 Depressed inpatients (6 psychotic, 2 bipolar)	Open with blind rater 4 or more weeks	Lithium added to desipramine or adinazolam or bupropion	Tranylcypromine (30–60 mg) and lithium	8/12 Much or very much improved
Georgotas et al. 1983	20 Depressed elderly patients	Open 2–7 weeks	Imipramine 150–300 mg or equivalent for 1–8 months	Phenelzine (15–75 mg)	11/20 Marked response
Nolen et al. 1985	26 Depressed patients	Open randomized crossover 4 weeks	Imipramine > 150 mg or equ. followed by trials of oxaprotiline, fluvoxamine, and sleep depriv.	Tranylcypromine (82 mg) or L-5HTP	MAOI: 7/14 responders L-5HTP: 0/12 responders

Study	Patients	Design/Duration	Antidepressant	MAOI/ECT	Results
Nolen et al. 1988	13 Depressed patients	Double blind randomized 4 weeks	Imipramine > 150 mg. or equ. followed by trials of oxaprotiline, fluvoxamine, and sleep depriv.	Tranylcypromine (71 mg) or nomifensine	MAOI: 4/8 responders nomifensine: 0/5 responders
Roose et al. 1986	14 Depressed nonpsychotic melancholic inpatients	Open ? duration	Imipramine or nortriptyline at therapeutic plasma levels	MAOI (phenelzine or tranylcypromine) or ECT	ECT: 9/10 responders MAOI: 5/5 responders (including 1 ECT failure)
McGrath et al. 1987	26 Outpatients atypical depression	Double-blind randomized crossover 6 weeks	Imipramine (200–300 mg) for 6 weeks	Phenelzine (60–90 mg) for 6 weeks	17/26 Responders
Thase and Kupfer 1988	32 Patients with recurrent depression	Open 6 weeks	Imipramine (257 mg) and interpersonal psychotherapy	Phenelzine (60 mg) or tranylcypromine (38.5 mg)	16/32 Responders

[a]Dosage refers to mean prescribed dosage, where provided, or to dosage range.
Source. Adapted from Devlin and Walsh 1990.

depressed patients to MAOIs used in lieu of, rather than in addition to, a previous regimen. Georgotas and colleagues (1983) studied a sample of 20 elderly (mean age 68) and for the most part endogenously (14 of 20) and chronically depressed patients who had failed treatment with various tricyclic antidepressants in the past. Their finding of marked improvement in 11 of 20 patients, although limited by the uncontrolled design of the study, nonetheless suggests that MAOIs may have a role in the treatment of elderly melancholic patients who are resistant to standard antidepressant treatment. An open study comparing the efficacy of L-5-hydroxytryptophan (L-5HTP) and tranylcypromine (Nolen et al. 1985) found a 50% response rate to tranylcypromine, significantly greater than the response to L-5HTP, which was virtually without effect. In addition to its open design, methodological problems in this study include the possible inadequacy of previous treatment, which was defined as >150 mg of imipramine or the equivalent followed by trials of several less orthodox treatments, and the failure to describe patient characteristics such as age and other diagnoses. A later study by the same group, with similar criteria for refractoriness but with a double-blind design, compared response to tranylcypromine with response to nomifensine. Once again, approximately half of the tranylcypromine group but none of the nomifensine group responded favorably (Nolen et al. 1988). Roose and colleagues (1986) studied a group of 17 inpatients with unipolar nondelusional depression who had failed tricyclic antidepressant treatment and were subsequently treated with MAOIs or electroconvulsive therapy (ECT) in an open fashion. All five of the patients who received MAOIs demonstrated a robust response. However, given the very small number of patients, the nonrandom assignment of patients to treatments, and the authors' failure to specify doses of MAOIs used, it is difficult to draw firm conclusions concerning the overall efficacy of MAOIs in refractory depression from this study.

Two recent studies that address the use of MAOIs in tricyclic antidepressant nonresponders deserve special notice. The first double-blind crossover study to address this issue was carried out by McGrath and colleagues (1987). These investigators studied a group of patients with atypical depression, defined according to criteria similar to those of Liebowitz and colleagues (1988). Of the 26 patients who failed treatment with imipramine, which they received either as their initial treatment or following failure on placebo, 17 responded to phenelzine. Conversely, 4 of 14 patients who had failed on phenelzine responded to treatment with imipramine. Because patients who had failed on either active drug were assigned to the other active treatment rather than to placebo, the response of tricyclic nonresponders to phenelzine was not rigorously controlled for the effects of time in this study. However, the difference between the response rates of the two crossover groups suggests that the robust response to phenelzine in atypically depressed tricyclic nonresponders is not simply an effect of time. The most recent study (Thase and Kupfer 1988) is an open trial of MAOI treatment in 32 patients with recurrent major depression who had failed adequate treatment with imipramine and interpersonal psychotherapy, and in some cases had failed to respond to augmentation with lithium, triiodothyronine (T3), or perphenazine. The response rate to MAOI treatment was 53%. Although this is an open trial, its relatively rigorous criteria for tricyclic nonresponse make it one of the more convincing pieces of evidence in support of the treatment of refractory depression with MAOIs.

The above studies address the treatment of refractory depression with standard doses of MAOIs; more recently, case reports have appeared describing the successful treatment of refractory depression with unusually high doses of MAOIs. Guze and colleagues (1987) have described the successful treatment of two refractory depressed patients, one with 60 mg bid of tranylcypromine added to a regimen of lithium and carbamazepine, and one with 100 mg bid of tranylcypromine added to an ongoing regimen of nortriptyline. Both patients had a favorable response with no major side effects, although the second patient discontinued the medication after a month due to dietary restrictions. The authors point out that these patients could have required high-dose treatment due to unusually rapid clearance; additional careful studies will be needed to answer such objections. Pearlman (1987) reported the case of a man with refractory depression and panic disorder who failed to respond to tranylcypromine at 50 mg/day with documented 90% platelet MAO inhibition at a lower dose, but who improved when his dosage reached 50 mg bid. Finally, Amsterdam and Berwish (1988) reported that four of seven patients who had failed to respond to at least three treatments for depression subsequently responded to high dose tranylcypromine, with responders receiving daily dosages of 90 to 130 mg. Although such reports are intriguing, controlled studies, preferably with some form of pharmacokinetic monitoring, will be required to establish whether treatment with high-dose MAOI is a safe and efficacious treatment option for refractory patients.

COMBINED MAOI AND TRICYCLIC TREATMENT

The treatment of depressed patients with a combination of a tricyclic antidepressant and an MAOI has been the subject of much controversy. It was well summarized by White and Simpson (1981) but has received few careful studies over the past three decades. Even fewer studies have specifically dealt with the use of this form of treatment in patients who have been refractory to other treatments. The literature to date (see Table 4-5) on combined treatment in refractory patients consists of several case reports, clinical series reports, and clinicians' testimonials; one prospective open study; and one randomized, controlled but nonblind study. Representative of the uncontrolled studies is an early clinical series reported by Gander (1965) that included 90 patients who had failed at least one treatment during the current episode. Detailed information concerning the adequacy of previous treatments is not provided. Patients received either amitriptyline, nortriptyline, imipramine, or desipramine in combination with phenelzine, iproniazid, or isocarboxazid, with both medications being given at relatively low dosage. Although a majority of patients showed complete recovery or considerable improvement, some caution is needed in the interpretation of this and other such studies due to their open, uncontrolled design and the possible inadequacy of the previous medication trials to which patients were unresponsive. In fact, it has been observed that many purportedly refractory patients who are included in studies such as these recover when tried on MAOI alone (White and Simpson 1981). A prospective open study of combined treatment with moderately low doses of phenelzine (45 mg) and very low doses of amitriptyline (75 mg) reported improvement in 9 of 12 patients (Sethna 1974). The patients whose clinical features were of the atypical variety described above had all failed treatment with MAOIs, tricyclic antidepressants, and ECT. Although suggestive of a role for combined treatment and intriguing in its description of the patients who were refractory to prior treatments but responsive to combined treatments, this study's uncontrolled design is an important limitation. Davidson and colleagues (1978) studied, in a randomized, controlled but nonblind fashion, a heterogeneous group of 17 depressed patients, 9 of whom were psychotic, who had failed "conventional psychotropic drugs in clinically adequate doses" (p. 639). Patients received either combined phenelzine (mean dose 34 mg) and amitriptyline (mean dose 71 mg) or bilateral ECT. The authors reported that ECT was superior to the combined drug treatment, especially in psychotic depressive patients. Although this study confirms the efficacy of ECT in delusional depression, it does not allow any clear conclusions regarding combined treatment due to high rate of psychosis in the sample, relatively low dose, and nonblind nature of the study.

Although the efficacy of combined tricyclic and MAOI treatment in refractory depression has not yet been established, the above studies have yielded some important information concerning the safety of this form of treatment. It appears that most serious adverse reactions, which are characterized by hyperpyrexia, hypertonicity, and delirium rather than hypertension, occur when a tricyclic is added to an ongoing regimen of an MAOI or when one MAOI is replaced by another without an adequate washout period. Most clinicians have employed relatively low doses of tricyclic and MAOI when using them in combination; the safety and efficacy of combining these two classes of drugs at full dose or high dose is as yet unknown.

Brief consideration should be given here to preliminary studies of MAOIs used in conjunction with agents other than tricyclics in the treatment of refractory depression. Feighner and colleagues (1985) compiled a series of 16 patients with major depression of at least 2 years' duration who had not responded to standard tricyclic, MAOI, or combined treatment or who could not tolerate MAOIs due to hypotension. These patients were treated with the direct stimulants d-amphetamine or methylphenidate in combination with an MAOI and, in some cases, a tricyclic. Several of these patients showed distinct improvement, and there were no hypertensive or hyperthermic crises, although there have been case reports of fatalities when high doses of these medications are used in combination (summarized in Feighner et al. 1985). In addition, the authors state that, in their experience, some patients cannot tolerate this combination due to elevated blood pressure. Further studies will be required to confirm the utility and safety of this treatment and to understand better the nature of the synergism between the different medications. Another combined treatment involving MAOIs that has been advocated in refractory depression is the use of alprazolam (Xanax) with an MAOI in treatment-refractory patients with both depression and panic disorder who do not respond to an MAOI alone. Two case reports (Deicken 1987; Ries and Wittkowsky 1986) have described such patients, one of whom was considered to have an atypical depression. Both patients responded well to the combined treatments, one with relatively low doses of both medications and one with more standard doses. Other combined treatments involving MAOIs, including augmentation with lithium or thyroid, are covered elsewhere in this volume.

CONCLUSION

In our view, based on the group of studies of MAOIs in atypical depression described above, there is good reason to believe that treatment with MAOIs is superior to treatment with tricyclic antidepressants in a subgroup of patients with atypical features, including

Table 4-5. Studies of combined MAOI and TCA treatment in refractory depression

Study	Sample	Design	Refractory to:[a]	Treatment[a]	Response
Gander 1965	90 Depressed outpatients	Open clinical series	MAOI or TCA (dose unspecified) or ECT or psychotherapy	Phenelzine (up to 45 mg) and amitriptyline (up to 150 mg)	49/90 Considerably improved or resolved
Dally 1965	8 Depressed outpatients	Open clinical series	Antidepressant drugs (dose unspecified) and/or ECT	Iproniazid (50–100 mg) or isocarboxazid (20–30 mg) plus amitriptyline (150 mg)	8/8 Improved
Winston 1971	20 Depressed outpatients	Open clinical series	ECT and, in 16/20, TCA trial and MAOI trial (doses unspecified)	Tranylcypromine (up to 30 mg) or isocarboxazid (20–30 mg) plus amitriptyline (up to 100 mg) or imipramine	14/20 Considerably improved or resolved

Ray 1973	73 Depressed inpatients, 11 depressed outpatients	Open clinical series	Psychotropic drugs (unspecified)	Tranylcypromine (20–30 mg) or phenelzine (30–45 mg) plus trimipramine or amitriptyline (25–150 mg) with preceding or concomitant ECT in most cases	52/84 Considerably improved
Sethna 1974	12 Depressed inpatients	Prospective consecutive series 16 months	Tricyclic antidepressant, MAOI (doses unspecified), and ECT	Phenelzine (45 mg) plus amitriptyline (50–75 mg)	10/12 Considerably improved
Davidson et al. 1978	17 Depressed patients (9 psychotic)	Randomized open with blind rater 5 weeks	"Conventional psychotropics in clinically adequate doses"	Phenelzine (34 mg) plus amitriptyline (71 mg) or bilateral ECT	ECT superior especially in psychotic patients

[a]Dosage refers to mean prescribed dosage, where provided, or to dosage range.

70

anxiety symptoms, mood reactivity, and reversed vegetative symptoms. This suggests that some patients with these features who are unresponsive to tricyclics may respond to MAOIs. The direct evidence in support of MAOI treatment of refractory depression is more meager. However, the studies reviewed herein suggest that MAOIs may be effective in some cases in which tricyclics have failed. Certain of these studies have begun to define the characteristics of patients who are likely to respond to MAOIs after having failed tricyclics. There is a need at this point for further double-blind, controlled studies of MAOI treatment in various well-defined groups of depressed patients who have not responded to tricyclic antidepressant treatment given in adequate dose and duration, and who preferably have failed lithium-augmented tricyclic treatment as well. Such studies will provide the most useful information for clinicians who are faced with the option of using MAOIs, with their sometimes problematic side effects, in these treatment-refractory patients.

REFERENCES

Amsterdam JD, Berwish NJ: High dose tranylcypromine therapy for refractory depression. Pharmacopsychiatry 22:21–25, 1989

Dally PJ: Combining the antidepressant drugs (letter). Br Med J 1:384, 1965

Davidson J, McLeod M, Law-Yone B, et al: A comparison of electroconvulsive therapy and combined phenelzine-amitriptyline in refractory depression. Arch Gen Psychiatry 35:639–642, 1978

Deicken RF: Combined alprazolam and phenelzine treatment of refractory depression with panic attacks. Biol Psychiatry 22:762–766, 1987

Derogatis LR, Lipman RS, Covi L: SCL-90: an outpatient psychiatric rating scale. Psychopharmacol Bull 9:13–28, 1973

Devlin MJ, Walsh BT: Use of monoamine oxidase inhibitors in refractory depression, in American Psychiatric Press Review of Psychiatry, Vol 9. Edited by Tasman A, Goldfinger SM, Kaufmann CA. Washington, DC, American Psychiatric Press, 1990, pp 74–90

Feighner JP, Herbstein J, Damlouji N: Combined MAOI, TCA, and direct stimulant therapy of treatment-resistant depression. J Clin Psychiatry 46:206–209, 1985

Gander DR: Treatment of depressive illnesses with combined antidepressants. Lancet 1:107–109, 1965

Georgotas A, Friedman E, McCarthy M, et al: Resistant geriatric depressions and therapeutic response to monoamine oxidase inhibitors. Biol Psychiatry 18:195–205, 1983

Georgotas A, McCue RE, Friedman E, et al: Response of depressive symptoms to nortriptyline, phenelzine, and placebo. Br J Psychiatry 151:102–106, 1987a

Georgotas A, McCue RE, Cooper T, et al: Clinical predictors for response to antidepressants in elderly patients. Biol Psychiatry 22:733–740, 1987b

Guze BH, Baxter LR, Rego J: Refractory depression treated with high doses of a monoamine oxidase inhibitor. J Clin Psychiatry 48:31–32, 1987

Himmelhoch JM, Detre T, Kupfer DJ, et al: Treatment of previously intractable depressions with tranylcypromine and lithium. J Nerv Ment Dis 155:216–220, 1972

Liebowitz MR, Quitkin FM, Stewart JW, et al: Antidepressant specificity in atypical depression. Arch Gen Psychiatry 45:129–137, 1988

McGrath PJ, Quitkin FM, Harrison W, et al: Treatment of melancholia with tranylcypromine. Am J Psychiatry 141:288–289, 1984

McGrath PJ, Stewart JW, Harrison W, et al: Phenelzine treatment of melancholia. J Clin Psychiatry 47:420–422, 1986

McGrath PJ, Stewart JW, Harrison W, et al: Treatment of tricyclic refractory depression with a monoamine oxidase inhibitor antidepressant. Psychopharmacol Bull 23:169–172, 1987

Nies A: Differential response patterns to MAO inhibitors and tricyclics. J Clin Psychiatry 45:70–77, 1984

Nies A, Robinson DS, Lamborn KR, et al: The efficacy of the monoamine oxidase inhibitor, phenelzine: dose effects and prediction of response, in Neuropsychopharmacology. Edited by Boissier JR, Hippius H, Pichot P. Amsterdam, Excerpta Medica, 1975, pp 765–770

Nolen WA, van de Putte JJ, Dijken WA, et al: L-5HTP in depression resistant to re-uptake inhibitors: an open comparative study with tranylcypromine. Br J Psychiatry 147:16–22, 1985

Nolen WA, van de Putte JJ, Dijken WA, et al: Treatment strategy in depression, II: MAO inhibitors in depression resistant to cyclic antidepressants: two controlled crossover studies with tranylcypromine versus L-5-hydroxytryptophan and nomifensine. Acta Psychiatr Scand 78:676–683, 1988

Paykel ES, Parker RR, Penrose RJJ, et al: Depressive classification and prediction of response to phenelzine. Br J Psychiatry 134:572–581, 1979

Paykel ES, Rowan PR, Parker RR, et al: Response to phenelzine and amitriptyline in subtypes of outpatient depression. Arch Gen Psychiatry 39:1041–1049, 1982

Pearlman C: High-dosage tranylcypromine in refractory depression. J Clin Psychiatry 48:424–425, 1987

Price LH, Charney DS, Heninger GR: Efficacy of lithium-tranylcypromine treatment in refractory depression. Am J Psychiatry 142:619–623, 1985

Quitkin FM, Stewart JW, McGrath PJ, et al: Phenelzine versus imipramine in the treatment of probable atypical depression: defining syndrome boundaries of selective MAOI responders. Am J Psychiatry 145:306–311, 1988

Ravaris CL, Nies A, Robinson DS, et al: A multiple-dose, controlled study of phenelzine in depression-anxiety states. Arch Gen Psychiatry 33:347–350, 1976

Ravaris CL, Robinson DS, Ives JO, et al: Phenelzine and amitriptyline in the treatment of depression: a comparison of present and past studies. Arch Gen Psychiatry 37:1075–1080, 1980

Ray I: Combinations of antidepressant drugs in the treatment of depressive illness. Can Psychiatr Assoc J 18:399–402, 1973

Ries RK, Wittkowsky AK: Synergistic action of alprazolam with tranyl-cypromine in drug-resistant atypical depression with panic attacks. Biol Psychiatry 21:519–521, 1986

Robinson DS, Nies A, Ravaris CL, et al: The monoamine oxidase inhibitor, phenelzine, in the treatment of depressive-anxiety states: a controlled clinical trial. Arch Gen Psychiatry 29:407–413, 1973

Robinson DS, Kayser A, Corcella J, et al: Panic attacks in outpatients with depression: response to antidepressant treatment. Psychopharmacol Bull 21:562–567, 1985

Roose SP, Glassman AH, Walsh BT, et al: Tricyclic nonresponders: phenomenology and treatment. Am J Psychiatry 143:345–348, 1986

Rowan PR, Paykel ES, Parker RR: Phenelzine and amitriptyline: effects on symptoms of neurotic depression. Br J Psychiatry 140:475–483, 1982

Sethna ER: A study of refractory cases of depressive illnesses and their response to combined antidepressant treatment. Br J Psychiatry 124:265–272, 1974

Spitzer RL, Endicott J, Robins E: Research Diagnostic Criteria: rationale and reliability. Arch Gen Psychiatry 35:773–783, 1978

Thase ME, Kupfer DJ: MAOI treatment of imipramine-resistant depression, in Syllabus and Scientific Proceedings, American Psychiatric Association 141st Annual Meeting, 1988

West ED, Dally PJ: Effects of iproniazid in depressive syndromes. Br Med J 2:1491–1494, 1959

White K, Simpson G: Combined MAOI-tricyclic antidepressant treatment: a reevaluation. J Clin Psychopharmacol 1:264–282, 1981

Winston F: Combined antidepressant therapy. Br J Psychiatry 118:301–304, 1971

Chapter 5

Carbamazepine and Other Antiepileptic Drugs in Refractory Depression

David Kahn, M.D.

Chapter 5

Carbamazepine and Other Antiepileptic Drugs in Refractory Depression

INTRODUCTION

Antiepileptic drugs (AEDs), a diverse group of compounds with numerous actions in the central nervous system, have often been of interest in the treatment of depression. Prior to the introduction of phenothiazines and tricyclic antidepressants (TCAs), barbiturates such as phenobarbital (PB) or amobarbital were employed in depression simply for their sedative effect, sometimes combined with a stimulant. Barbiturates were even used as an active control treatment in some early trials of TCAs (Wheatley 1969). Phenytoin (PHT) was investigated as an antidepressant soon after it became available in 1938 (e.g., Kalinowsky and Putnam 1943) and garnered a renewed following in the 1960s (Turner 1967; reviewed by Smith et al. 1988), though its utility was never proven systematically and remains uncertain. Klein (1967), reviewing the available data, remarked that PHT may have subtle antidepressant effects on occasional patients, "not to be compared with the massive effects seen with the phenothiazines or major antidepressants" (p. 563).

Carbamazepine (CBZ), in use internationally since 1963, was approved for epilepsy in the United States in 1974. Structurally related to TCAs and chlorpromazine, it has numerous physiological and biochemical effects but no single proven mechanism in epilepsy or affective disorders. It is neither a dopamine blocker nor a strong inhibitor of catecholamine reuptake (Post 1988). Following reports of mood improvement in neurological patients (reviewed by Dalby 1975), Okuma and colleagues (1973) in Japan found CBZ effective in acute mania. Ballenger and Post (1980) at the National Institute of Mental Health (NIMH) pioneered its use for bipolar illness in this country, building on neurobiological models of limbic system instability. Since then, a limited body of research suggests some efficacy in depression. Two more AEDs of interest in mania, clonazepam (CNZP), a high-potency benzodiazepine, and sodium valproate (VA) (valproic acid; n-dipropylacetic acid), a potentiator of GABA transmission (Bernasconi et al. 1984; Chapman et al. 1982), may also possess antidepressant activity (Kishimoto et al. 1988; McElroy et al. 1987).

The two remaining AEDs commonly used in the United States, primidone (PMD) and ethosuximide (ESX), have not been studied for psychotropic potential. ESX, in fact, may produce psychosis as a side effect (Dreifuss 1982). Though often prescribed for affective disorders (in general medical practice), benzodiazepines available in the United States other than CNZP will not be considered in this review as they are not useful AEDs except in status epilepticus. Novel 1,5-benzodiazepines such as clobazam, used in Europe, are potent AEDs (Swinyard 1982) but have not been evaluated in depression.

This chapter will focus primarily on CBZ, the only AED extensively studied in depression. Though a detailed discussion of possible mechanisms would be too lengthy, the heterogeneity of actions among AEDs will be explored briefly for implications in understanding potential biological subtypes of refractory depression. Finally, new directions in epilepsy drug research that may hold promise for depression and other psychiatric illnesses will be reviewed.

A word about nomenclature: the Epilepsy Branch of the National Institute of Neurological Disorders and Stroke has adopted the term AED for a drug that has been approved for treating seizures in humans, and the term anticonvulsant drug (ACD) for a compound thus far shown only to inhibit experimental convulsions in animals. This distinction would also be useful in the growing psychiatric literature on the subject.

CARBAMAZEPINE

Efficacy Studies in Acute Depression

Table 5-1 summarizes data from the major available studies of CBZ in acute depression other than single case reports; the latter are described below in the text. Most studies were small and uncontrolled or naturalistic; several focused on bipolar mania but included depressed patients who have been extracted for the table. Shown also are two small studies comparing CBZ with TCAs.

Post and colleagues (1986b) at NIMH performed the only placebo-controlled, double-blind study in patients said to be refractory. Post and associates (1983) and the Kishimoto group (1983) both initially found that during maintenance treatment of bipolar

Table 5-1. Acute trials of carbamazepine in depression grouped by type of design

Source	Design	Diagnosis	Positive response	Percentage
Post et al. 1986b	Blind vs. PLA	24 BP* 11 UP*	15 (10 mkd) 5 (2 mkd)	63 45
Cowdrie and Gardner 1988	Blind vs. PLA, TRA, ALP, or TFP	15 Borderline in CBZ group	Groups: CBZ = TRA, > PLA, ALP, TFP on depression scores, only to observers	NA
Okuma et al. 1973 and Okuma 1984	Open	9 BP*	3 (1 sl, 2 mkd)	33
Folks et al. 1982	Open**	2 BP* 2 Organic*	1 sl 2 mkd	50 100
Wunderlich et al. 1983	Open	5 BP 8 UP	11 mkd (no break-down of UP vs. BP)	85
Kwamie et al. 1984	Open**	3 BP* 1 UP*	3 (1 sl, 2 mod) 1 sl	100
Prasad 1985	Open	12 UP*	11 mkd	92
Neumann et al. 1984	Open vs. TRI	10 Unknown	5 on CBZ = 5 on TRI, all mkd	NA
Sethi and Tiwari 1984	Open vs. IMI	10 UP	5 on CBZ mod 5 on IMI mkd	NA

Note. Includes all reports of more than one patient. Single case studies described in text. Percentage of positive response includes all responders regardless of degree. BP = bipolar. UP = unipolar. * = refractory to various prior treatments. ** = other medications used concomitantly. PLA = placebo. ALP = alprazolam. TFP = trifluoperazine. TRA = tranylcypromine. CBZ = carbamazepine. TRI = trimipramine. IMI = imipramine. sl = slight. mod = moderate. mkd = marked. NA = not available.

patients, CBZ was nearly as protective against recurrence of depression as mania, leading to the acute study of depression.

The NIMH group reported on 35 inpatients with bipolar (24) or unipolar (11) depression. All were "relatively treatment resistant" to unspecified prior regimens. Twelve more patients have since been studied with unpublished results (Ballenger 1988a). Although schizoaffective patients were excluded, the authors did not mention whether any patients had delusional depression. No patient had a neurological disease, although some had mild EEG abnormalities.

After a long placebo period with no spontaneous remissions, all patients received CBZ alone in double-blind fashion for 6 weeks, followed by discontinuation with placebo resubstitution. Overall, 20 of 35 patients (57%) improved to some degree, 12 (34%) markedly, and the remainder mildly. Response was noticeable after 1 week, especially for sleep disturbance, and maximal by 4 to 6 weeks. The time course was similar to that seen with conventional antidepressants. Upon discontinuation, 60% of the marked responders relapsed, compared with only 21% of the mild responders.

A number of clinical and biological variables were monitored prospectively and then correlated with response (Table 5-2). Among the predictors of positive response, responders tended to be more severely depressed at baseline, especially the subgroup of marked responders. Bipolar patients were slightly more likely to respond than unipolar patients, although dramatic improvements were seen in some unipolar patients. Responders were significantly more likely than nonresponders to have had more prior hospitalizations for mania (3 vs. 0.5), to be rapid cyclers (2.9 vs. 1 episode per year), and to have fewer lifetime weeks of depression (138 vs. 238). Age, sex, family history, agitation versus retardation, and presence of minor EEG abnormalities were not predictive. Other prospective variables are summarized in Table 5-2.

During treatment, neither plasma levels (range: 3–12.5 mcg/ml) nor cerebrospinal fluid (CSF) levels of CBZ correlated with dose (average 1070 mg/day) or outcome, although CSF levels of the 10,11-epoxide metabolite (an active AED used outside the United States) did appear predictive (Post et al. 1984b). Motor activity increased more in responders, and no patients were sedated (Joffe et al. 1987). Of interest, all patients showed declines in serum total and free thyroxine (T_4), with the greatest fall in responders. Changes in other measures—hematological, electrolyte, and neuroendocrine— did not differ between groups. Rash (11%) was the only major adverse reaction.

The NIMH report remains the basis for prescribing CBZ for acute treatment of depression. The only serious criticism that can be made is that the outcome measure used, a nursing global rating from the Bunney-Hamburg scale (Bunney and Hamburg 1963), is not nearly as detailed as more widely used structured scales such as the Hamilton Depression Rating Scale (although the investigators' impression was that their Bunney-Hamburg scoring would have correlated well with Hamilton scores). As to its applicability to refractory patients, the absence of detailed medication histories is of concern; one must accept the investigators' assertion that patients referred to NIMH had had good trials of other drugs.

The only other double-blind, placebo-controlled study concerned borderline personality disorder rather than major depression. However, because this group often presents with depression, the study deserves note here. Cowdrie and Gardner (1988) compared four groups, each with 12 to 15 patients. Groups received CBZ, alprazolam, the neuroleptic trifluoperazine, or the monoamine

Table 5-2. Potential predictors and nonpredictors of acute antidepressant response to carbamazepine

Predictors of positive response	Nonpredictors of positive response
More severely depressed	Age
Rapid cycling	Sex
More previous hospitalization for mania	EEG
	Family history
Fewer prior weeks of depression (lifetime)	Duration of current episode
Bipolar depressions more than unipolar	Agitation vs. retardation[b]
Positive response to sleep deprivation	CSF GABA, MHPG, NE, SOM
Higher CSF opiate binding activity	
Lower CSF levels of cyclic GMP and HVA[a]	

Note. GABA = gamma-aminobutyric acid. GMP = guanosine monophosphate. HVA = homovanillic acid. MHPG = 3-methoxy-4-hydroxyphenylethyleneglycol. NE = norepinephrine. SOM = somatostatin.
[a]Post et al. 1986a. [b]Joffe et al. 1987.
Source. Adapted from Ballenger, 1988a. Reprinted with the permission of Physicians Postgraduate Press.

oxidase inhibitor (MAOI) tranylcypromine, each in placebo cross-over. As a group, the 15 patients who received CBZ improved significantly in physicians' global ratings of depression, anxiety, anger, impulsivity, rejection sensitivity, and suicidality, comparable to changes seen with tranylcypromine and superior to alprazolam, trifluoperazine, or placebo. However, patient ratings indicated improvement only on tranylcypromine. This result was interpreted to suggest that CBZ failed to lift subjective feelings of depression in this chronic group, but helped in observable mood and behavior.

The remaining studies shown in Table 5-1 vary greatly in design and quality. All of these were open; several provided only sketchy details concerning prior treatments and outcome measures. Results between bipolar and unipolar patients were not always separated.

There have been a few well-detailed, single-case reports. Barker and Eccleston (1984) described a 60-year-old woman with unipolar depression who responded to CBZ alone and remained well after twice relapsing on different MAOIs. Schaffer et al. (1985) reported a case of delusional depression refractory to tricyclics and MAOIs each with neuroleptics and lithium, and responsive briskly to CBZ alone. Length of follow-up was brief, however. Nurnberg and Finkel (1985) treated depression without precipitating mania by adding CBZ to lithium in a 31-year-old bipolar female with a history of tricyclic manic switching. There is only one case of mania due to CBZ, which occurred in a bipolar child (Reiss and O'Donnell 1984).

CBZ may be helpful in organic affective syndromes presenting as depression. Mood improves in many seizure patients taking CBZ (Dalby 1975; Trimble 1988). Indeed, the Okuma group's initial study (1973) stated that improvement in "symptomatic depression" secondary to epilepsy was the basis for trying CBZ in purely psychiatric patients. CBZ may, however, make some neurological patients worse. Reiss and O'Donnell (1984) described a depressed epileptic boy who became manic on CBZ but not PHT. The rare phenomenon of "forced normalization" has been seen with several AEDs including CBZ (Pakalnis et al. 1987). In this situation, normalization of the EEG with seizure control is accompanied by *de novo* psychosis, at times with affective symptoms, that may respond to the addition of a neuroleptic. Psychosis occurring only during periods of spontaneous EEG normalization has been seen in drug-free epileptics (Schiffer 1987). This suggests that the problem is not drug toxicity, but rather a biochemical antagonism between epilepsy and psychosis in these particular patients. Thus, there may be a small subset of patients who present with refractory intermittent depression and underlying neurologic disease who become paradoxically worse on CBZ.

A statistically meaningful meta-analysis of all the above reports is impossible due to their great diversity. Excluding single cases and neurological and borderline patients, these studies show some response in 50 of 75 patients, or 67%. A more realistic and conservative consensus in recent reviews (105 patients by Stromgren and Boller 1985 [they appear to have counted some studies more than once]; 54 patients by Kravitz and Fawcett 1987; Ballenger 1988a) is that when stringent criteria are applied, half the patients showed some improvement, with one third experiencing marked response or recovery. This is lower than the efficacy rates reported for CBZ in mania.

Not all studies included treatment-refractory cases, making it hard to generalize to this population. The study by Post and colleagues (1986b) gives the most relevant picture. However, the trend toward more robust responses in those studies that may not have rigidly excluded refractory cases (Prasad 1985; Wunderlich et al. 1983), as well as response rates comparable to TCAs in two studies (Neumann et al. 1984; Sethi and Tiwari 1984), if valid, may indicate that CBZ has a spectrum of efficacy similar to that of TCAs, particularly for unipolar patients. This might explain the lower rates reported by Post and associates (1986b), Okuma and colleagues (1973), and Okuma (1984), whose patients had had more prior treatment, as well as the poor long-term outcomes in refractory patients suggested in a recent study described below (Frankenburg et al. 1988).

Efficacy Studies in Long-Term Treatment

Long-term maintenance or prophylactic treatment with CBZ appears useful in most studies, although, again, it is not always clear whether the patient who has relapsed on other treatments will do better with CBZ. A general observation is that CBZ is somewhat less effective in preventing depression than mania.

Despite poor acute antidepressant response to CBZ in the patients followed by Okuma and colleagues (1973), in open follow-up over periods of up to 3 years, 14 of 27 patients (52%) were free of depression, somewhat less favorable than the 74% protected from mania. Furthermore, 20% of patients without mania suffered depressive relapse, whereas no patients had only mania without depression. Lithium nonresponders tended to respond more favorably to CBZ. In a longer follow-up study (Kishimoto et al. 1983) including these and other patients over a mean treatment period of more than 6 years preceded by a mean baseline period of 5 years, 75% of patients were protected against mania and 62% against depression, both improvements over baseline. Patients who continuously cycled during the baseline period showed the best responses.

In a 1-year controlled study of maintenance in 22 patients, more than half of the patients on CBZ were free of both depression and mania, compared with only about 20% on placebo for both phases (Okuma et al. 1981). Post and co-workers (1983) observed in seven of their original group of rapid cyclers a sharp and equal reduction in the severity and frequency of both mania and depression over an average period of 17 months (6 months to 4 years). The Placidi group (1986), collaborating with Akiskal, compared CBZ with lithium over a 3-year period in 83 recurrently ill patients with DSM-III (American Psychiatric Association 1980) affective, schizoaffective, or schizophreniform disorders who had not been selected for lithium resistance. Both drugs afforded similar protection, although there was some tendency for more depression in the CBZ group. Watkins and associates (1987) randomly assigned 37 patients, equally unipolar and bipolar, to lithium or CBZ following remission from an episode. Lithium-treated patients remained well an average of 15 months, compared to 10 months for CBZ, a significant difference. Breakdown by diagnosis or type of recurrence was not given.

Reviewing studies before 1985, Stromgren and Boller (1985) concluded that among 192 patients, 51% to 65% had a prophylactic effect against depression, depending on whether "slight" responses were counted. Kravitz and Fawcett (1987) calculated a 63% antidepressant prophylactic effect in their review of 78 cases. In both reviews, the rate of prophylaxis in depression was only slightly lower than the rate against mania; consistent predictive factors, such as prior lithium failure or bipolar diagnosis, could not be established. As in the acute studies, diversity of design and frequent absence of pretreatment information limit generalizability to patients known to be refractory to standard antidepressant prophylactic regimens. A particular gap in knowledge is an absence of comparison with tricyclics or MAOIs in unipolar patients.

Casting doubt on the long-term value of CBZ in the average clinician's practice is a recent report from Frankenburg and co-workers at McLean Hospital (1988). Of 50 patients, 65% with bipolar disorder and 13% with other disorders responded acutely to CBZ. All patients had had adequate trials of lithium or antidepressants, if indicated. However, over 3 to 4 years later, only 2 of the initial responders (out of 20 available), both bipolar, experienced clear benefit. Although such a study has clear limitations, it raises important concerns.

Thus, in maintenance and prophylactic treatment of refractory depression, the role of CBZ cannot be firmly established. The discrepancy between early research reports and later experience is difficult to reconcile. CBZ may be of value in bipolar patients, especially if rapidly or continuously cycling, who have failed on lithium. For the unipolar patient who has relapsed on tricyclics or MAOIs, there is scant evidence supporting the use of CBZ, although an occasional patient may unpredictably respond.

Clinical Guidelines

Side effects and toxicity. Although most studies report that CBZ is well tolerated, Frankenburg and associates (1988) reported that nearly one quarter of patients had to stop the medication within the first 2 months due to a variety of side effects that could not be attributed to other medications. This corresponds to the impression of the author and other colleagues on a general inpatient service. On the positive side, anticholinergic effects, a bane of TCAs, are rare with CBZ.

CBZ mainly affects the skin, liver, bone marrow, heart, hormones, and central nervous system. Estimates of rash are from 5% to 16% in the neurological and psychiatric literature (Pellock 1987; Warnock and Knesevich 1988). If essential, it may be safe to continue CBZ while treating the rash with dermatological consultation (Warnock and Knesevich 1988). Liver enzymes are transiently elevated in 5% to 10% of patients but are seldom a cause for concern (Pellock 1987).

Hematologic toxicity is differentiated into transient, benign leukopenia commonly seen over the first 4 weeks of treatment, and rare but potentially fatal agranulocytosis or aplastic anemia (Joffe et al. 1985a; Porter 1987). The former is not of concern as long as total white counts remain above 2,500/cu.mm to 3,000/cu.mm and neutrophils above 1,000/cu.mm to 1,500/cu.mm (Hart and Easton 1982, Joffe et al. 1985a; Porter 1987). If white counts fall below these parameters, cessation of CBZ is recommended, although reintroduction at a lower dose may be safe (Regan 1987). Platelet counts may also show benign falls, rarely serious unless platelets are clumped and destroyed in association with immunological hypersensitivity.

The frequency of hematologic monitoring is no longer rigidly specified by the Food and Drug Administration. Some sources advise repeated CBCs weekly for the first 2 to 3 months, and relatively frequently thereafter. The author's impression is that many neurologists who frequently use CBZ are much less strict. Indeed, agranulocytosis and aplastic anemia remain controversial, with some evidence that they are only marginally more common on CBZ than in the general population (Pellock 1987) and no more frequent than with chlorpromazine (Hart and Easton 1982). There is no evidence that frequent blood counts allow early detection of this sudden event.

Cardiac conduction disease may prompt the search for an alternative treatment to TCAs for the depressed patient. Unfortunately, CBZ must be used cautiously here because there have been several case reports of atrioventricular block and slow ventricular escape rhythm in patients with and without prior known cardiac disease (Beerman et al. 1975; Benassi et al. 1987; Durelli et al. 1985; Gasperetti 1987). These observations are confirmed by conduction studies in animals, which also show that CBZ is a type I antiarrhythmic, resembling quinidine and tricyclics in delaying phase 4 depolarization (Giardina et al 1979; Singh and Hauswirth 1974; Steiner et al. 1970). Orthostatic hypotension, common with tricyclics, is rare with CBZ (Post et al. 1986b).

Hormonally, CBZ reduces free and bound T_4 and triiodothyronine (T_3) levels and slightly raises thyroid-stimulating hormone (TSH). These effects are greatest in manic and depressed responders for unknown reasons. Clinical hypothyroidism is rare; the change in levels may reflect altered hepatic metabolism rather than dysfunction of the gland (Roy-Byrne et al. 1984). Testosterone may decline by the same mechanism and prolactin may rise, leading to male sexual dysfunction (Macphee et al. 1988). Decreased serum sodium is seen in up to one fourth of neurological and psychiatric patients, reflecting increased renal sensitivity to vasopressin (Yassa et al. 1987). Resulting symptomatic hyponatremia with confusion or lethargy may resemble depression. Elevated urinary free cortisol and dexamethasone escape occur, invalidating the dexamethasone suppression test in monitoring depression (Rubinow et al. 1984).

Central nervous system side effects are well documented in epileptic patients, who may experience increased seizures (especially absence), as well as a number of dose-related problems early in treatment, including drowsiness, ataxia, diplopia, nausea, and vomiting (Masland 1982; Porter 1987). Fewer cognitive difficulties occur with CBZ than with other AEDs (Trimble 1987), although comparison with standard psychotropic agents has not been made. A variety of mental status abnormalities have been described, some related to forced normalization of the EEG, as discussed earlier, but others more idiosyncratically tied to CBZ (Mathew 1988). CBZ does not appear especially more toxic in elderly patients (Hockings et al. 1986).

Overdose is a risk with any drug in a depressed population. Nine cases of CBZ overdose have been published (Leslie et al. 1983; Sullivan et al. 1981; Weaver et al. 1988), none fatal with ingestion of up to 20 g (about a 1-month supply). Prolonged coma and stupor, delirium, seizures, and ataxia are seen. Delayed gut absorption and saturation of conjugating enzymes may prolong symptoms; charcoal lavage or hemoperfusion are useful. Sinus tachycardia is seen unless there is complete heart block, in which case there will be bradycardia due to slow ventricular escape. Ventricular ectopy is rare. Neither physostigmine nor atropine reverse tachy- or brady- heart rates (Leslie et al. 1983; Sullivan et al. 1981), as these changes are not cholinergically mediated. Overdose with CBZ appears different from, and less dangerous than, that with TCAs in the limited numbers of patients seen.

Metabolism and drug interactions. CBZ induces proliferation of the microsomal cytochrome P-450 oxidase enzyme pathway in the liver, by which CBZ is initially metabolized itself. At the start of the treatment, its half-life is 30 to 40 hours; after several weeks this declines to 10 to 15 hours, requiring increasing doses to maintain a steady state concentration (Porter 1987). Other drugs oxidatively metabolized will be converted more rapidly when given concomitantly with CBZ. Several such interactions are of importance to psychiatrists treating refractory depression. Accelerated metabolism of TCAs may decrease the level of the parent compound, while simultaneously causing a build-up of unexcreted hydroxylated metabolites, not usually measured. The metabolites may be both therapeutically active and cardiotoxic. If metabolite levels are unavailable, ECGs should be more closely monitored (Baldessarini et al. 1988). Alprazolam and clonazepam concentrations are lowered enough to provoke reemergent anxiety or even withdrawal (Arana et al. 1988). Neuroleptic levels fall as well (Jann et al. 1985). The calcium blockers verapamil and nifedipine, which may be used in affective illness (Chapter 7) can elevate CBZ levels by competing for cytochrome P-450 (Beattie et al. 1988).

Idiosyncratic cases of central nervous system toxicity, perhaps unrelated to altered blood levels, have been reported for combinations of CBZ with lithium (Andrus 1984; Shukla et al. 1984), neuroleptics (Brayley and Yellowlees 1987; Kanter et al. 1984), and TCAs (Lesser 1984). The rarity of such reactions is encouraging. In fact, an unpublished study (Kramlinger and Post, cited in Ballenger 1988b) suggests that adding lithium potentiates antidepressant action in CBZ nonresponders, similar to some observations made for conventional antidepressants. CBZ has been used safely with tranylcypromine (Joffe et al. 1985b; Lydiard et al. 1987). The author has not observed hypertensive or hyperthermic reactions in combination with MAOIs, regardless of the order in which the two drugs were started (unpublished). The Physician's Desk Reference, however, warns against using CBZ with MAOIs.

As clinicians may wish to continue CBZ during a course of electroconvulsive therapy (ECT), potential interactions should be considered. Cantor (1986) described a successful course of ECT while continuing CBZ, although one might expect any AED to interfere with seizure elicitation. In the author's inpatient unit, if a patient needs to continue CBZ during ECT, either because of epilepsy or to prevent rapid cycling, dosage the evening before is lowered or held.

Summary and Recommendations

The clearest indications for CBZ derive from the 1986 NIMH study (Post et al. 1986b). The patient with severe but episodic depression, especially if bipolar and at risk for more rapid cycling with conventional antidepressants, may be the best candidate for receiving CBZ acutely and prophylactically. Treatment-refractory, chronically depressed unipolar patients are less likely to do well. There may be synergistic advantage to adding CBZ to an existing regimen, especially if it includes lithium, provided an eye is kept toward potential drug interactions. A 6-week trial is adequate.

Dosing usually begins with 100 mg or 200 mg bid, although administration of as little as 50 mg hs only may be adequate at the start if sedation is a problem. The dose may be increased as tolerated every few days; higher doses will be needed as hepatic enzymes are induced. More than 800 mg to 1,200 mg/day divided in two or three doses is rarely needed; much less may suffice. Blood levels are chiefly of value in preventing side effects; otherwise clinical response is the determinant of dose.

Prior to treatment, CBC, liver chemistries, and in older patients baseline ECG should be obtained. The CBC should be repeated every 1 to 2 weeks for the first 6 weeks and periodically thereafter. Unfortunately, bone marrow failure will declare itself abruptly and should be ruled out by emergency CBC at signs of fever, infection, petechiae, or unusual lethargy. Other tests may be repeated after a therapeutic dose is established. Blood levels of concomitantly administered psychotropic and other drugs should be monitored, or clinical manifestations of altered levels should be checked.

VALPROATE

Synthesized over a century ago, VA was discovered in the mid-1960s to be an ACD and has been used since then to treat most types of epilepsy. In the 1970s Lambert, a French neuropsychiatrist, described its efficacy against mania and, to a lesser extent, depression, in a large, open trial of about 300 patients with various diagnoses (reviewed in English by Lambert 1984). A retrospective report by McElroy and colleagues (1987) describing positive results in mania has spawned renewed interest. Two depressed patients mentioned in their survey showed no response. However, anecdotal experience suggests VA may occasionally produce gratifying responses in some depressed patients. Another report also describes rapid-cycling bipolar patients refractory to CBZ but responsive to VA (McElroy et al. 1988a).

The author has used VA for acute treatment in a small open series of nine patients with primary diagnoses of depression. Retrospective data were collected informally by chart review (Kahn and Low, unpublished). Three of the patients were unipolar and six were bipolar. Most had had well-documented prior treatments with both TCAs and MAOIs resulting in no or partial response, intolerance, or mania. Many had also received lithium, stimulants, thyroid, and/or neuroleptics.

Overall, three of the nine (2/3 unipolar, 1/6 bipolar) appeared to have unequivocal positive responses to VA. One of the unipolar responders relapsed when VA was stopped and recovered again when it was restarted. Improvement was seen over 1 to 3 weeks with blood levels greater than 50 mcg/ml.

Four of the nine patients, including one of the unipolar responders, had adverse reactions severe enough to warrant stopping the medication. One had thrombocytopenia on a combination of VA and chlorpromazine; one had sharply elevated liver enzymes but had had this reaction to numerous other medications as well; and two were oversedated, but they also were on numerous other medications.

In addition to the above nine patients with primary affective disorders, one patient with borderline personality disorder and atypical depression had no improvement on VA. Two patients with affective syndromes and demyelinating disease did well after failure on other medications. One had an acute syndrome resembling depression. The other, with preexisting bipolar disorder including annual depressions, has remained well on VA during 18 months of prophylaxis (Kahn et al. 1988; additional unpublished follow-up data).

Guidelines for the use of VA in psychiatry have been recently reviewed (McElroy et al. 1988b). It is generally well tolerated in neurological patients. Weight gain, hair loss, tremor, and sedation may be seen (Bourgeois et al. 1987; Brown 1988). The author's impression is that combination with usual doses of benzodiazepines or neuroleptics may be unusually sedating. A variety of gastrointestinal side effects are reportedly milder with the divalproex sodium (Depakote) formulation (Wilder et al. 1983). Platelet count may decrease in dose-related fashion (Sussman and McLain 1979).

Fatality due to liver failure has been of great concern but occurs almost exclusively in children, many with inborn errors of metabolism who are receiving other AEDs simultaneously. In the United States, there have been no incidents of fatal liver necrosis in adults receiving VA monotherapy. Toxic metabolites produced in the presence of microsomal enzyme-inducing AEDs such as CBZ appear responsible (Dreifuss et al. 1987; Rettie et al. 1987). VA itself does not induce liver enzymes (Oxley et al. 1978) and may raise the levels of some other drugs by either competitive protein binding or inhibition of metabolic pathways (Levy and Koch 1982).

The usual starting dosage is 250 mg two or three times daily, increased every few days to a total of 750 mg to 3,000 mg, aiming for blood levels of 50 mcg/ml to 100 mcg/ml.

Large-scale, controlled studies will be necessary to delineate the role of VA in refractory depression and to determine its profile of safety and efficacy in comparison to CBZ.

CLONAZEPAM

CNZP is the only benzodiazepine in the United States approved for ongoing treatment of seizures. It is used adjunctively in several types of seizures, primarily absence and myoclonic. In addition to having high affinity for the central type of benzodiazepine receptor, it also may increase the activity of serotonin (Chouinard 1987), although its exclusivity among benzodiazepines in this regard has not been shown. Preliminary evidence of efficacy in acute mania (Chouinard et al. 1983) led to several case reports of value for unipolar, bipolar, and organically related depression (Alvarez and Freinhar 1987; Jones and Chouinard 1985; Pande 1988; Zetin and Freedman 1986).

In the only careful, although uncontrolled study (Kishimoto et al. 1988), an average dose of 3.4 mg of CNZP was used to treat 27 bipolar and unipolar depressed patients. Moderate to marked improvement occurred in 21 of 25 completers (84%), although patients known to be drug resistant did slightly less well. Breakdown by diagnostic groups was not given. On a less sanguine note, some have noticed treatment-emergent depression in patients receiving CNZP and other benzodiazepines for anxiety disorders (reviewed by Pollack 1987). The author has found CNZP useful for initial symptomatic relief in depressed patients with agitation or severe anxiety, but only transient improvement in depressive symptoms. CNZP is thus of interest in refractory depression but is in need of further study.

MECHANISMS OF AEDs AND FUTURE DIRECTIONS

Research Challenges

The mechanisms by which AEDs help at least some depressed patients are of great interest: are they related to anticonvulsant mechanisms? Such knowledge would not only suggest more specific treatments but ultimately shed light on the etiology of depression as a whole, or of subtypes. However, it is a great leap from knowing some of the effects of a drug to identifying its mechanism in a particular disease, especially depression, whose etiology is unknown. For brevity, this section will not review the voluminous biochemical data concerning each AED, but will focus on a small number of observations relevant to categorizing AEDs.

Neuropsychiatric drug effects may be direct or indirect. Direct effects result almost immediately from interactions with specific receptors. Indirect effects may emerge acutely or chronically, resulting from activation of distal neuronal pathways or adaptive changes in membranes, receptors, or enzymes (Chapman et al. 1982). A further confound is the fact that many psychotropic drugs are "dirty," causing a plethora of direct effects, with indirect effects that geometrically cascade to the point where numerous systems are altered. Clearly, drugs of diverse classes may appear similar or different depending on whether an experiment is designed to measure direct or indirect effects, acutely or chronically.

Research into the mechanisms of AEDs and antidepressants is extremely difficult for these reasons, and results must be interpreted very cautiously. The finding that different types of drugs have similar clinical effects may not mean they work by the same mechanism, and the finding that a particular neurotransmitter system changes cannot be viewed in isolation as evidence that the change is curative. Furthermore, from the perspective of pathophysiology a disease like depression may have multiple etiological subtypes, and each subtype may be amenable to cure by multiple mechanisms.

Clinical Results and Mechanisms

As an example of how difficult it is to move backward from observations of efficacy to explanations of mechanism, one might consider the following illustration. Selected drugs from the apparently diverse classes of AEDs, TCAs, calcium channel blockers, and antiarrhythmics

overlap in anticonvulsant, thymoleptic, and antiarrhythmic properties. These classes share the ability to alter the function of excitable
membranes to varying degrees in varying organ systems, yet it is
premature to hypothesize a final common mechanistic pathway. The
following are specific examples of overlapping properties.

PHT and CBZ, in addition to effects on epilepsy and perhaps
mood, are both antiarrhythmics (Singh and Hauswirth 1974; Steiner
et al. 1970), although with different electrophysiological profiles.

Tricyclic antidepressants not only are antiarrhythmics (Giardina et
al. 1979), but also possess anticonvulsant properties in animals (Lange
et al. 1976; Reigel et al. 1986) and humans (Fromm et al. 1972, 1978;
Ojemann et al. 1983). As an aside, the common impression that
tricyclics lower seizure threshold at therapeutic doses (Edwards et al.
1986) is probably mistaken. In fact, tricyclics show a biphasic pattern,
becoming proconvulsive only at high doses in animals (Lange et al.
1976). Seizures in humans are associated with tricyclics at toxic levels
or rarely and idiosyncratically at higher therapeutic doses, similar to
AEDs (Decina et al. 1983).

Calcium blockers, in addition to vascular and cardiac effects, are
reported to stabilize mood, help movement disorders (Buck and
Havey 1988), and be anticonvulsant in animals (Vezzani et al. 1988)
and humans (Overweg et al. 1984; Sander and Shorvon 1988).
Different subtypes of this class, however, differ markedly in the types
of experimental seizures they block in animals (Vezzani et al. 1988).

The antiarrhythmic lidocaine, like tricyclics, is anticonvulsant at low
doses and proconvulsant at higher levels (Julien 1973). Mexiletine, a
congener of lidocaine, inhibits seizures in animals and may be mildly
antiepileptic in humans (Cereghino 1982). Although lidocaine can
produce psychosis, antiarrhythmics have not been evaluated for
beneficial psychotropic effects to the best of the author's knowledge.

Heterogeneous Mechanisms of AEDs

Before considering applications of epilepsy research to depression, it
is important to outline the heterogeneous nature of AEDs, as shown
by their varying spectra of efficacy in animals and humans. Epilepsy is
a term encompassing a wide range of clinical entities that result from
numerous proposed defects in either membrane structure or synaptic
networks (Delgado-Escueta et al. 1986), similar to the case for the
broad category of affective illnesses.

Historically, AEDs have been identified by two basic animal screen-
ing tests: 1) inhibition of convulsions from maximal electroshock
(MES) and 2) elevation of threshold for chemically induced seizures
by pentylenetetrazol (PTZ [Metrazol], also used by Meduna earlier

this century for convulsive therapy) (Fink 1984). Inhibition of MES indicates effect on spread of a seizure from a focus and correlates with clinical efficacy in humans against tonic-clonic seizures. Elevation of PTZ threshold appears to reflect processes in the initiation of a seizure and correlates with clinical efficacy in absence seizures (Swinyard 1982).

Available AEDs differ widely in these tests. PHT, CBZ, and primidone are effective only against MES and useful only for partial complex and generalized tonic-clonic seizures. PB, CNZP, and VA are effective in both tests; CNZP and VA are useful in both absence and convulsive seizures. ESX works only against PTZ and is used only to treat absence seizures (MacDonald and McLean 1986; Swinyard 1982).

The kindling model of epilepsy also illustrates the heterogeneity of AEDs. Kindling is a model of neuronal plasticity in which experience of frequent subthreshold stimulation alters neuronal function such that paroxysmal events become more frequent with less provocation over time (Post et al. 1984a). Albright and Burnham (1980) and Post and colleagues (1984a, 1986c) have identified the varying potencies of AEDs in preventing different phases of kindling that develop with various kinds of convulsive stimuli.

At the cellular and molecular levels, there are several theories of the mechanisms of AEDs. DeLorenzo (1988) suggests that the PTZ test is linked to the "central" benzodiazepine receptor and the gamma-aminobutyric acid (GABA-A) receptor that together in an allosteric complex regulate neuronal excitability by controlling chloride ion flux. The MES test is thought to reflect activity of the "peripheral," lower affinity benzodiazepine site, not affiliated with GABA-A receptors, that appears to be involved in calcium channel and calmodulin regulation.

Ferrendelli (1987) proposes that CBZ, PHT, VA, and primidone all inhibit MES by binding to specific sites on the inside of cell membranes regulating sodium channels, slowing reactivation after a stimulus.

Explaining the action of ESX in the PTZ test has been problematic for these models, as it neither alters the GABA-A/benzodiazepine receptor/chloride-ionophore complex (DeLorenzo 1988) nor affects cation transport (Ferrendelli 1987). It may act by enhancing dopaminergic output from the ventral tegmental nuclei (Mirski and Ferrendelli 1986), which could also explain its propensity to cause psychosis. Dopamine and other catecholamines have been suggested as endogenous anticonvulsants (Beas-Zarate et al. 1985; Schiffer 1987).

From Epilepsy Research to Psychiatry

The above caveats notwithstanding, the question of whether anti-depressant effects of AEDs are related to their anticonvulsant mechanisms is of great practical interest. If anticonvulsant mechanisms were related to antidepressant mechanisms, then animal models of epilepsy, which are readily available compared with animal models of depression, could be used to find new antidepressants and perhaps classify subtypes or stages of depression. This is essentially the strategy Post et al. (1984a) first employed in choosing to test CBZ in affective illness, based on the kindling model of epilepsy.

Post and colleagues (1984a, 1986c) proposed limbic system kindling as a model of the accelerating frequency of episodes in cyclic affective illness. They sought to correlate mood-stabilizing properties of AEDs, particularly CBZ, with potency in preventing the development of various stages of kindling. For example, in the rat, diazepam was found to be potent in preventing the development of amygdaloid kindling, whereas CBZ and PHT were not. However, after kindling had developed, CBZ was the most effective drug in preventing the spread of a seizure, whereas diazepam was ineffective. Accordingly, they proposed that CBZ might be effective only in later stages of bipolar illness (Post et al. 1986c). There is some evidence that bipolar illness overall contains subgroups differentially responsive to lithium or CBZ, based primarily on the presence of rapid cycling, a phenomenon seen late in the course (Lerer et al. 1985; Post and Uhde 1985).

Dovetailing with this model, Paul (1988) proposed that early stages of depression are characterized by dysfunction of the GABA-A/benzodiazepine receptor/chloride ionophore complex and are manifested by anxiety, whereas later stages are related to subsequent exhaustion of catecholamines. Paul's theory might justify trials of benzodiazepines and AEDs that prevent PTZ-induced seizures (such as VA, CNZP, or even PB) early in the illness, or for prophylaxis between episodes.

Recently, however, Post (1988) has suggested that anticonvulsant and thymoleptic actions of CBZ may be separated by time course and pharmacological dissection. Specifically, anticonvulsant properties are of rapid onset and appear tied to effects on "peripheral" benzodiazepine receptors and cation channels, whereas mood-stabilizing effects are delayed and may be related to adenosine or GABA-B receptors. The GABA-B receptor is pharmacologically distinct from the GABA-A receptor, not associated with benzodiazepine receptors (Bowery et al. 1983), and probably not a site of anticonvulsant activity (Post 1988).

In conclusion, it can be seen that AEDs are a diverse group of drugs, differentially effective in various types of experimental convulsions and human disease. Their biochemical mechanisms are only starting to be understood. Until these are clarified, together with a better understanding of the biochemistry of depression, it will not be possible to attribute antidepressant properties to specific anticonvulsant mechanisms. Because AEDs are not a monolithic group, it may also be that different types will be shown effective in different subgroups of depression. There are already well-documented cases of rapid-cycling bipolar patients sensitive to CBZ but not VA or PHT (Post et al. 1984c) or to VA but not CBZ (McElroy et al. 1988a).

New Approaches to Epilepsy and Depression

GABA, the principal inhibitory neurotransmitter in the brain, and excitatory amino acids (EAAs) are both of current research interest in the pathogenesis and treatment of neurologic and psychiatric disorders. Roberts (1986) has outlined a "reins and whip" model to describe the opposing, regulatory effects of GABA and EAAs on the spontaneous firing rates of virtually every cell in the central nervous system. Accumulating evidence emphasizes the importance of intact GABA projections (Gale 1988) and adequate local GABA concentrations (Lloyd et al. 1986a) in controlling seizures in many, although not all (MacDonald and McLean 1986), types of epilepsy.

A team of researchers in France led by Bartholini and colleagues (1986) has put forward the GABA deficiency hypothesis of depression. In recent reviews, they have summarized indirect evidence, for example, that blockade with bicuculline of the GABA-A receptor reverses many effects of TCAs in animal models of depression, and that GABA-B receptors are up-regulated by all antidepressant treatments, including ECT (Bartholini et al. 1985b; Lloyd et al. 1986b).

The development of specific GABA agonists and their applications in neurology and psychiatry are exciting prospects. Progabide, an analog of GABA, is the first mixed GABA-A, GABA-B direct agonist to be tested in humans as an AED and antidepressant. In preliminary studies of seizure control in animals and humans progabide appeared promising (Bartholini et al. 1985a). In depression preliminary studies also suggest progabide is as effective as TCAs (Bartholini et al. 1986). Unfortunately, progabide has been withdrawn from further study due to difficulty replicating its antiepileptic effects in refractory U.S. populations and concerns over hepatotoxicity (Leppik et al. 1987; Rudick et al. 1987). Fengabine, a similar compound that is hoped to be safer, appears effective in preliminary studies of depression (Bartholini et al. 1986) and currently is undergoing a trial in Great Britain.

Baclofen is a GABA-B agonist in use for a number of years both as an antinociceptive in trigeminal neuralgia and as an antispasmodic. It is structurally similar to CBZ, although it is not a useful anticonvulsant in animals or humans (Post et al. 1986d). In the rat, it accelerates the down-regulation of beta-adrenergic receptors induced by imipramine and, therefore, has been proposed as a potential adjunctive antidepressant treatment (Enna et al. 1986). It may have antidepressant effects by itself, according to a single study in mild depression (Badr et al. 1983) and case reports of its inducing mania (Wolf et al. 1982; Yassa and Iskandar 1988). The discovery of a specific GABA-B antagonist should speed research into this receptor (Dutar and Nicoll 1988).

A different approach to enhance GABA activity is seen with the ACD vigabatrin (gamma-vinyl-GABA; GVG), a selective, irreversible inhibitor of GABA transaminase, the principal degradative enzyme of GABA (Tartara et al. 1986). American and European studies have shown GVG to be effective in complex partial seizures in treatment-refractory human subjects (Browne et al. 1987; Schechter et al. 1984; Tartara et al. 1986). GVG is available in Europe, although American approval has been delayed pending resolution of safety questions. High doses have caused brain vacuoles in subprimates but not primates; safety experience in humans has been excellent (Gram et al. 1985; Schechter 1988, unpublished manuscript). GVG is of interest in depression, both on theoretical grounds and because of reported mood improvement or "mood swings" in some seizure patients (Browne et al. 1987; Schechter et al. 1984; Tartara et al. 1986).

Clinical research involving EAAs is at a much earlier stage. Excess activity of EAAs has been implicated in anxiety, epilepsy, anoxic brain damage, and neurodegenerative diseases (Meldrum 1985; Watkins 1988). Several specific EAA receptors and ligands have been identified that stimulate calcium influx and increase sodium and potassium conductance (Watkins 1988). Intense study is being applied to the receptor identified by the synthetic agonist N-methyl D-aspartic acid (NMDA) and the corresponding antagonist MK-801. In addition to potential anticonvulsant effects (Watkins 1988), MK-801 may have non–benzodiazepine-mediated anxiolytic properties (Liebmann and Bennet 1988). In the only psychiatric study of it so far, Wender and co-workers reported that MK-801 had a significant beneficial effect on mood in adults with attention deficit disorder (Reimherr et al. 1986).

SUMMARY

CBZ may be effective for some depressed patients as suggested by one controlled study and several uncontrolled and anecdotal reports.

Until further studies have compared it against standard treatments in refractory and nonrefractory populations, its true spectrum of efficacy remains undetermined. Preliminary evidence supports its use in treat-ment-refractory bipolar patients with severe, frequent, discrete affec-tive episodes; it may be less effective in refractory patients with unipolar or chronic depression.

PHT, VA, and CNZP have all been reported to help some refrac-tory patients, although none has been subjected to a rigorous trial.

It is unclear whether the anticonvulsant mechanisms of AEDs are also responsible for potential antidepressant effects. Given the diver-sity in likely mechanisms of different AEDs, it may be useful to try more than one AED in the refractory depressed patient, with the hope of serendipitously treating a possible subtype.

Finally, the roles of GABA and EAAs are among the targets of current epilepsy research. These substances may also be involved in depression. Thus, it may prove fruitful to explore the antidepressant potential of future AEDs that are specifically designed to interact with GABA and EAAs. Baclofen, a nonanticonvulsant GABA-B agonist, might also be a useful adjunct in refractory depression.

REFERENCES

Albright PS, Burnham WM: Development of a new pharmacological seizure model: effects of anticonvulsants on cortical- and amygdala-kindled seizures in the rat. Epilepsia 2:681–689, 1980

Alvarez WA, Freinhar JP: Clonazepam: an antidepressant? (letter). Am J Psychiatry 144:536–537, 1987

American Psychiatric Association: Diagnostic and Statistical Manual of Mental Disorders, 3rd Edition. Washington, DC, American Psychiatric Association, 1980

Andrus PF: Lithium and carbamazepine (letter). J Clin Psychiatry 45:525, 1984

Arana GW, Epstein S, Molloy M, et al: Carbamazepine-induced reduction of plasma alprazolam concentrations: a clinical case report. J Clin Psychiatry 49:488–449, 1988

Badr GG, Matusek M, Frederiksen PK: A quantitative EEG analysis of the effects of baclofen on man. Neuropsychobiology 10:13–18, 1983

Baldessarini RJ, Teicher MH, Cassidy JW, et al: Anticonvulsant cotreatment may increase toxic metabolites of antidepressants and other psychotropic drugs (letter). J Clin Psychopharmacol 8:381, 1988

Ballenger JC: The clinical use of carbamazepine in affective disorders. J Clin Psychiatry 49 (suppl 4):13–19, 1988a

Ballenger JC: The use of anticonvulsants in manic-depressive illness. J Clin Psychiatry 49 (suppl 11):21–24, 1988b

Ballenger JC, Post RM: Carbamazepine in manic-depressive illness: a new treatment. Am J Psychiatry 137:782–790, 1980

Barker WA, Eccleston D: The treatment of chronic depression: an illustrative case. Br J Psychiatry 144:317–319, 1984

Bartholini G, Bossi L, Lloyd KG, et al (eds): Epilepsy and GABA Receptor Agonists: Basic and Therapeutic Research. New York, Raven Press, 1985a

Bartholini G, Lloyd KG, Scatton B, et al: The GABA hypothesis of depression and antidepressant drug action. Psychopharmacol Bull 21:385–388, 1985b

Bartholini G, Lloyd KG, Morselli PG (eds): GABA and Mood Disorders. New York, Raven Press, 1986

Beas-Zarate C, Arauz-Contreras J, Velazquez A, et al: Monosodium L-glutamate-induced convulsions, II: changes in catecholamine concentrations in various brain areas of adult rats. Gen Pharmacol 16:489–493, 1985

Beattie B, Biller J, Mehlhaus B, et al: Verapamil-induced carbamazepine neurotoxicity. Eur Neurol 28:104–105, 1988

Beerman B, Edhag O, Vall H: Advanced heart block aggravated by carbamazepine. Br Heart J 37:668–671, 1975

Benassi E, Bo G, Cocito L, et al: Carbamazepine and cardiac conduction disturbances. Ann Neurol 22:280–281, 1987

Bernasconi R, Hauser K, Martin P, et al: Biochemical aspects of the mechanism of action of valproate, in Anticonvulsants in Affective Disorders. Edited by Emrich HM, Okuma T, Muller AA. Amsterdam, Elsevier, 1984, pp 14–32

Bourgeois B, Beaumanoir A, Blajer B, et al: Monotherapy with valproate in primary generalized epilepsies. Epilepsia 28 (suppl 2):S8–S11, 1987

Bowery NG, Hill DR, Hudson AL: Characteristics of GABA-B receptor binding sites in rat whole brain synaptic membrane. Br J Pharmacol 78:191–206, 1983

Brayley J, Yellowlees P: An interaction between haloperidol and carbamazepine in a patient with cerebral palsy. Aust N Z J Psychiatry 21:605–607, 1987

Brown JK: Valproate toxicity. Dev Med Child Neurol 30:115–125, 1988

Browne TR, Hattson RH, Penry JK, et al: Vigabatrin for refractory complex partial seizures. Neurology 37:184–189, 1987

Buck OD, Havey P: Treatment of tardive dyskinesia with verapamil. J Clin Psychopharmacol 8:303–304, 1988

Bunney WE, Hamburg DA: Methods for reliable longitudinal observation of behavior. Arch Gen Psychiatry 9:280–294, 1963

Cantor C: Carbamazepine and ECT: a paradoxical combination. J Clin Psychiatry 47:276–277, 1986

Cereghino JJ: Potential antiepileptic drugs: mexiletine, in Antiepileptic Drugs. Edited by Woodbury DM, Penry JK, Pippenger LE. New York, Raven Press, 1982, pp 825–830

Chapman A, Keane DE, Meldrum BS, et al: Mechanism of anticonvulsant action of valproate. Prog Neurobiol 19:315–359, 1982

Chouinard G: Clonazepam in acute and maintenance treatment of bipolar affective disorder. J Clin Psychiatry 48(suppl 10):29–36, 1987

Chouinard G, Young SN, Annable L: Antimanic effect of clonazepam. Biol Psychiatry 18:451–466, 1983

Cowdrie RW, Gardner DL: Pharmacotherapy of borderline personality disorder. Arch Gen Psychiatry 45:111–119, 1988

Dalby MA: Behavioral effects of carbamazepine. Adv Neurol 11:331–334, 1975

Decina P, Sackeim HA, Mukherjee S, et al: Tricyclic antidepressant risks and benefits (letter). J Clin Psychopharmacol 3:389, 1983

Delgado Escueta AV, Ward AA, Woodbury DM, et al: New wave of research in the epilepsies. Adv Neurol 44:3–55, 1986

DeLorenzo RJ: Mechanisms of actions of anticonvulsant drugs. Epilepsia 29(suppl 2):S35–S47, 1988

Dreifuss FE: Ethosuximide toxicity, in Antiepileptic Drugs. Edited by Woodbury DM, Penry JK, Pippenger LE. New York, Raven Press, 1982, pp 647–653

Dreifuss F, Santilli N, Langer D, et al: Valproic acid hepatic fatalities: a retrospective review. Neurology 37:379–385, 1987

Durelli L, Mutani R, Sechi GP, et al: Cardiac side effects of phenytoin and carbamazepine. Arch Neurol 42:1067–1068, 1985

Dutar P, Nicoll RA: A physiological role for GABA-B receptors in the central nervous system. Nature 332:156–158, 1988

Edwards JG, Long SK, Sedgwick EM, et al: Antidepressants and convulsive seizures: clinical, electroencephalographic and pharmacological aspects. Clin Neuropharmacol 9:329–360, 1986

Enna SJ, Karbon EW, Duman RS: GABA-B agonists and imipramine-induced modifications in rat brain beta-adrenergic receptor binding and function, in GABA and Mood Disorders. Edited by Bartholini G, Lloyd KG, Morselli PL. New York, Raven Press, 1986, pp 23–32

Ferrendelli JA: Pharmacology of antiepileptic drugs. Epilepsia 28(suppl 3):S14–S16, 1987

Fink M: Meduna and the origins of convulsive therapy. Am J Psychiatry 141:1034–1041, 1984

Folks DG, King LD, Dowdy SB, et al: Carbamazepine treatment of selected affectively disordered inpatients. Am J Psychiatry 139:115–117, 1982

Frankenburg FR, Tohen M, Cohen BM, et al: Long term response to carbamazepine: a retrospective study. J Clin Psychopharmacol 8:130–132, 1988

Fromm GH, Amires CY, Thies W: Imipramine in epilepsy. Arch Neurol 27:198–204, 1972

Fromm GH, Wessel HB, Glass JD, et al: Imipramine in absence and myoclonic-astatic seizures. Neurology 28:953–957, 1978

Gale K: Progression and generalization of seizure discharge: anatomical and neurochemical substrates. Epilepsia 29(suppl 2):S15–S34, 1988

Gasperetti CM: Conduction abnormalities complicating carbamazepine therapy (letter). Am J Med 82:381, 1987

Giardina EG, Bigger JT Jr, Glassman AH, et al: The electrocardiographic and antiarrhythmic effects of imipramine hydrochloride at therapeutic plasma concentrations. Circulation 60:1045–1052, 1979

Gram L, Klosterskov P, Dam M: gamma-Vinyl GABA: A double-blind placebo-controlled trial in partial epilepsy. Ann Neurol 17:262–266, 1985

Hart RG, Easton JD. Carbamazepine and hematological monitoring. Ann Neurol 11:309–312, 1982

Hockings N, Pall A, Moody J, et al: The effects of age on carbamazepine pharmacokinetics and adverse effects. Br J Clin Pharmacol 22:725–728, 1986

Jann MW, Ereshefsky L, Saklad SR, et al: The effects of carbamazepine on plasma haloperidol levels. J Clin Psychopharmacol 5:106–109, 1985

Joffe RT, Post RM, Roy-Byrne PP, et al: Hematological effects of carbamazepine in patients with affective illness. Am J Psychiatry 142:1196–1199, 1985a

Joffe RT, Post RM, Uhde TW: Lack of pharmacokinetic interaction of carbamazepine with tranylcypromine (letter). Arch Gen Psychiatry 42:738, 1985b

Joffe RT, Uhde TW, Post RM, et al: Motor activity in depressant patients treated with carbamazepine. Biol Psychiatry 22:941–946, 1987

Jones BD, Chouinard G: Clonazepam in the treatment of recurrent symptoms of depression and anxiety in a patient with systemic lupus erythematosus. Am J Psychiatry 142:354–355, 1985

Julien RM: Lidocaine in experimental epilepsy: correlation of anticonvulsant effect with blood concentrations. Electroencephalogr Clin Neurophysiol 34:639–645, 1973

Kahn D, Stevenson E, Douglas C: Effect of sodium valproate in three patients with organic brain syndromes. Am J Psychiatry 145:1010–1011, 1988

Kalinowsky LB, Putnam TJ: Attempts at treatment of schizophrenia and other non-epileptic psychoses with Dilantin. Archives of Neurology and Psychiatry 49:414–420, 1943

Kanter GL, Yerevanian BI, Ciccone R: Case report of a possible interaction between neuroleptics and carbamazepine. Am J Psychiatry 141:1101–1102, 1984

Kishimoto A, Ogura C, Hazama H, et al: Long term prophylactic effects of carbamazepine in affective disorder. Br J Psychiatry 143:327–331, 1983

Kishimoto A, Kamatu K, Sugihara T, et al: Treatment of depression with clonazepam. Acta Psychiatr Scand 77:81–86, 1988

Klein DF: Discussion of psychotropic effect of diphenylhydantoin. International Journal of Neuropsychiatry 3(suppl 2):S63, 1967

Kravitz HM, Fawcett J: Carbamazepine in the treatment of affective disorders. Medical Science Research 15:1–8, 1987

Kwamie Y, Persad E, Stancer H: The use of carbamazepine as an adjunctive medication in the treatment of affective disorders: a clinical report. Can J Psychiatry 29:605–608, 1984

Lambert PA: Acute and prophylactic therapies of patients with affective disorders using valpromide (dipropylacetamide), in Anticonvulsants in Affective Disorders. Edited by Emrich HM, Okuma T, Muller AA. Amsterdam, Elsevier, 1984, pp 33–43

Lange SC, Juline RM, Fowler GW: Biphasic effects of imipramine in experimental models of epilepsy. Epilepsia 17:183–196, 1976

Leppik IE, Dreifuss FE, Porter MD, et al: A controlled study of progabide in partial seizures. Neurology 37:963–968, 1987

Lerer B, Moore N, Meyendorff E, et al: Carbamazepine and lithium: different profiles in affective disorders? Psychopharmacol Bull 21:18–22, 1985

Leslie PJ, Heyworth R, Prescott LF: Cardiac complications of carbamazepine intoxication: treatment by haemoperfusion. Br Med J 286:1018, 1983

Lesser I: Carbamazepine and desipramine: a toxic reaction. J Clin Psychiatry 45:360, 1984

Levy RH, Koch KM: Drug interactions with valproic acid. Drugs 24:543–556, 1982

Liebmann JM, Bennet DA: Anxiolytic actions of N-methyl-D-aspartate antagonists, in Frontiers in Excitatory Amino Acid Research. Edited by Cavalheiro EA, Lehmann J, Tuski L. New York, Alan R Liss, 1988, pp 301–308

Lloyd KG, Bossi L, Morselli PL, et al: Alterations of GABA-mediated synaptic transmission in human epilepsy. Adv Neurol 44:1033–1044, 1986a

Lloyd KG, Thuret F, Pilc A: GABA and the mechanism of antidepressant drugs, in GABA and Mood Disorders. Edited by Bartholini G, Lloyd KG, Morselli PL. New York, Raven Press, 1986b, pp 33–42

Lydiard RB, White D, Harvey B, et al: Lack of pharmacokinetic interaction between tranylcypromine and carbamazepine (letter). J Clin Psychopharmacol 7:360, 1987

Macphee GJA, Larkin JG, Butler E, et al: Circulating hormones and pituitary responsiveness in young epileptic men receiving long-term antiepileptic medication. Epilepsia 29:468–475, 1988

Masland RL: Carbamazepine neurotoxicity, in Antiepileptic Drugs. Edited by Woodbury DM, Penry JK, Pippenger CE. New York, Raven Press, 1982, pp 521–531

Mathew G: Psychiatric symptoms associated with carbamazepine. Br Med J 296:1071, 1988

MacDonald RL, McLen MJ: Anticonvulsant drugs: mechanisms of action. Adv Neurol 44:713–736, 1986

McElroy SL, Keck PE, Pope HG: Sodium valproate; its use in primary psychiatric disorders. J Clin Psychopharmacol 7:16–24, 1987

McElroy SL, Keck PE, Pope HG, et al: Valproate in the treatment of rapid-cycling bipolar disorder. J Clin Psychopharmacol 8:275–279, 1988a

McElroy SL, Keck PE, Pope HG, et al: Valproate in primary psychiatric disorders: literature review and clinical experience in a private psychiatric hospital, in Use of Anticonvulsants in Psychiatry: Recent Advances. Edited by McElroy SL, Pope HG. Clifton, NJ Oxford Health Care, 1988b, pp 25–42

Meldrum B: Possible therapeutic applications of antagonists of excitatory amino acid neurotransmitters. Clin Sci 68:113–122, 1985

Mirski MA, Ferrendelli JA: Selective metabolic activation of the mamillary bodies and their connections during ethosuximide-induced suppression of pentylenctetrazol seizures. Epilepsia 27:194–203, 1986

Neumann J, Seidel K, Wunderlich HP: Comparative studies of the effect of carbamazepine and trimipramine in depression, in Anticonvulsants in Affective Disorders. Edited by Emrich HM, Okuma T, Muller AA. Amsterdam, Elsevier, 1984, pp 160–166

Nurnberg HG, Finkel JA: Carbamazepine in bipolar-depressed disorder complicated by tricyclic antidepressant switching: case report. J Clin Psychiatry 46:487–488, 1985

Ojemann LM, Friel PN, Trejo WJ, et al: Effect of doxepin on seizure frequency in depressed epileptic patients. Neurology 33:646–648, 1983

Okuma T: Therapeutic and prophylactic efficacy of carbamazepine in manic depressive psychosis, in Anticonvulsants in Affective Disorders. Edited by Emrich HM, Okuma T, Muller AA. Amsterdam, Elsevier, 1984, pp. 76–87

Okuma T, Kishimoto A, Inoue K, et al: Anti-manic and prophylactic effects of carbamazepine (Tegretol) in manic depressive psychosis. Folia Psychiatr Neurol Jpn 27:283–297, 1973

Okuma T, Inanaga K, Otsuki S, et al: A preliminary study on the efficacy of carbamazepine in the prophylaxis of manic-depressive illness. (Berlin) Psychopharmacology 73:95–96, 1981

Overweg J, Binnie CD, Meijer JWA, et al: Double-blind placebo-controlled trial of flunarizine as add-on therapy in epilepsy. Epilepsia 25:217–222, 1984

Oxley J, Hedges A, Makki KA, et al: Lack of enzyme inducing effect of sodium valproate. Br J Clin Pharmacol 8:189–190, 1978

Pakalnis A, Drake ME, Kuruvilla J, et al: Forced normalization: acute psychosis after seizure control in seven patients. Arch Neurol 44:289–292, 1987

Pande AC: Clonazepam treatment of atypical bipolar disorder. Psychosomatics 29:333–335, 1988

Paul SM: Anxiety and depression: a common neurobiological substrate? J Clin Psychiatry 49(suppl 10):13–16, 1988

Pellock JM: Carbamazepine side effects in children and adults. Epilepsia 28(suppl 3):S64–S70, 1987

Placidi GF, Lenzi A, Lazzerini F, et al: The comparative efficacy and safety of carbamazepine vs lithium: a randomized, double-blind 3 year trial in 83 patients. J Clin Psychiatry 47:490–494, 1986

Pollack MH: Clonazepam: a review of open clinical trials. J Clin Psychiatry 48(suppl 10):12–14, 1987

Porter RJ: Initiating carbamazepine therapy. Epilepsia 28(suppl 3):S59–S63, 1987

Post RM: Time course of clinical effects of carbamazepine: implications for mechanisms of action. J Clin Psychiatry 49(suppl 4):35–48, 1988

Post RM, Uhde TW: Carbamazepine in bipolar illness. Psychopharmacol Bull 21:8–17, 1985

Post RM, Uhde TW, Ballenger JC, et al: Prophylactic efficacy of carbamazepine in manic-depressive illness. Am J Psychiatry 140:1602–1604, 1983

Post RM, Rubinow DR, Ballenger JC: Conditioning, sensitization and kindling: implications for the course of affective illness, in Neurobiology of Mood Disorders. Edited by Post RM, Ballenger JC. Baltimore, MD, Williams & Wilkins, 1984a, pp 432–466

Post RM, Uhde TW, Wolff EA: Profile of clinical efficacy and side effects of carbamazepine in psychiatric illness: relationship to blood and CSF levels of carbamazepine and its 10,11-epoxide metabolite. Acta Psychiatr Scand 313(suppl):104–120, 1984b

Post RM, Berrettini W, Uhde TW, et al: Selective response to the anticonvulsant carbamazepine in manic-depressive illness: a case study. J Clin Psychopharmacol 4:178–185, 1984c

Post RM, Rubinow DR, Uhde TW, et al: Dopaminergic effects of carbamazepine. Arch Gen Psychiatry 43:392–396, 1986a

Post RM, Uhde TW, Roy-Byrne PP, et al: Antidepressant effects of carbamazepine. Am J Psychiatry 143:29–34, 1986b

Post RM, Uhde TW, Rubinow DR, et al: Antimanic effects of carbamazepine: mechanisms of action and implications for the biochemistry of manic-depressive illness, in Mania: New Research and Treatment. Edited by Swann AC. Washington, DC, American Psychiatric Press, 1986c, pp 95–176

Post RM, Uhde TW, Rubinow DR, et al: Carbamazepine in affective illness: implications for GABA mechanisms, in GABA and Mood Disorders. Edited by Bartholini G, Lloyd KG, Morselli PG. New York, Raven Press, 1986d, pp 201–214

Prasad AJ: Efficacy of carbamazepine in chronic resistant depressives. J Indian Med Assoc 83:235–237, 1985

Regan WM: Successful treatment course with carbamazepine despite initial significant leukopenia: case report. J Clin Psychiatry 48:338–339, 1987

Reigel CE, Dailey JW, Jobe PC: The genetically epilepsy-prone rat: an overview of seizure prone characteristics and responsiveness to anticonvulsant drugs. Life Sci 39:763–774, 1986

Reimherr FW, Wood DR, Wender PH: The use of MK-801, a novel sympathomimetic, in adult attention deficit disorder, residual type. Psychopharmacol Bull 22:237–242, 1986

Reiss AL, O'Donnell DJ: Carbamazepine-induced mania in 2 children: case report. J Clin Psychiatry 45:272–274, 1984

Rettie AE, Rettenmeier AW, Howald WN, et al: Cytochrome P-450-catalyzed formation of delta-4-VPA, a toxic metabolite of valproic acid. Science 235:890–893, 1987

Roberts E: Failure of GABAergic inhibition: a key to local and global seizures. Adv Neurol 44:319–342, 1986

Roy-Byrne PP, Joffe RT, Uhde TW, et al: Carbamazepine and thyroid function in affectively ill patients. Arch Gen Psychiatry 41:1150–1153, 1984

Rubinow DR, Post RM, Gold PW, et al: The relationship between cortisol and clinical phenomenology of affective illness, in Neurobiology of Mood Disorders. Edited by Post RM, Ballenger JC. Baltimore, MD, Williams & Wilkins, 1984, pp 271–289

Rudick RA, Breton D, Krall RL: The GABA agonist progabide for spasticity in multiple sclerosis. Arch Neurol 44:1033–1036, 1987

Sander J, Shorvon SD: Nifedipine for epilepsy? (letter). Br Med J 296:1070, 1988

Schaffer CB, Mungas D, Rockwell E: Successful treatment of psychotic depression with carbamazepine. J Clin Psychopharmacol 5:233–235, 1985

Schechter PJ, Hanke NFJ, Grove J, et al: Biochemical and clinical effects of gamma-vinyl GABA in patients with epilepsy. Neurology 34:182–186, 1984

Schiffer RB: Epilepsy, psychosis and forced normalization (editorial). Arch Neurol 44:253, 1987

Sethi BB, Tiwari SC: Carbamazepine in affective disorders, in Anticonvulsants in Affective Disorders. Edited by Emrich HM, Okuma T, Muller, AA. Amsterdam, Elsevier, 1984, pp 167–176

Shukla S, Godwin CD, Long L, et al: Lithium-carbamazepine neurotoxicity and risk factors. Am J Psychiatry 141:1604–1606, 1984

Singh BN, Hauswirth O: Comparative mechanisms of action of antiarrhythmic drugs. Am Heart J 87:367–382, 1974

Smith BH, Bogoch S, Dreyfus J: The Broad Range of Clinical Use of Phenytoin. New York, Dreyfus Medical Foundation, 1988

Steiner C, Witt AL, Weiss MB, et al: The antiarrhythmic action of carbamazepine. J Pharmacol Exp Ther 173:323–335, 1970

Stromgren LS, Boller S: Carbamazepine in treatment and prophylaxis of manic-depressive disorder. Psychiatr Dev 4:349–367, 1985

Sullivan JB, Rumack BH, Peterson RG: Acute carbamazepine toxicity resulting from overdose. Neurology 31:621–624, 1981

Sussman NM, McLain LW: A direct hepatotoxic effect of valproic acid. JAMA 242:1173–1174, 1979

Swinyard EA: Introduction, in Antiepileptic Drugs. Edited by Woodbury DM, Penry JK, Pippenger CE. New York, Raven Press, 1982, pp 1–9

Tartara A, Manni R, Galimberti CA, et al: Vigabatrin in the treatment of epilepsy: a double-blind, placebo controlled study. Epilepsia 27:717–723, 1986

Trimble MR: Anticonvulsant drugs and cognitive function: a review of the literature. Epilepsia 28(suppl 3):S37–S45, 1987

Trimble MR: Carbamazepine and mood: evidence from patients with seizure disorders. J Clin Psychiatry 49(suppl 4):7–11, 1988

Turner WJ: The usefulness of diphenylhydantion in treatment of non-epileptic emotional disorders. International Journal of Neuropsychiatry 3(suppl 2):S8–S20, 1967

Vezzani A, Wu JQ, Stasi MA, et al: Effect of various calcium channel blockers on 3 different models of limbic seizures in rats. Neuropharmacology 27:451–458, 1988

Warnock JK, Knesevich JW: Adverse cutaneous reactions to antidepressants. Am J Psychiatry 145:425–430, 1988

Watkins JC: Thirty years of excitatory amino acid research, in Frontiers in

Excitatory Amino Acid Research. Edited by Cavalheiro EA, Lehmann J, Tuski L. New York, Alan R Liss, 1988, pp 3–10

Watkins SE, Callendar K, Thomas DR, et al: The effect of carbamazepine and lithium on remission from affective illness. Br J Psychiatry 150:180–182, 1987

Weaver DF, Camfield P, Fraser A: Massive carbamazepine overdose. Neurology 38:755–759, 1988

Wheatley D: A comparative trial of imipramine and phenobarbital in depressed patients seen in general practice. J Nerv Ment Dis 148:542–549, 1969

Wilder BJ, Karas BJ, Penry JK: Gastrointestinal tolerance of divalproex sodium. Neurology 33:808–811, 1983

Wolf ME, Almy G, Toll M, et al: Mania associated with the use of baclofen. Biol Psychiatry 17:757–759, 1982

Wunderlich HP, Grunes JU, Neumann J, et al: Antidepressive therapie mit carbamazepin (Finelspin). Schweiz Arch Neurol Neurochir Psychiatr 133:363–371, 1983

Yassa R, Iskandar H, Nastase C, et al: Carbamazepine and hyponatremia in patients with affective disorder. Am J Psychiatry 145:339–342, 1987

Yassa RY, Iskandar HL: Baclofen-induced psychosis: two cases and a review. J Clin Psychiatry 49:318–320, 1988

Zetin M, Freedman MJ: Clonazepam in bipolar affective disorder (letter). Am J Psychiatry 143:1055, 1986

Chapter 6

Refractory Depression and Electroconvulsive Therapy

Joan Prudic, M.D.
Harold A. Sackeim, Ph.D.

Chapter 6

Refractory Depression and Electroconvulsive Therapy

U se of electroconvulsive therapy (ECT) in depression long preceded the development of pharmacologic treatments. The original reports on the efficacy of ECT were derived from populations who are heterogeneous by today's diagnostic criteria and who were untreated by the spectrum of antidepressant drugs now available. With the introduction of these agents, practice patterns have increasingly reserved ECT for patients who have failed to respond to antidepressants and may be regarded as treatment resistant in varying degrees. In medicine, it is generally the case that patients who fail initial treatments for an illness may be at greater risk of failing subsequent treatments. Thus, the extent to which treatment resistance affects the efficacy of ECT in depressed patients becomes a critical issue. Three areas will be reviewed here. First, what predictive value does antidepressant resistance have for response to subsequent ECT? Second, does antidepressant resistance affect relapse rates following response to ECT? Third, what can be recommended for effective treatment of patients failing a course of ECT?

ANTIDEPRESSANT MEDICATION RESISTANCE AND RESPONSE TO ECT

Shortly after the introduction of ECT as a somatic treatment for psychiatrically ill populations, reports were published suggesting its antidepressant effects. In the subsequent decades, the response rate of untreated depressed populations was estimated to be 70% to 90% (Fink 1979). Currently, the primary indication for the use of ECT is failure of a course of antidepressant medications (American Psychiatric Association 1978), but remarkably few data are available about the response rates of these patients to ECT. We will review the findings of two retrospective and two prospective studies, and we will report a controlled comparison of the effect of antidepressant resistance on ECT response.

Among the most recent information to appear are two retrospective reports of the experience of two institutions with antidepressant-resistant patients who subsequently received ECT. Mandel and colleagues (1977), at McLean Hospital, reviewed the records of 100 patients and addressed the question of the predictive value of medication resistance for ECT response. In this report, tricyclic resistance was defined as lack of response to imipramine at 200 mg or its equivalent for at least 3 weeks or side effects precluding the use of this dosage. Diagnostic groups included primary affective disorder by Feighner criteria (Feighner et al. 1972), but also secondary affective disorder. Patients received nondominant (right) unilateral ECT without further specification of technical conditions. Patients were considered responders if they received a global rating of substantial improvement 3 to 6 months after ECT. Treatment received following ECT, if any, was not documented. The response rate was reported as 71%.

Factors that make interpretation of the response rate difficult include the heterogeneous diagnostic mix, a nonuniform level of tricyclic resistance by inclusion of medication-intolerant patients, the use of a type of ECT that may not have been the most efficacious, and the focus on outcome several months after ECT. Most critically, no comparison group of nonresistant patients was included. Nonetheless, the authors viewed the obtained response rate of 71% positively and supported the role of ECT in treatment of medication-resistant patients.

Paul and colleagues (1981) reported on the outcome of nine treatment-resistant depressed patients given ECT at the National Institute of Mental Health (NIMH). All nine met Research Diagnostic Criteria (RDC) (Spitzer et al. 1978) for major depression and manifested severe symptoms. However, only seven had antidepressant trials prior to ECT; the other two patients had such serious symptoms that medication trials were bypassed. Of the patients receiving antidepressant trials, only four patients were documented to have received at least a dose of tricyclic antidepressant at 150 mg for 3 weeks; the medication status of the remainder was unreported. All patients except one rapid cycler responded to ECT. In addition to the question of small sample, the question of degree of medication resistance was again at issue. The results are consistent with the Mandel and co-workers (1977) report and do not point to a differential predictive value of antidepressant resistance for subsequent ECT response in the same episode.

Although not specifically designed to address the issue of the outcome with ECT for medication-resistant patients, two prospective studies conducted in Europe in the 1960s contain pertinent data. The first study was conducted by DeCarolis and associates (1964) and later reevaluated by Avery and Lubrano (1979). A large sample ($N = 437$) received imipramine 200 mg to 350 mg for a 25-day minimum. Diagnostic groups were quite heterogeneous and included the following: manic-depressive illness; endogenous unipolar depression; cycloid psychosis; atypical depressive psychosis, similar to delusional depression; secondary depressions, for example, to schizophrenia; organic depression; neurotic depression; and reactive depression. Patients may have received a phenothiazine or barbiturate concurrently with imipramine treatment. Those who did not respond to imipramine were given 8 to 10 treatments with ECT. Response was determined at 1 month post-ECT and ranged from return to premorbid state to "reintegrated socially." Manic-depressive ($n = 8$) and unipolar depressive ($n = 5$) patients who were medication resistant had 100% and 83% response rates, respectively. Atypical depressive patients ($n = 43$) had a 72% response rate. These diagnoses are most likely to be comparable to current concepts of major depression. Severity criteria were not reported, but medication-resistant neurotic and reactive depressive patients had only 27% and 22% response rates to subsequent ECT. These latter groups could meet modern criteria for major depression of varying severity. Again, unfortunately, no comparison group of patients treated with ECT and not known to be medication resistant was included. Despite these limitations, the authors concluded that depressed patients with severe symptomatology had an excellent chance for recovery with ECT following medication nonresponse.

The Medical Research Council (MRC) (1965) conducted a prospective study in Britain comparing the efficacy of four to eight ECT, imipramine at 100 mg to 200 mg, phenelzine at 30 mg to 60 mg, and placebo in a sample of 250 depressed patients. The authors reported that patients receiving ECT as their first treatment had a 71% response rate. Thirty-two percent of the imipramine group and 59% of the phenelzine group received ECT after failing the random assignment, for a total of 59 patients. The response rates among these two groups of patients were 55% and 50%, respectively. This crossover group had received pre-ECT pharmacological treatments that would not meet current standards for establishing medication resistance. ECT practice may not be comparable either. More critically, it was not reported whether drugs were continued concurrently with ECT. Nevertheless, the comparison of medication-resistant patients with a group in whom medication resistance was not determined suggests a difference in response rates by as much as 20%.

Prudic et al. (in press) reported on the relationship of antidepressant medication resistance to response to ECT in patients participating in an ongoing prospective study of the affective and cognitive consequences of ECT. Fifty-three patients received bilateral ECT under circumstances described elsewhere (Sackeim et al. 1987). The sample was restricted to bilateral ECT to minimize the question of the efficacy of the different types of ECT and to ensure that the ECT trial was sufficient. The sample also excluded patients who had received ECT earlier in the current episode in order to restrict the question to the predictive value of medication resistance alone. All patients met the RDC for major depressive episode, unipolar or bipolar, and had a score on the Hamilton Rating Scale for Depression (Hamilton 1960) of 18 or greater, with an average score of 33. Antidepressant medication trials prior to ECT were examined and their strength rated on a 0 to 5 scale. Adequacy was determined to be at least one trial of tricyclics at 200 mg to 300 mg or greater for a minimum of 4 weeks. Adequacy criteria for psychotic patients required concomitant treatment with the equivalent of chlorpromazine at 400 mg. The power of the best trial and the sum potency, sum of ratings for each trial, were also used in the analyses. Response to ECT was rated blind to medication resistance and treatment conditions.

Patients were classified in the overall study as ECT responders if scores on the Hamilton Rating Scale for Depression 1 week post-ECT were at least 60% lower than pretreatment, with a maximum of 16. Although these patients could be considered to have benefited from ECT and to be relatively well compared to pretreatment, a group of more fully reconstituted patients was also defined. This second classification of response required a final maximum Hamilton score posttreatment of at most nine in addition to the 60% reduction. Of the patients rated as having had inadequate pre-ECT antidepressant trials, 89% met the less stringent response criteria, and 69% met the more restrictive criteria. The medication-resistant group who met criteria for adequate pre-ECT trials had a 50% response for the less stringent criteria and a 42% response for the more stringent criteria. Medication-resistant patients did not differ demographically from the less resistant group, although they did have a longer depressive episode at the time of referral for ECT and an earlier age of onset of affective disorder. Examining the issue in reverse, ECT responders (stricter criteria) received an average pre-ECT medication rating of 2.09 (2.02); ECT nonresponders received a comparable rating of 3.19 (2.96). These findings were consistent whether adequacy, most potent trial, or sum potency was used in the analyses. A substantially lower rate of short-term response to ECT was found in medication-resistant patients relative to patients who had not failed an adequate medication trial prior to ECT.

In summary, two retrospective reports in which patients had modest, if any, levels of resistance and a prospective study with unusual diagnostic groups and no comparison medication-nonresistant group led to the expectation that patients who had already received antidepressants would have ECT response rates in the same range as untreated patients. In the two studies that used a prospective design and had comparison groups of untreated or inadequately treated (i.e., medication nonresistant) patients, response rates were substantially lower with medication resistance. We should probably alter our views and expect that approximately 50% of medication-resistant patients will respond to ECT, as opposed to 70% to 80% for nonresistant patients.

Dosage of tricyclic equivalents may be quite critical in predicting subsequent ECT response as well as defining antidepressant medication resistance. Trials of less than 200 mg of a tricyclic for several weeks in most of the reports appear to yield an ECT response rate comparable to that found in populations whose medication resistance is unknown. Most medication-intolerant patients will fall into this category, as will many patients whose trials are discontinued because of severe symptomatology requiring rapid intervention. Medication trial above these levels, in a prospective controlled setting as reported by Prudic et al. (in press), was the only factor found to be predictive of nonresponse to ECT. This study also suggests that failure after one adequate antidepressant trial is as informative for subsequent ECT response as failure after many trials. Although findings from the DeCarolis study conflict, it is difficult to make a comparison because of the unique diagnostic categories used, particularly the question of whether to view neurotic and/or reactive depressions as major depression, and the nonquantitative character of the response criteria.

Finally, a treatment that yields 50% recovery for antidepressant-resistant patients, although falling short of the expectation of 80%, is still impressive. One may argue that this rate likely compares favorably to other treatment options, mostly in the pharmacologic armamentarium, although prospective controlled comparisons have not been published.

ANTIDEPRESSANT DRUG RESISTANCE, RELAPSE, AND CONTINUATION TREATMENTS FOLLOWING RESPONSE TO ECT

When patients with major depression respond to antidepressant medications with remission of an acute episode, relapse rates over the ensuing 6 months approach 50% if antidepressants are discontinued

(Prien et al. 1973). If medications are continued, these rates are significantly reduced (Klein et al. 1980; Prien et al. 1973). Patients whose major depressive episode responds to ECT show similar rates of relapse if there is no continuation treatment following ECT (Imlah et al. 1965; Seager and Bird 1962; Snaith 1981). Current practice now increasingly reserves the use of ECT to populations of patients whose major depressive episode fails adequate antidepressant medication trials and may be regarded as treatment resistant (American Psychiatric Association 1978). ECT continues to be used in less resistant populations also. These populations include: medication-intolerant patients whose side-effects preclude adequate drug trials; patients with prior depressive episodes responsive to ECT; and patients whose acute symptoms are so severe (for example, suicide risk) as to necessitate an accelerated treatment response. Psychotically depressed patients are thought to constitute a population whose illness may be relatively more resistant to single or combined medication treatments and whose syndrome predisposes them to higher risk of suicide and severe symptomatology, as well as lengthy medication trials (Glassman et al. 1975). For all these groups of patients, recommendations for continuation treatment following ECT are similar and include the use of tricyclic antidepressants and lithium (Klein et al. 1980). With the evolution of the population of depressed patients receiving ECT, reexamination of the available evidence on the efficacy of continuation treatments becomes an increasingly critical issue. This is particularly so because the medications often used for continuation treatment are of the same class to which patients may have been nonresponsive during the acute episode.

In England in the 1960s, three prospective studies bearing on the issue of continuation treatment were conducted (Imlah et al. 1965; Kay et al. 1970; Seager and Bird 1962). The trials were designed to examine whether combining antidepressant medications with ECT would decrease the number of ECT required for response. At the time of the studies, ECT was frequently a treatment of first choice for major depressive illness. The issue of prior antidepressant resistance was not examined, and prior pharmacotherapy was not documented. The subject population most likely included a heterogeneous group with respect to these characteristics. Most patients were treated with both antidepressant medications and ECT concurrently during the acute episode. The number of patients who benefited from treatment of the acute phase with antidepressants is unknown and may have been significant. Following resolution of depressive symptoms, patients were assigned to continuation antidepressant, placebo, or no medications. Due to the design of these trials, it is likely that patients who benefited from antidepressant medications during the acute episode may also have benefited from their use as continuation therapy. All three studies reported that use of a tricyclic antidepressant or monoamine oxidase inhibitor (MAOI) after response to ECT was associated with a relapse rate of approximately 20% over 6 months, compared to approximately 50% in placebo or no medication conditions. However, the use of pharmacological treatment concurrent with ECT and the use of the combination as a first-line treatment seriously limits the relevance of this work for the patient who is medication resistant during the acute phase of illness.

Coppen and associates (1981) conducted a prospective, placebo-controlled study of the use of lithium as a continuation therapy for unipolar depressive patients responding to ECT. As in older studies, pre-ECT pharmacotherapy was not documented. In the first 6 months, there was no difference between placebo and lithium in relapse rates. Differences favoring lithium emerged at 6 months and 1 year, a pattern suggestive of prevention of recurrence of new episodes, as opposed to relapse. These findings are similar to those of the NIMH collaborative study (Prien et al. 1984), in which there was no difference between lithium and placebo as maintenance treatments for unipolar patients responding to antidepressant medications in the acute depressive episode. Although lithium may be helpful in prevention of new episodes, its value in prevention of relapse in unipolar patients is uncertain, and its usefulness in medication-resistant patients responding to ECT is not established.

Perry and Tsuang (1979) conducted a retrospective review of the course of unipolar patients responding to ECT and then treated with tricyclic prophylaxis or lithium prophylaxis. Medication resistance again was not documented. No differences in outcome measures were detected between the two groups; however, the tricyclic group consisted of patients taking low doses of imipramine equivalents, whereas the lithium group was maintained at levels of 0.8 to 1.2 mEq/L, a more standard regimen.

To examine how resistance to antidepressant medications during the acute episode and adequacy of pharmacotherapy following response to ECT bear on relapse rates, Sackeim et al. (in press) reported a prospective, naturalistic study. Fifty-eight patients were followed 1 year or until relapse. Pre-ECT pharmacotherapy was rated with respect to adequacy, strength, and number of trials. Post-ECT pharmacotherapy was rated for adequacy. Demographic variables, clinical characteristics, and form of ECT had no significant relationship to relapse rates. Adequacy of pre-ECT pharmacotherapy for depression, strength of the best trial pre-ECT, and total strength of all trials had significant negative relationships with relapse rates, that is, those who relapsed were more likely to have had adequate and/or stronger trials. The relation between the adequacy of post-ECT pharmacotherapy and relapse rate was marginal. There was no significant relation between adequacy of pre-ECT medication and adequacy of continuation medication post-ECT.

The interaction of medication resistance, that is, nonresponse to adequate pre-ECT pharmacotherapy for depression, and of adequacy of continuation antidepressant treatment on relapse rates was examined further. There was no significant difference in relapse rates between medication-resistant patients who had adequate continuation therapy (53% relapsed), and those who did not have adequate continuation therapy (64% relapsed). These rates, in addition, are comparable to rates of relapse for placebo or no medication follow-up treatment in the British studies cited above and to the rate of relapse in patients of this study whose pre-ECT and post-ECT pharmacotherapy was inadequate (48% relapsed). The group that derived most benefit from adequate continuation treatment post-ECT consisted of those patients (8%) who had inadequate pre-ECT antidepressant trials. An additional finding was that 80% of relapse over the year occurred in the first 4 months regardless of medication status post-ECT.

To summarize, older studies addressed themselves to a population of depressed patients likely to include both antidepressant medication-resistant patients and those who were not. The early studies pointed to the usefulness of continuation treatment, especially with tricyclic antidepressants, in the group of patients whose responsiveness to medications is unknown, regardless of demographic or clinical characteristics. For those patients with proven antidepressant resistance, the same conclusions cannot be asserted without qualification. The one prospective study addressing itself to this group did not use a controlled design and may be subject to biases due to medication compliance and heterogeneity of continuation treatments. Nevertheless, the expectation of 20% to 25% relapse with continuation treatment following ECT response for antidepressant-resistant patients did not materialize, and the rates were closer to those seen with placebo, that is, approximately 60% of medication-resistant patients relapsed. Although 40% of medication-resistant patients remained euthymic for long periods, it is uncertain whether standard continuation treatments are contributing much beyond the effects of ECT alone. It may not be true that ECT changes the neurobiology of medication-resistant patients sufficiently to make them susceptible to standard antidepressant drugs as continuation treatments. It may be true that acute control of depressive symptoms and subsequent maintenance of euthymia are not so intrinsically different. Prospective, placebo-controlled trials of standard continuation treatments are needed in the ECT-responsive, medication-resistant patient.

Because 50% to 60% of medication-resistant patients can be expected to relapse in the early months post-ECT, and standard antidepressants may be unlikely to ameliorate this outcome, it becomes imperative to consider alternative strategies for post-ECT continuation treatments. The only related study addressing the use of MAOIs administered phenelzine concurrently with ECT to patients whose medication resistance was unknown and then continued the phenelzine post ECT (Imlah et al. 1965). Whether this strategy would be useful in medication-resistant patients remains unknown. A prospective, placebo-controlled trial evaluating continuation lithium therapy for unipolar patients found no benefit for lithium in the first 6 months, the period of greatest risk for relapse (Coppen et al. 1981). Benefit was obtained between 6 months and 1 year, a circumstance that might be better characterized as preventing recurrence (Abou-Saleh 1987). Unlike other somatic treatments for depression, ECT is typically discontinued once the patient has responded. For medication-resistant patients, it may be worthwhile to consider continuation ECT. Again, no controlled prospective investigations have been done, but reported clinical experience is available and encouraging (Decina et al. 1987; Stevenson and Geoghegan 1951). Finally, other types of continuation treatments require evaluation. The usefulness of such strategies as combination medications (e.g., lithium augmentation of antidepressants, MAOI-tricyclics) is unknown. If ECT does, in fact, exert its antidepressant properties through enhancing endogenous inhibitory processes that terminate the seizure (Sackeim et al. 1983), antidepressant anticonvulsants (e.g., progabide) that enhance (GABAergic) processes may prove useful as continuation treatments and warrant investigation.

ECT RESISTANCE AND SUBSEQUENT TREATMENT OUTCOME

Depressed patients who are treatment resistant may receive a variety of antidepressants or ECT. Often the minimum standard applied to establish pharmacological resistance is a course of a tricyclic antidepressant of a defined minimum dosage (e.g., 150 mg to 300 mg) for a defined minimum period (e.g., 3 to 6 weeks) (Quitkin et al. 1984). Almost all of the available literature on treatment-resistant depressed patients concerns circumstances in which pharmacological treatment fails to induce short-term response. Perhaps because of

ECT's reputation for efficacy, with expectations of 80% to 90% response in previously untreated samples, little has been reported on the ECT-resistant patient. However, ECT is being increasingly reserved for patients failing antidepressant medications, a group in whom the response rate may more realistically be estimated at 40% to 70%, leaving 30% to 60% of patients in need of further treatment.

Prospective, controlled trials of treatment following failure to respond to ECT have not been reported. Reports of cases, often included in studies addressing other issues, have suggested the usefulness of such treatments as a course of MAOI-tricyclic combination (Davidson 1974) or lithium augmentation of a tricyclic (Price et al. 1983). Often, conditions of ECT treatment were not reported, and ECT adequacy was unknown. Shapira and co-workers (1988) recently reported their experience with 12 patients refractory to ECT. Refractory was defined as a decrease in Hamilton ratings of less than 50% over the course of treatment, with a final score greater than 18. All patients were diagnosed by DSM-III (American Psychiatric Association 1980) as having a major depressive episode. Psychotic patients had mood congruent delusions; patients with medical illness, organic mental syndromes, or substance abuse were excluded. Adequacy of ECT methods was documented.

One patient's course of ECT was terminated at seven treatments because of a severe organic brain syndrome. This patient had received ECT as a first treatment for psychotic depression and was a partial responder when ECT ended. Eight of the patients had failed at least one trial of tricyclics at 200 mg/day or greater. All patients subsequently responded to psychopharmacological treatment. Eight patients responded to a tricyclic in doses ranging from 50 mg to 200 mg/day; seven of these received clomipramine. Three more patients responded to lithium augmentation of a tricyclic, with two of the patients receiving clomipramine. The remaining patient responded to clomipramine at 200 mg/day with lithium augmentation and haloperidol at 15 mg/day. The authors postulated that ECT had sensitized serotonergic systems, resulting in improved tricyclic antidepressant efficacy. However, they could not rule out spontaneous remission. Late effects of ECT seemed unlikely, as all remissions occurred more than 1 month post-ECT. The relative refractoriness of patients to antidepressant medications could be at issue. Three patients had no pre-ECT medication trials; two patients responded to doses 25 mg to 50 mg/day higher than that administered pre-ECT. However, five patients responded to the same or lower tricyclic equivalents than pre-ECT, and the remaining two patients required lithium augmentation.

To examine this issue further, we reviewed cases of nonresponse to ECT in patients participating in an ongoing study of the affective and cognitive consequences of ECT. All patients met the RDC for major depressive disorder, endogenous subtype. The study has had two phases. In the first phase, patients were assigned randomly to either right unilateral ECT or bilateral ECT, both administered with electrical stimulus intensities just above threshold (Sackeim et al. 1987). In the second phase, two different types of ECT were contrasted, right unilateral or bilateral ECT at electrical dosage 150% above threshold or at dosage just above threshold. Some patients who failed to respond to the random assignment condition were then given the higher dosage bilateral ECT on an open basis. Raters of clinical response were blind to the randomly assigned treatment modality. To be classified a responder, a 60% decrease in Hamilton score from pretreatment and an absolute Hamilton score of less than 16 had to be maintained for 1 week post-ECT. A minimum of 8 to 10 ECT were administered in the random, blindly rated assignment before patients were classified as nonresponders. If patients showed clinical improvement, ECT was continued until no further improvement was observed over two or three treatments. For patients receiving subsequent openly assigned and rated treatment, a minimum of six bilateral treatments were given before the second course could be discontinued as ineffective. If depressive symptoms were decreasing, treatment continued until no further improvements were noted over two to three sessions.

Here we considered only patients who failed a course of bilateral ECT. Nineteen such patients were identified and are considered here as ECT resistant (see Table 6-1). Antidepressant treatments received prior to entry into the ECT study were documented. Sixteen patients (84%) had received pharmacological treatment equivalent to at least 200 mg/day of a tricyclic for at least 4 weeks prior to ECT and could be classified as relatively medication resistant as well as nonresponsive to ECT. Thirteen had failed bilateral ECT at doses near threshold. Of these, 11 had been blindly evaluated and 2 had been openly evaluated. Six patients had failed bilateral ECT at doses 150% above threshold. Of these, two had been blindly evaluated and four had been openly evaluated.

Patients had already been rigorously examined for medical causes of depression prior to entry into the study, and no new causes had been determined at the time ECT resistance emerged. Two patients whose psychiatric diagnoses were reconsidered had a shift of treatment focus. One patient (#2) was rediagnosed as having narcissistic personality disorder and later responded to analytically oriented psychotherapy as an inpatient. The other (#13) had deteriorated

Table 6-1. Nonresponders to a course of bilateral ECT

Patient	Diagnosis	Pre-ECT treatment	ECT Number/Type	Subsequent treatments Unsuccessful	Subsequent treatments Successful
1	Unipolar	Amitriptyline 400 mg +Trifluoperazine 60 mg Imipramine 300 mg +Trifluoperazine 60 mg	13 Lo Bi	Imipramine 400 mg Doxepin 300 mg Phenelzine 60 mg + $LiCo_3$(0.6) Carbamazepine Amitriptyline 200 mg + Phenelzine 60 mg	Amitriptyline 200 mg + $LiCo_3$(0.9)
2	Unipolar	Maprotiline hydrochloride 150 mg 7 ECT	2 Lo Uni +10 Lo Bi	Rediagnosed	
3	Unipolar	Amoxapine 250 mg	11 Lo Bi	Phenelzine 75 mg	Nortriptyline 50 mg
4	Unipolar	Trazodone 300 mg	10 Lo Bi		Phenelzine 60 mg
5	Unipolar psychotic	None	10 Lo Uni 9 Lo Bi	Nortriptyline 75 mg Haloperidol 20 mg Liothyronine sodium Dextroamphetamine sulfate	
6	Unipolar	Phenelzine 90 mg Imipramine 300 mg	11 Lo Uni 10 Lo Bi		Mesoridazine 200 mg + Nortriptyline[a]
7	Unipolar	Doxepin 250 mg Phenelzine 60 mg	11 Lo Uni 7 Lo Bi	Sedatives	
8	Unipolar	Nortriptyline[a]	10 Lo Bi		5 Hi Bi
9	Bipolar	Trazodone 400 mg	10 Lo Bi		3 Hi Bi
10	Unipolar psychotic	Doxepin 300 mg	10 Hi Uni	7 Hi Bi Nortriptyline[a]	

11	Unipolar	Amitriptyline 150 mg + $LiCo_3$ 600 mg Isocarboxazid 50 mg + $LiCo_3$ 600 mg	8 Lo Uni	6 Hi Bi	16 Hi Bi
12	Unipolar psychotic	Desipramine 250 mg + Haloperidol 25 mg	12 Hi Bi	Desipramine	Trazodone 600 mg + Haloperidol 15 mg
13	Unipolar	Desipramine 350 mg + Perphenazine 32 mg	7 Hi Bi	Rediagnosed	
14	Bipolar	Nortriptyline[a] + $LiCo_3$ 8 ECT	9 Hi Bi		14 Hi Bi
15	Unipolar	Desipramine 250 mg Imipramine 200 mg + Thioridazine 150 mg	9 Lo Bi		Nortriptyline[a] + Perphenazine 40 mg 7 Hi Bi
16	Bipolar	Nortriptyline[a] + $LiCo_3$	10 Lo Bi		10 Hi Bi
17	Unipolar psychotic	Tranylcypromine 60 mg	14 Lo Bi		10 Hi Bi
18	Unipolar	Desipramine 150 mg	10 Lo Bi		4 Hi Bi
19	Unipolar	Desipramine 100 mg	9 Hi Bi		7 Hi Bi

Note. Lo = Low-dose electrical stimulus intensity; Hi = High-dose electrical stimulus intensity; Uni = Right unilateral electrode placement; Bi = Bilateral electrode placement.

[a] 50–150 ng/ml plasma level.

Source. Adapted from Sackeim et al. 1990.

during the course of ECT and showed symptoms of schizophrenia, including thought control and insertion. This patient responded to a moderately high dose of neuroleptic and supportive environmental manipulations, for example, placement in a structured setting. Other occult causes of depression such as dementia and substance abuse had been excluded at the outset.

Seventeen patients retained the diagnosis of major depression, resistant to ECT. Of these, 16 were also considered resistant to antidepressants. Treatment beyond this point was determined by each individual clinician, a heterogeneous group ranging from first-year residents under supervision to clinical researchers whose main area of work was the ongoing ECT study. The successful and unsuccessful treatments given are listed in Table 6-1. Of these, one patient received only sedatives and was transferred for long-term hospitalization. Of the remaining 16 cases, 9 received further ECT, and 8 received further antidepressant medications. One was considered ECT resistant to bilateral ECT at threshold and to subsequent bilateral ECT 150% above threshold. Of the nine patients receiving further ECT, six had failed bilateral ECT at threshold and received further bilateral ECT at 150% above threshold; five responded. The other three patients failed or were intolerant to an initial course of bilateral ECT at 150% above threshold, and all three responded to a subsequent course of bilateral ECT at 150% above threshold after a 2–7 day intervening period. Eight patients failing ECT received antidepressants subsequently; five patients had failed bilateral ECT at threshold; three patients had failed bilateral ECT at 150% above threshold. Six of these eight patients responded to four different medication regimens: 1) amitriptyline plus lithium, 2) nortriptyline, 3) phenelzine, and 4) combination neuroleptic-tricyclics. One failed a variety of trials, nortriptyline, haloperidol, dextroamphetamine, and thyroid augmentation. The other failed nortriptyline.

In reviewing these reports, one characteristic stands out: the ECT-resistant depressed patient has frequently been resistant to antidepressant medications as well. Under these circumstances, reexamination of cases for diagnosis and contributory medical or psychiatric conditions is warranted. Beyond this, generalizations are difficult, but it appears that patients are resistant but not refractory to treatments, although in our experience subsequent response to traditional tricyclics is not commonly seen. The case for clomipramine made by Shapira and colleagues (1988) is an interesting exception.

The usual caveats concerning biases introduced by open evaluations and lack of control groups must be mentioned. Nevertheless, patients in these reports may also be resistant to ECT and not refractory. When 50% of ECT nonresponders in our sample were given further ECT, all but one responded. Because of the numbers reported here, it may appear that there is a greater resistance to bilateral ECT at threshold, but cell sizes are unequal and response rates are currently about the same for both types of bilateral ECT. There is a small minority of patients who do not respond to the usual number of ECT treatments, regardless of type, and require courses of 15 to 25 treatments before recovery. Such patients, at times, do not show substantial clinical improvement until after 10 treatments. It may well be that ECT is typically discontinued in such cases and that these patients are considered ECT refractory. In summary, nonresponse to the usual course of ECT defines an ECT-resistant population. This group is likely to be characterized by a very high rate of medication resistance during that depressive episode. Nonetheless, it is encouraging that, in our experience, almost all such patients subsequently respond to further ECT or to nonstandard pharmacologic approaches.

SUMMARY

There is very limited information on the efficacy of ECT in medication-resistant patients. Our experience indicates that such patients are more likely to fail a standard course of ECT than patients who have not failed an adequate trial of antidepressant medication prior to ECT. However, the overall rate of short-term ECT response is, nonetheless, quite substantial in medication-resistant patients, with approximately 50% benefiting from ECT. Perhaps of greater concern is the issue of long-term benefit. At present, it appears that relapse following ECT is about twice as likely in medication-resistant patients regardless of whether traditional continuation pharmacotherapy is used. This area requires considerably more attention.

There is also limited information available on how best to treat the patient who does not respond to ECT. The report by Shapira and associates (1988) suggests that a subgroup of such patients may respond to clomipramine. Our experience suggests that continuing ECT, despite lack of response at what has traditionally been an adequate number of treatments, often results in marked clinical response. It may be that there are extremely few patients who are truly refractory to ECT, but some patients may require unusually prolonged treatment courses. Thus, ECT may be akin to tricyclic antidepressants, where it also appears that a subgroup requires long exposure before showing clinical improvement (Quitkin et al. 1984).

REFERENCES

Abou-Saleh MT: How long should drug therapy for depression be maintained? Am J Psychiatry 144:1247–1248, 1987

American Psychiatric Association: Electroconvulsive Therapy (Task Force Report 14). Washington, DC, American Psychiatric Association, 1978

American Psychiatric Association: Diagnostic and Statistical Manual of Mental Disorders, 3rd Edition. Washington, DC, American Psychiatric Association, 1980

Avery D, Lubrano A: Depression treated with imipramine and ECT: the DeCarolis study reconsidered. Am J Psychiatry 136:559–562, 1979

Coppen A, Abou-Saleh MT, Milln P, et al: Lithium continuation therapy following electroconvulsive therapy. Br J Psychiatry 139:284–287, 1981

Davidson J: Management of resistant depression. Br J Psychiatry 124:219–220, 1974

DeCarolis V, Gilberti F, Roccatagliata G, et al: Imipramine and electroshock in the treatment of depression: a clinical statistical analysis of 437 cases. Dis Nerv Syst 16:29–42, 1964

Decina P, Guthrie EB, Sackeim HA, et al: Continuation ECT in the management of relapses of major affective episodes. Acta Psychiatr Scand 75:559–562, 1987

Feighner JP, Robins E, Guze SB, et al: Diagnostic criteria for use in psychiatric research. Arch Gen Psychiatry 26:57–63, 1972

Fink MF: Convulsive Therapy: Theory and Practice. New York, Raven Press, 1979

Glassman AH, Roose SP: Delusional depression: a distinct clinical entity? Arch Gen Psychiatry 38:424–427, 1981

Hamilton M: Development of a rating scale for primary depressive illness. Br J Soc Clin Psychol 6:278–296, 1960

Imlah NW, Ryan E, Harrington JA: The influence of antidepressant drugs on the response to electroconvulsive therapy and on subsequent relapse rates. Neuropsychopharmacology 4:438–442, 1965

Kay DWK, Kahy T, Garside RF: A 7-month double-blind trial of amitriptyline and diazepam in ECT-treated depressed patients. Br J Psychiatry 117:667–671, 1970

Klein DF, Gittelman R, Quitkin F, et al: Diagnosis and Drug Treatment of Psychiatric Disorders: Adults and Children. Baltimore, MD, Williams & Wilkins, 1980

Mandel MR, Welch CA, Mieske M, et al: Prediction of response to ECT in tricyclic-intolerant or tricyclic-resistant depressed patients. McLean Hosp J 2:203–209, 1977

Medical Research Council: Clinical trial of the treatment of depressive illness. Br Med J 5439:881–886, 1965

Paul SM, Extein I, Calil HM, et al: Use of ECT with treatment resistant depressed patients at the National Institute of Mental Health. Am J Psychiatry 138:486–489, 1981

Perry P, Tsuang MT: Treatment of unipolar depression following electroconvulsive therapy: relapse rate comparisons between lithium and tricyclic therapies following ECT. J Affective Disord 1:123–129, 1979

Price LH, Conwell Y, Nelson JC: Lithium augmentation of combined neuroleptic-tricyclic treatment in delusional depression. Am J Psychiatry 140:318–322, 1983

Prien RF, Klett CJ, Caffey EM Jr: Lithium carbonate and imipramine in prevention of affective episodes: a comparison in recurrent affective illness. Arch Gen Psychiatry 29:420–425, 1973

Prien RF, Kupfer DJ, Mansky PA, et al: Drug therapy in the prevention of recurrences in unipolar and bipolar affective disorder. Arch Gen Psychiatry 41:1096–1104, 1984

Prudic J, Sackeim HA, Devanand DP: Medication resistance and clinical response to electroconvulsive therapy. Psychiatry Res (in press)

Quitkin FM, Rabkin JG, Ross D, et al: Duration of antidepressant drug treatment: what is an adequate trial? Arch Gen Psychiatry 41:238–245, 1984

Sackeim HA, Decina P, Prohovnik I, et al: Anticonvulsant and antidepressant properties of ECT: a proposed mechanism of action. Biol Psychiatry 18:1301–1310, 1983

Sackeim HA, Decina P, Prohovnik I, et al: Seizure threshold in electroconvulsive therapy: effects of sex, age, electrode placement, and treatment number. Arch Gen Psychiatry 44:355–360, 1987

Sackeim HA, Prudic J, Devanand DP: Treatment of medication-resistant depression with electroconvulsive therapy, in American Psychiatric Press Review of Psychiatry, Vol 9. Edited by Tasman A, Goldfinger SM, Kaufmann CA. Washington, DC, American Psychiatric Press, 1990, pp 91–115

Sackeim HA, Prudic J, Devanand DP, et al: The impact of medication resistance and continuation pharmacotherapy on relapse following response to electroconvulsive therapy in major depressive disorder. J Clin Psychopharm (in press)

Seager CR, Bird RL: Imipramine with electrical treatment in depression—a controlled trial. J Ment Sci 108:704–707, 1962

Shapira B, Kindler S, Lerer B: Medication outcome in ECT-resistant depression. Convulsive Ther 4:192–199, 1988

Snaith RP: How much ECT does the depressed patient need? in Electroconvulsive Therapy: An Appraisal. Edited by Palmer RL. New York, Oxford University Press, 1981, pp 61–64

Spitzer RL, Endicott J, Robins E: Research Diagnostic Criteria: rationale and reliability. Arch Gen Psychiatry 35:773–782, 1978

Stevenson GH, Geoghegan JJ: Prophylactic electroshock: a five-year study. Am J Psychiatry 107:743–748, 1951

Chapter 7

Calcium Channel Blockers in Treatment-Resistant Bipolar and Unipolar Affective Disorders

Richard Brown, M.D.

Chapter 7

Calcium Channel Blockers in Treatment-Resistant Bipolar and Unipolar Affective Disorders

There is a clear need for alternatives to lithium and standard antidepressants. Perhaps 20% or more of bipolar patients do not respond to or cannot tolerate lithium (Jamison et al. 1979; Takehashi et al. 1975). Some unipolar depressed patients do not respond well to the most adequate trials of chemical antidepressants. Calcium channel blockers may offer potential treatment for some of these patients.

Calcium channel blockers, also known as calcium channel inhibitors or calcium antagonists, are drugs that typically decrease the entry of calcium into cells by interfering with the function of calcium channels. This class of medications was first developed as coronary vasodilators and is now in clinical use for treatment of angina, cardiac arrhythmias, and hypertension. This article reviews the physiology of calcium and calcium channels in nerve function, discusses the pharmacology of currently available calcium channel blockers, reviews studies of their usefulness in affective disorders, and suggests what future studies should be done.

PHYSIOLOGY OF CALCIUM

Changes in extracellular calcium have been associated with psychiatric symptoms for some time (Petersen 1968; Weston and Howard 1922). Decreased serum calcium has been linked with mania, agitation, delirium, and psychosis (Bowden et al. 1988). Hypercalcemia has been associated with depression, lethargy, and coma (Bowden et al. 1988). Decreases in serum and cerebrospinal fluid (CSF) calcium have been found following successful antidepressant treatment with tricyclic medications, lithium, and electroconvulsive therapy (ECT)

131

(Carman and Wyatt 1979a; Carman et al. 1977; Jimerson et al. 1979). Decrease in CSF calcium has been associated with depression by some investigators.

Calcium is integral to many activities of nerves, such as neurotransmitter release, regulation of enzyme activity, and axonal transport (Greenberg 1987). Calcium levels inside the cell are tightly controlled. Excess calcium is exchanged from inside the cell to outside the cell in place of sodium such that the concentration of calcium inside the cell is approximately one ten thousandth of that on the outside. Calcium inside the cell is compartmentalized within the mitochondria, smooth endoplasmic reticulum, and synaptic vesicles. Increases in the free intracellular level of calcium can activate a variety of enzymes and structural proteins important in nerve function. Calcium may enter the cell through specific lipoprotein pores in the cell membrane. In nerves, free intracellular calcium can be increased by the opening of calcium channels through electrical depolarization or by the binding of an agonist and a cell surface receptor. The latter releases calcium from its stores within the cell. Inside the cell, calcium usually binds to a protein such as calmodulin, which then changes in such a way that protein kinases activate a cascade of reactions.

There are three types of calcium channels in cell membranes in the body. The most well studied is the "slow channel," so called because it carries a current that lasts the longest. There are also three receptors for the slow channel, one each for drugs like verapamil, nifedipine, and diltiazem.

EARLY ATTEMPTS TO CHANGE CALCIUM IN PSYCHIATRY

Earlier observations of increases in serum calcium and decreases in CSF calcium level in psychotic agitation and mania led to a double-blind, placebo-controlled trial of calcitonin (Carman and Wyatt 1979b). Calcitonin decreased serum calcium, increased CSF calcium, and produced brief increases in depression with decrease in arousal.

Conversely, dihydrotachysterol (DHT), related to vitamin D, increased serum calcium and decreased CSF calcium. It was associated with the appearance or worsening of manic behavior in eight patients over a 2- to 6-week period (Carman and Wyatt 1979b). Although these preliminary studies did not lead to clinically useful treatments, they did lay a conceptual groundwork for the manipulation of calcium physiology in the treatment of affective disorders.

The class of calcium channel blockers includes more than 20 therapeutic compounds. In the past 20 years, they have been tested in therapy for migraine, dysmenorrhea, asthma, esophageal spasm,

Raynaud's phenomenon, and myocardial ischemia. Investigations continue in the use of calcium channel blockers in treatment of subarachnoid hemorrhage, cerebral vascular disorders such as seizures and migraine, other cardiac disorders, atherosclerosis, peripheral vascular disorders, and iatrogenic renal failure.

Human and animal studies have established that there are specific binding sites for calcium channel blockers in the brain (Greenberg 1987). Furthermore, in addition to blocking calcium channels, these drugs may either inhibit or activate nerves and the release of catecholamines. Verapamil, for example, inhibits alpha, beta, and opiate receptors as well as central sympathetic outflow.

CALCIUM CHANNEL BLOCKERS IN TREATMENT OF AFFECTIVE DISORDERS

Acute Mania

Dubovsky and colleagues expanded their report (1982) of a first case of an acutely manic patient responding to verapamil with a study of three acutely manic patients treated in a double-blind, placebo-controlled study of verapamil with each patient as his own control (Dubovsky and Franks 1983). Manic symptoms decreased significantly with dosages of verapamil from 160 mg to 480 mg per day. Symptoms returned on placebo.

Giannini and colleagues (1984) treated 10 mildly manic patients with verapamil in dosages of 320 mg per day compared to lithium or placebo in a single-blind, crossover design. Verapamil and lithium were both equally effective in reducing mania and superior to placebo.

Hoschl and Kozeny (1989) treated 12 manic inpatients with verapamil, 24 with neuroleptics, and 11 with both neuroleptics and lithium. All three treatments were significantly effective, even though the verapamil group was more severely ill at baseline before treatment.

Brotman and associates (1986) reported an open trial of verapamil in dosages of 160 mg to 320 mg per day in six acutely manic and psychotic patients who either had stopped lithium because of intolerance or had recurrences despite lithium compliance. All patients had a prompt reduction in their significant manic symptoms in 2 to 3 weeks.

Dubovsky and colleagues (1986) found that five of seven acutely manic patients treated over 24 days in a double-blind, crossover study responded to verapamil in dosages up to 480 mg per day and had no response to placebo. In that study, two patients in whom mania was associated with dementia improved on verapamil.

Caillard (1985) treated seven acutely manic patients with diltiazem in dosages from 120 mg to 360 mg per day. He reported that five patients improved over a 2-week period, although three of these were also treated with neuroleptics. The interpretation of this study must be limited because the trial of diltiazem was briefer than prior studies. Placebo was not used, and the three patients were treated with concomitant neuroleptics. (This was also true for the Brotman study.) The two nonresponders may have had organic affective syndromes.

Giannini and associates (1985) reported a double-blind, crossover study of 20 lithium-resistant manic patients with verapamil in dosages of 320 mg per day or clonidine with crossover to the other drug. Results indicated that verapamil had more effect on manic symptoms as measured by Brief Psychiatric Rating Scale (BPRS) scores (Overall and Gorham 1962), subjective reports, and global ratings; however, actual numbers on BPRS scores were not reported, and it is difficult to compare the severity of these patients' illnesses with other patients in the literature.

In contrast to these findings of Dubovsky, Giannini, and others, Barton and Gitlin (1987) reported more negative results from an open trial of verapamil in lithium-resistant mania. None of eight patients treated for acute mania responded. In fact, two became depressed. Two of four other patients showed partial or good response when treated with verapamil prophylactically. However, doses of verapamil used for acute mania (up to 240 mg daily) were lower than in most other studies.

Continuation in Manic-Depressive Illness

Giannini and colleagues (1987) reported on the use of verapamil in a 1-year, double-blind, crossover study of verapamil versus lithium in 20 manic patients. Subjects received lithium and verapamil for 6 months each. Both groups improved on the initial drug, verapamil or lithium, before crossover. However, verapamil-treated patients showed sufficient improvement sooner than lithium-treated patients, and lithium-treated patients continued to improve after being switched over to verapamil. This study indicated that verapamil might be a useful agent in the preventive treatment of bipolar illness. However, the sample size is small, the only rating scale used was the BPRS, and numbers were not reported. The number of relapses during the year was not reported for the two groups.

Blockade of Antidepressant-Induced Mania

Several case reports have supported the use of verapamil to prevent antidepressant-induced mania in bipolar patients. Gitlin and Weiss (1984) described a bipolar woman with a history of mania precipitated by antidepressants, including trazodone, despite lithium. Verapamil at 160 mg per day prevented manic symptoms when the patient was again treated with trazodone. She was able to remain euthymic on verapamil at 240 mg per day. Dubovsky and colleagues (1985) also described a double-blind, placebo crossover trial of verapamil in a patient with a history of phenelzine-induced mania. The patient refused to take lithium or carbamazepine. After pretreatment with verapamil, 400 mg per day, mania was not induced by the reintroduction of phenelzine. Solomon and Williamson (1986) reported two cases of manic-depressive patients who were unable to take lithium due to hyperparathyroidism in one case and noncompliance in the other. Their hypomania was successfully treated with verapamil, but treatment-emergent depression required the addition of trazodone. Both patients were stable for 4 months on the combination of verapamil and trazodone. Barton and Gitlin (1987) and Gitlin and Weiss (1984) described three cases in which verapamil blocked antidepressant-induced mania (in two cases, due to isocarboxazid).

Treatment of Unipolar Depression

Hoschl (1983) first reported a hypertensive woman with recurrent endogenous depression who had failed treatment with tricyclic antidepressants, lithium, neuroleptics, and ECT and whose depressive symptoms responded to a placebo crossover trial of verapamil. Hoschl and associates further reported (1986) that 15 of 19 endogenous or neurotic depressed patients showed slight to marked improvement when given a 2-week trial of verapamil in dosages from 240 mg to 400 mg per day. Clinical significance of the improvement was unclear, however, and further studies must be done.

Pollack and Rosenbaum (1987) reported verapamil treatment of a 35-year-old woman with recurrent, unipolar depression. This patient had a complicated and unusual history. On her first inpatient admission for depression, she responded to treatment with lithium carbonate and then experienced a recurrence that responded to the addition of imipramine. Due to renal side effects, lithium was discontinued, and the patient again relapsed despite continued adequate doses of imipramine. A 2-week trial of verapamil titrated up to 320 mg per day resulted in resolution of major depression and recurrent atypical migraine headaches. Imipramine was discontinued, and the patient remained well for over a year on verapamil.

Kramer and associates (1988) treated six male inpatients with major depression with 60 mg daily of nifedipine in a double-blind, placebo-controlled, crossover study of 8 weeks duration. Depression ratings worsened in both placebo and nifedipine groups.

Hoschl and Kozeny (1989) randomized 64 depressed inpatients to treatment with verapamil, amitriptyline, or placebo. Verapamil was no different from placebo in efficacy, and amitriptyline was superior to both.

Eckmann (1985) reported a double-blind, placebo-controlled comparison of flunarizine with placebo in 32 patients with diagnosis of involutional depression and cerebral circulatory disturbances. The study showed an 82% rate of improvement in the flunarizine group compared to 26% in the placebo group.

CLINICAL USE

Verapamil or other calcium channel blockers might be considered in the acute treatment of mania in patients unresponsive to or unable to tolerate lithium or anticonvulsants. Patients with organic brain syndromes, particularly cerebrovascular problems or cardiovascular problems such as ischemic heart disease or hypertension, might also be considered for treatment. Patients with migraine or peripheral vascular disease might benefit from verapamil if they have concomitant affective disorder. Another use of calcium channel blockers in affective disorder is in adjunctive use in patients who have had mania induced by treatment with antidepressants.

Patients with preexisting heart block or congestive heart failure have relative contraindications to the use of calcium channel blockers. Verapamil is perhaps the best studied of the calcium channel blockers in psychiatry or medicine. Dosages of 240 mg to 480 mg per day, are used in the treatment of angina. Major cardiovascular effects include relaxation of coronary arteries and peripheral blood vessels and decreased conduction through the atrioventricular node. Side effects may include atrioventricular block, bradycardia, constipation, edema, heartburn, nausea and flushing, dizziness, and headache. Side effects of parkinsonism, akathisia, and delirium have been rarely reported (Chouza et al. 1986; Jacobs 1983), especially in combination with the neuroleptics. Verapamil has been reported to be well tolerated in the long-term study of patients with supraventricular tachycardia (Mauritson et al. 1982).

Diltiazem is used in the treatment of angina in dosages from 120 mg to 240 mg daily. Both verapamil and diltiazem may increase digoxin levels and result in toxicity.

Nifedipine is used in the treatment of angina in dosages from 30 mg to 90 mg daily. It is associated with a greater frequency of significant hypotension and reflex tachycardia as well as interactions with the metabolism of cimetidine.

Calcium channel blockers and beta adrenergic blocking drugs, such as propranolol, may produce significant bradycardia or conduction defects in some vulnerable patients; therefore, these drugs should be combined cautiously, if at all (Johnston et al. 1985). Caution must be exercised when combining lithium and verapamil, because they share cardiac effects; Dubovsky and colleagues (1987) reported two elderly manic patients who experienced significant cardiotoxicity from this combination.

Price and Giannini (1986) reported a syndrome of neurotoxicity characterized by nausea, vomiting, weakness, ataxia, and tinnitus. This syndrome recurred upon rechallenge with verapamil and lithium in a 42-year-old woman.

Carbamazepine, a drug that has become an important second line of treatment in bipolar illness, also has a significant metabolic interaction with verapamil and diltiazem such that carbamazepine toxicity may be caused by the combinations (Brodie and MacPhee 1986; MacPhee et al. 1986).

SUMMARY

The above studies of verapamil, diltiazem, and nifedipine in the treatment of mania and depression suggest that calcium channel blockers have a modest antimanic effect acutely and a modest effect on prevention of mania. Treatment of depression with verapamil would only be considered after other more standard or innovative treatments, such as those discussed in this monograph, have failed. There may be a minority of patients whose depression would respond well to calcium channel blockers, but we do not know how to identify those patients.

Another significant issue is whether calcium channel blockers might predispose to recurrences of depression in some vulnerable bipolar or unipolar depressive patients. My own experience with verapamil is similar to that of Barton and Gitlin (1987) and Fogelman (1988) who noted switches into depression. Hullett and colleagues (1988) reported four cases of unipolar depression associated with nifedipine. Further prospective studies of larger numbers of patients with more comprehensive rating scales need to be done in this area.

Speculation on the mechanism of action of calcium channel blockers is interesting but not definitive. We still do not understand the cause of manic-depressive illness nor the mechanism of action of lithium in those patients who do respond (Aronoff et al. 1971). We still do not know whether the bipolar patients who respond to lithium or anticonvulsants are physiologically and clinically similar to those patients who respond to verapamil. One hypothesis would be that calcium channel blockers produce improvement in manic symptoms by blocking calcium influx or otherwise preventing increased intracellular calcium. This would in turn decrease activation of related neurotransmitters and receptors. However, the indirect evidence that decreasing intraneural levels of calcium may predispose to depression should make us wary of indiscriminately using these agents in treatment-resistant depressions. One piece of supportive evidence for the use of calcium channel blockers in the treatment of depression is that most effective antidepressant agents have been reported to induce mania. There is a report of mania as a side effect of diltiazem in one patient (Brink 1984). Furthermore, Itil and colleagues (1984) reported that nimodipine had an electrophysiologic profile on electroencephalogram similar to the activity of antidepressants.

Therefore, verapamil and other calcium channel blockers may be useful in the acute treatment of manic patients as an alternative to lithium, anticonvulsants, or ECT. Using calcium channel blockers to prevent antidepressant-induced mania may be an innovative but esoteric use. They may be helpful in a small number of patients with refractory depression, but we do not yet know how to identify such patients. More studies are needed of their efficacy and side effects in acute depression, acute mania, and the long-term maintenance of bipolar disorder.

Such studies are not easily done because patients who would benefit from such a third line alternative are uncommon. It is often difficult to obtain consent in the acute affective episode, and to get agreement from family to embark on double-blind, placebo-controlled trials of such patients. There has been little consistency in the rating scales for affective symptoms that have been used in published studies.

Calcium channel blockers may offer more potential in the future. Different tissues have different types of calcium channels with different responses to the same calcium channel blocker. Animal models of mania and depression may prove the most efficient way to screen for potential usefulness of various calcium channel blockers with greater specificity for nerve channels in the brain.

REFERENCES

Aronoff MS, Evens RG, Durell J: Effect of lithium salts on electrolyte metabolism. J Psychiatr Res 8:139–159, 1971

Barton BM, Gitlin ML: Verapamil in treatment-resistant mania: an open trial. J Clin Psychopharmacol 7:101–103, 1987

Bowden CL, Huang LG, Javors MA, et al: Calcium function in affective disorders in healthy controls. Biol Psychiatry 23:367–376, 1988

Brink DD: Diltiazem and hyperactivity (letter). Ann Intern Med 100:459, 1984

Brodie MJ, MacPhee GJA: Carbamazepine neurotoxicity precipitated by diltiazem. Br Med [Clin Res] 292:1170–1171, 1986

Brotman AW, Fahardi AM, Gelenberg AJ: Verapamil in treatment of acute mania. J Clin Psychiatry 47:136–138, 1986

Caillard V: Treatment of mania using a calcium antagonist—preliminary trial. Neuropsychobiology 14:23–26, 1985

Carman JS, Post RM, Teplitz TA, et al: Calcium and electroconvulsive therapy of severe depressive illness. Biol Psychiatry 12:5–17, 1977

Carman JS, Wyatt RJ: Calcium: bivalent cation in the bivalent psychoses. Biol Psychiatry 14:295–336, 1979a

Carman JS, Wyatt RJ: Use of calcitonin in psychotic agitation or mania. Arch Gen Psychiatry 36:72–75, 1979b

Chouza C, Scaramelli A, Caamano JL, et al: Parkinsonism, tardive dyskinesia, akathisia and depression induced by flunarizine. Lancet 1:1303–1304, 1986

Dubovsky SL, Franks RD: Intracellular calcium in affective disorders: a review and an hypothesis. Biol Psychiatry 18:781–787, 1983

Dubovsky SL, Franks RD, Lifschitz M, et al: Effectiveness of verapamil in the treatment of a manic patient. Am J Psychiatry 139:502–504, 1982

Dubovsky SL, Franks RD, Schrier D: Phenelzine-induced hypomania: effect of verapamil. Biol Psychiatry 20:1009–1014, 1985

Dubovsky SL, Franks RD, Allen S, et al: Calcium antagonists in mania: a double-blind study of verapamil. Psychiatry Res 18:309–320, 1986

Dubovsky SL, Franks, RD, Allen S: Verapamil: a new antimanic drug with possible interactions with lithium. J Clin Psychiatry 48:371–372, 1987

Eckmann F: Clinical double blind study with the calcium antagonist flunarizine in cerebral circulatory disturbances. Arzneimittelforschung 35:1276–1279, 1985

Fogelman J: Verapamil caused depression, confusion, and impotence (letter). Am J Psychiatry 145:380, 1988

Giannini AJ, Houser WL, Loisell RH, et al: Antimanic effects of verapamil. Am J Psychiatry 141:1602–1603, 1984

Giannini AJ, Loisell RH, Price WA, et al: Comparison of antimanic efficacy of clonidine and verapamil. J Clin Pharmacol 25:307–308, 1985

Giannini AJ, Taraszewski R, Loisell H: Verapamil and lithium in maintenance therapy of manic patients. J Clin Pharmacol 27:980–982, 1987

Gitlin MJ, Weiss J: Verapamil as maintenance treatment in bipolar illness: a case report. J Clin Psychopharmacol 4:341–343, 1984

Greenberg DA: Calcium channels and calcium channel antagonists. Ann Neurol 21:317–330, 1987

Hoschl C: Verapamil for depression? (letter). Am J Psychiatry 140:1100, 1983

Hoschl C, Kozeny J: Verapamil in affective disorders: a controlled, double-blind study. Biol Psychiatry 25:128–140, 1989

Hoschl C, Blahos J, Kabes J: The use of calcium channel blockers in psychiatry, Biological Psychiatry 1985. Edited by Shagass CE, Josiassen RC, Bridger WH, et al. New York, Elsevier, 1986, pp 330–332, 1986

Hullett FJ, Potkin SG, Levy AB, et al: Depression associated with nifedipine-induced calcium channel blockade. Am J Psychiatry 145:1277–1279, 1988

Itil TM, Michael ST, Hoffmeister F, et al: Nimodipine, a calcium antagonist vasodilator with psychotropic properties (a controlled quantitative pharmaco-EEG study). Curr Therapeutic Res 35:405, 1984

Jacobs MB: Diltiazem and akathisia. Ann Intern Med 99:794–795, 1983

Jamison KR, Gerner RH, Goodwin FK: Patient and physician attitudes towards lithium. Arch Gen Psychiatry 36:866–869, 1979

Jimerson DC, Post RM, Carman JS, et al: CSF calcium: clinical correlates in affective illness and schizophrenia. Biol Psychiatry 14:37–51, 1979

Johnston DL, Lesoway R, Humen DP, et al: Clinical and hemodynamic evaluation of propranolol in combination with verapamil, nifedipine and diltiazem in exertional angina pectoris: a double-blind, randomized, crossover study. Am J Cardiol 55:680–687, 1985

Kramer MS, Caputo K, DiJohnson C, et al: Negative trial of nifedipine in depression (letter). Biol Psychiatry 24:958–959, 1988

MacPhee GJA, Thompson GG, McInnes GT, et al: Verapamil potentiates carbamazepine neurotoxicity: a clinically important inhibitory interaction. Lancet 1:700–703, 1986

Mauritson DR, Winniford MD, Waler WS, et al: Oral verapamil for paroxysmal supraventricular tachycardia: a long-term, double-blind randomized trial. Ann Intern Med 96:409–412, 1982

Overall JE, Gorham DR: The Brief Psychiatric Rating Scale. Psychol Rep 10:799–812, 1962

Patterson JF: Treatment of acute mania with verapamil (letter). J Clin Psychopharmacol 7:206–207, 1987

Petersen P: Psychiatric disorders in primary hyperparathyroidism. J Clin Endocrinol Metab 28:1491–1495, 1968

Pollack MH, Rosenbaum JF: Verapamil in the treatment of recurrent unipolar depression. Biol Psychiatry 22:779–782, 1987

Price WA, Giannini AJ: Neurotoxicity caused by lithium-verapamil synergism. J Clin Pharmacol 26:717–719, 1986

Solomon L, Williamson P: Verapamil in bipolar illness. Can J Psychiatry 31:442–444, 1986

Takehashi R, Sakuma A, Itoh K, et al: Comparison of efficacy of lithium carbonate and chlorpromazine in mania. Arch Gen Psychiatry 32:1310–1318, 1975

Weston PG, Howard MQ: The determination of sodium, potassium, calcium, and magnesium in the blood and spinal fluid of patients suffering from manic-depressive insanity. Archives of Neurology and Psychiatry 8:179–183, 1922

Chapter 8

Serotonergic Agents in the Treatment of Refractory Depression

J. Sidney Jones, M.D.
Michael Stanley, Ph.D.

Chapter 8

Serotonergic Agents in the Treatment of Refractory Depression

This chapter will review the use of serotonergic agents in the treatment of refractory depression. The introduction will define the term *refractory depression*, describe the characteristics of patients with refractory depression, and summarize the importance of serotonin in relation to psychiatric clinical conditions. The reader will then be provided with a summary of the literature involving the use of serotonergic agents in the treatment of depression and a review of those studies that have used serotonergic agents in the treatment of refractory depression. Specific agents to be reviewed will include the serotonin precursors tryptophan and 5-hydroxytryptophan in addition to the serotonergic reuptake inhibitors chlorimipramine, zimelidine, fluvoxamine, and fluoxetine.

INTRODUCTION

Definition and Description of Patients With Refractory Depression

There are a number of methodological problems involved in the study of refractory depression, including clarification as to whether the patient is nonresponsive or noncompliant, variability in the patient's response to treatment from episode to episode of depression, and general lack of specificity of the term. In the psychiatric literature, refractory depression is often interchanged with treatment-resistant depression, and they have been operationally defined along a continuum of stringency. Kielholz and associates (1979) defined treatment-resistant depression as a depressed patient's lack of response to two correctly selected tricyclic antidepressants at adequate dosages. This lower threshold for treatment-resistant status has generally been

Supported in part by USPHS grants MH42242 and MH41847.

rejected in favor of more stringent criteria. Shaw (1977) have proposed that consecutive trials of different agents for specified minimal lengths of time be utilized before the terms refractory or treatment-resistant depression are employed. Specifically, this would include one or more trials of a tricyclic antidepressant at doses equivalent to 300 mg of a tertiary amine, an adequate trial of a monoamine oxidase inhibitor (MAOI), and an adequate course of electroconvulsive therapy (ECT) (up to 12 to 16 bilateral treatments). The most stringent criteria offered by others (Links and Akiskal 1987), entails a history of treatment failure with two standard tricyclic antidepressants, an MAOI, lithium carbonate, ECT, and a newer heterocyclic agent. In this chapter, the term *refractory depression* will be utilized to describe patients who fail to respond to two or more adequate courses of treatment with tricyclic antidepressants, MAOIs, or ECT.

The concept of refractory depression is meaningful and relevant if only because of the number of patients with major depressive disorders who do not respond satisfactorily to any given somatic treatment (Ayd 1983). Failure of patients to respond to antidepressant treatments (ADT) including MAOIs or tricyclic antidepressants (TCAs) has been estimated to range from 10% to 20% (Ananth and Ruskin 1974). Despite the differences in definitions, it is possible to ascertain what treatment-refractory patients are like and how they differ from the majority of depressive patients who respond to established somatic treatments of depression. Most of the literature concerning lack of response to treatment is based on lack of response to TCAs (Nelson and Charney 1981), MAOIs (Nies and Robinson 1982), or ECT (Kiloh 1982). A significantly smaller group of depressed patients fail to respond to two or more of these treatment modalities. These patients have generally been included in the literature as case reports rather than participants in controlled clinical trials. While there are no definitive collections of descriptors to provide distinguishing profiles regarding these patients, they are generally described as incapacitated by their depressions (e.g., high Hamilton depression scores), more likely to have a history of a greater number of psychiatric hospitalizations, and more likely to have suffered a chronic course with recurrent episodes. Whether these patients are more likely to have an earlier age of onset or a history of suicide attempts has not been systematically investigated.

Serotonin and Disorders Relevant to Psychiatry

Serotonin was first isolated in 1948 by Rapport and colleagues. This characterization of serotonin was followed by the discovery of serotonin in the central nervous system (Twarog and Page 1953). Depression was the first of the major psychiatric disorders to have disturbances in the serotonergic system identified. In humans the primary method of assessing serotonergic function has been to measure cerebrospinal fluid (CSF) levels of 5-hydroxyindoleacetic acid (5-HIAA), the metabolite of serotonin.

Cerebrospinal fluid 5-HIAA has been found to be decreased in approximately 30% to 40% of depressed patients by several investigators (for review see van Praag 1982a). In addition, low CSF 5-HIAA has been implicated in the study of suicide. Specifically, serotonin and/or 5-HIAA levels were found to be lower in the brainstem regions in postmortem studies of suicide completers (Pare et al. 1969; Shaw et al. 1967). Suicide attempter studies also reported lower CSF 5-HIAA levels in depressed patients who had attempted suicide before admission in comparison with depressed patients who had not attempted suicide. Eight of ten studies of depressed patients confirm the relationship between suicidal behavior and decreased CSF 5-HIAA (see Table 8-1) (Stanley and Stanley 1988).

Serotonergic dysfunction also has been noted in suicide attempters (as evidenced by decreased CSF 5-HIAA) with other diagnoses including schizophrenia and personality disorders (Asberg et al. 1986b). In addition, serotonergic dysfunction extends beyond depression and suicide research; it is also involved in anxiety disorder research (Kahn et al. 1988). Finally, the serotonergic system may also be important in modulation of pain, weight loss, and alcohol consumption (Murphy et al. 1985). Thus, continuing research on the

Table 8-1. In vivo CSF studies of suicide attempters with a diagnosis of depression

Source	CSF 5-HIAA effect
Asberg et al. (1976)	Decreased CSF 5-HIAA
Agren (1980)	Decreased CSF 5-HIAA
Banki et al. (1981)	Decreased CSF 5-HIAA
Oreland et al. (1981)	Decreased CSF 5-HIAA
van Praag (1982a)	Decreased CSF 5-HIAA
Agren (1983)	Decreased CSF 5-HIAA
Palanappian et al. (1983)	Decreased CSF 5-HIAA
Lopez-Ibor et al. (1985)	Decreased CSF 5-HIAA
Secunda et al. (1986)	No effect on CSF 5-HIAA
Vestergaard et al. (1978)	No effect on CSF 5-HIAA

Note. CSF = cerebrospinal fluid. 5-HIAA = 5-hydroxyindoleacetic acid.

serotonergic system expands knowledge regarding serotonergic dysfunction and depression as well as the serotonergic dysfunction relationship to other conditions.

SEROTONIN PRECURSORS

One area of this research has focused on the treatment of depression with serotonin precursors and the development of specific serotonergic reuptake inhibitors for the treatment of depression. Systematic administration of precursors of neurotransmitters to increase brain levels of neurotransmitters and potentially increase presynaptic activity has been employed in a number of disorders. This approach has been successful in the treatment of Parkinson's disease, using dopamine's precursor L-dopa, which crosses the blood-brain barrier (Barbeau and McDowell 1970). Tryptophan and 5-hydroxytryptophan (5-HT) also cross the blood-brain barrier. These precursors have been shown to increase the rate of synthesis of brain serotonin in humans, as evidenced by increased production of CSF 5-HIAA, the main degradation product of serotonin (Goodwin et al. 1973; van Praag 1980). Biochemical evidence that precursors increase brain levels of serotonin served as the rationale for using tryptophan and 5-HT in the treatment of depression. This section will review the literature regarding these agents in the treatment of depression, with particular emphasis on studies involving refractory depression.

Tryptophan

Tryptophan has been used alone and in combination with other antidepressants, including serotonergic antidepressants and MAOIs. Numerous trials comparing the use of tryptophan alone (3 g to 10 g/day) with placebo have failed to establish tryptophan's efficacy in the treatment of depression (van Praag 1980). A review by Cole et al. (1980) revealed that the use of tryptophan alone as a treatment for depression was effective in only 4 of 12 trials and among only 48 of 136 patients (35%), which is comparable to placebo responses in many antidepressant trials in depression (Baldessarini 1983).

Broadhurst (1970) explored the combination of 6 g of tryptophan with 60 mg of pyridoxine hydrochloride (vitamin B6), in the treatment of a group of 36 patients with refractory depression. Vitamin B6 was added to decrease the hepatic metabolism of tryptophan before it crossed the blood-brain barrier. At the time of entry for L-tryptophan, patients had received trials of unspecified dosage regimens for an unspecified duration of a TCA and/or MAOIs. After a 4-week trial, 22 patients, 61% of the sample, responded to tryptophan/pyridoxine, as evidenced by a 75% reduction in their pretreatment Hamilton Depression scores. An additional 6 patients responded more slowly; however, the authors did not specify the extent of the improvement. Follow-up data indicated that 20 of those patients who responded to treatment sustained improvement for at least 1 year. Reported side effects were generally mild and included nausea and lightheadedness.

Given the low percentage of studies that corroborate tryptophan's efficacy as an antidepressant (Cole et al. 1980), the fact that tryptophan was found to be efficacious in a group of patients who had failed to respond to trials of a TCA and an MAOI is noteworthy. However, the bulk of evidence does not support the role of tryptophan alone in the treatment of depression. In addition, the results by Broadhurst have not been replicated, nor was the author able to explain the discrepancy between his findings and those of others investigating the antidepressant properties of tryptophan.

Whether addition of tryptophan to antidepressants that are relatively potent serotonin reuptake inhibitors or to MAOIs enhances the antidepressant activity of these medications has also received research attention. Consistent with theoretical expectations that precursor loading with tryptophan or 5-HTs could increase levels of brain serotonin in an additive way with selective reuptake of serotonin (and antidepressant response), reports indicate that clomipramine response has been augmented by tryptophan (Roos 1976; Walinder et al. 1976). In the latter study, 24 endogenously depressed women, consecutively admitted, were treated in a double-blind study with chlorimipramine plus placebo, or tryptophan given at a daily dosage of 100 mg/kg body weight. There was a significantly better response in the clomipramine with tryptophan group on the basis of changes in the Cronholm and Ottosson criteria. The clinical effect of adding tryptophan to clomipramine measured during a 21-day trial was consistent in that response in the combined treatment group was more rapid, but the experiment was too short in duration to claim definitively a superior response. Shaw and associates (1972) also failed to demonstrate the efficacy of clomipramine and tryptophan, although in their study, only five patients were treated with this regimen.

In a more recent study by the Walinder group (1981), tryptophan failed to potentiate zimelidine, another potent 5-HT uptake inhibitor. In this double-blind study, 26 inpatients with a diagnosis of endogenous depression were randomly assigned to a combined treatment of zimelidine and tryptophan or zimelidine and placebo. The addition of tryptophan, administered in the same dosage as in earlier studies by Walinder and colleagues, did not alter the efficacy of treatment with zimelidine. Finally, toxic reactions have occurred when a selective serotonin uptake inhibitor, fluoxetine, and tryptophan (up to 10 g/day) were given concurrently (Steiner and Fontaine 1986). Thus, there is less than adequate evidence in support of tryptophan's capacity to enhance the efficacy of tricyclic antidepressants that block serotonin uptake.

The addition of tryptophan to MAOIs has also received attention. Coppen and associates (1967) first reported the potentiation of antidepressant effects of an MAOI by tryptophan. In this double-blind study, those patients who received an MAOI and tryptophan improved significantly more than the group receiving MAOI and placebo. Pare (1963) corroborated these results in a study without controls; 6 of 14 patients responded to the addition of tryptophan to an MAOI, relapsing when placebo was substituted for tryptophan. A 21-day study by Glassman and Platman (1969) involved 20 patients randomly assigned to phenelzine sulfate, an MAOI, with or without the addition of tryptophan. At the end of the third week, the group receiving tryptophan had shown a trend toward substantially better response, with the differences between the tryptophan and placebo groups falling between the .1 and .05 levels of significance. Ayuso-Gutierrez and Lopez-Ibor (1971) conducted a study of the effects of adding tryptophan to an MAOI. This 20-day study also demonstrated positive results. Despite apparently positive results, however, all of the above studies involving the potentiation of MAOIs with tryptophan are limited by short duration of treatment. In addition, there have been several reports of toxicity when MAOIs and tryptophan were used concurrently (Brotman and Rosenbaum 1984). As first noted by Thomas and Rubin (1982), toxic reactions resembled "serotonin syndrome" in experimental animals, which includes tremor, myoclonus, hyperactivity, and hypertonicity (Squires 1978).

Given the absence of evidence supporting the use of tryptophan alone, and reports of toxic reactions when tryptophan and serotonin reuptake inhibitors or tryptophan and MAOIs were given concurrently, it is not surprising that no consensus has emerged regarding the efficacy of tryptophan in the treatment of depression. (See Note to the reader, below.)

5-HTP

Studies in depression have also examined the therapeutic efficacy of 5-HTP, the immediate precursor of serotonin. Like tryptophan, this

Note to the reader: As of 1990, the FDA has withdrawn L-tryptophan from the market due to its association with eosinophilia-myalgia syndrome, which has lead, in several cases, to death. At this time, L-tryptophan is available only to Investigational New Drug (IND) applicants.

precursor has been used alone and in combination with other antidepressants.

Use of 5-HTP has been associated with problematic gastrointestinal side effects, including nausea, emesis, and diarrhea (Sourkes 1983), which can be partially alleviated in a number of ways. To minimize these side effects, van Praag (1987) suggests slow increases in dosage on a divided schedule. The addition of carbidopa, a peripheral decarboxylase inhibitor that diminishes the conversion of 5-HT to serotonin before it crosses the blood-brain barrier, increases the amount of centrally available 5-HTP and lowers the necessary oral dosage. This also reduces gastrointestinal side effects. Finally, encapsulation of 5-HTP has been suggested to allow medication release at a lower point in the gastrointestinal tract, thus limiting the nausea attributed to direct effect of 5-HTP on the stomach.

Six studies have been conducted involving the use of 5-HTP in the treatment of depressive patients who did not respond to reuptake inhibitors. Four of these have utilized 5-HTP alone or in combination with a peripheral decarboxylase inhibitor in groups of patients who had failed to respond to other antidepressant treatments. Takahashi and co-workers (1975) studied 24 depressed inpatients. Sixteen of them had been placed on unspecified doses of TCAs "months" prior to beginning the study. Six (38%) of the 16 patients with prior treatment failures improved on 5-HTP, as evidenced by a seven-point posttreatment reduction in mean Hamilton Depression scores (X > 17 to X < 10). In an open study, Angst and colleagues (1977) treated 10 severely depressed inpatients with a history of treatment failures on unspecified doses of TCAs. There was an absence of significant improvement in any of the patients in this study, which used a mean dosage of 190 mg/day of 5-HTP combined with 375 mg of benzerazide, a decarboxylase inhibitor. Van Praag and colleagues (1974) reported the effects of 5-HTP in conjunction with a decarboxylase inhibitor in a group of seven patients with refractory depressions that had persisted continuously from 9 to 60 months. Only one of the seven patients responded dramatically to 5-HTP, and two dropped out of the study due to gastrointestinal side effects. Nolen and colleagues (1985) compared the efficacy of 5-HTP versus tranylcypromine, an MAOI, in a study of 26 patients with refractory depression. Participants were randomly assigned to treatment with 5-HTP or tranylcypromine for 4 weeks in a crossover design. None of the 17 given 5-HTP responded, whereas 15 of the 26 receiving tranylcypromine responded to treatment, as demonstrated by a significant reduction in their Hamilton Depression scores. Thus, 5-HTP, both alone and in combination with decarboxylase inhibitors, does not appear to be a therapeutically effective alternative in the treatment of refractory depressive patients nor depressive patients who have failed to respond to even one trial of a reuptake inhibitor.

Another approach to the treatment of refractory depression has involved the combined use of 5-HTP and other antidepressant agents. Van Praag and colleagues (1974) added 50 mg of clomipramine per day for 2 or more weeks to the regimen of five patients who had originally been placed only on 5-HTP and a peripheral decarboxylase inhibitor. He noted additional improvements in two patients after adding clomipramine. This led Van Hiele (1980) to add 50 mg to 600 mg/day of 5-HTP (a wide range in dosage) in combination with carbidopa to the antidepressant regimen of 99 outpatients. Addition of 5-HTP resulted in "complete recovery" in 43 patients, with another 8 showing at least some improvement. Thus, approximately 50% of patients were successfully treated (without side effects) as evidenced by ratings in clinical improvement. However, past treatment history and characteristics of the sample were varied, including patients with a history of nonresponse to reuptake inhibitors alone or in combination with antipsychotics and lithium carbonate. Thus, the open design of the study and the varied characteristics of the sample limit the generalizability of the results.

Kline and Sacks (1980) reported a marked response in 11 of 25 patients where 100 mg to 300 mg/day of 5-HTP was added to the medication regimen of patients who had failed to respond to MAOIs alone. An additional eight patients were described as partial responders. However, the method of assessing improvement was not specified.

Thus, upon review of the available data, it remains unclear whether tryptophan or 5-HTP is useful in the treatment of refractory depression. On the basis of current evidence, it appears that 5-HTP alone or in combination with a decarboxylase inhibitor is not an efficacious alternative in patients who have not responded to one or more reuptake inhibitors. The use of 5-HTP with MAOIs may be useful in patients who have failed to respond to MAOIs alone. However, additional research is needed to resolve this issue. (See Note to the reader, below.)

SEROTONIN REUPTAKE INHIBITORS

The development of specific serotonin reuptake inhibitors was based at least in part on the rationale that a subgroup of depressive patients,

Note to the reader: As of 1990, the FDA has withdrawn L-tryptophan from the market due to its association with eosinophilia-myalgia syndrome, which has lead, in several cases, to death. At this time, L-tryptophan is available only to Investigational New Drug (IND) applicants.

those with low CSF 5-HIAA levels (approximately 30% to 40% of depressive patients) might respond preferentially to serotonin reuptake inhibitors. In addition, the most serotonergic of the tricyclic antidepressants, clomipramine, was found to be useful in the treatment of obsessive-compulsive disorder as well as depression, suggesting a potentially unique set of actions for serotonergic reuptake inhibitors. However, the main desmethylated metabolite of clomipramine is also a potent inhibitor of norepinephrine reuptake. These findings led to the development of more specific serotonin reuptake inhibitors. The first of these to reach the market was zimelidine. Some specific serotonin reuptake inhibitors, such as fluoxetine, are currently on the market, and others, such as fluvoxamine, are at various stages of development. The efficacy of these drugs in the treatment of depression and refractory depression and their side-effect profiles will be reviewed in this section.

Clomipramine

Clomipramine, a tricyclic antidepressant with a preferential but nonspecific ability to block the reuptake of serotonin, has been used in Europe for the last two decades. As stated earlier, clomipramine is a strong serotonin reuptake inhibitor; however, its metabolite, desmethylimipramine, preferentially blocks the reuptake of norepinephrine. Thus, the receptor-blocking qualities of this drug are similar to other TCAs such as imipramine and amitriptyline (Gram 1983).

The antidepressant efficacy of clomipramine has been established in numerous clinical trials. Studies have demonstrated that clomipramine is as efficacious as other antidepressants including imipramine, amitriptyline, and maprotiline (Zarifian and Rigal 1983). Research has also been conducted comparing clomipramine with more selective serotonin uptake inhibitors. One study compared clomipramine and citalopram in a group of 114 depressed inpatients (Danish University Antidepressant Group 1986). A significantly higher percentage of clomipramine responders were classified as complete responders (posttreatment week 3, 4, 5 Hamilton Depression scores of less than or equal to 7) than were citalopram responders. Posttreatment differences in outcome were particularly related to sleep items in the Hamilton Depression Scale. In addition to clomipramine's well established efficacy in the treatment of depression, this medication was also discovered to be effective in alleviating obsessive symptoms in depressed patients (Lopez-Ibor 1966).

Dudley and colleagues (1980) reported the benefit of intravenous clomipramine in a group of 12 refractory patients who had been depressed for a number of months and who had failed to respond to treatment with two or more TCAs. Four of the 12 patients had failed to respond to treatments including ECT. The patients in this study received infusions of 75 mg over the first 3 days. Medication was then increased by 25-mg increments, reaching a maximum dose of 150 mg/day. This treatment resulted in a decrease in mean Hamilton Depression scores from 35 to 18. Infusion therapy was described as free of serious side effects. Although the posttreatment Hamilton Depression score in this study is as high as pretreatment scores for inclusion in other studies of antidepressants, the authors reported the patients' subjective satisfaction with intravenous clomipramine. These patients had significant histories of response failure with other anti-depressant treatments.

In conclusion, clomipramine is an effective TCA with established efficacy in the treatment of depression (Collins 1973). Unlike more specific serotonergic reuptake inhibitors, such as fluoxetine, clomipramine causes the typical autonomic side effects, orthostatic hypotension, and sedation that is seen with TCAs.

Zimelidine

Zimelidine was marketed in Europe between 1982 and 1983. It was the first of the selective serotonin uptake inhibitors to be studied extensively in large populations of depressed patients. Biochemical findings demonstrated that the drug's metabolite, norzimelidine, was 10 times more potent than the parent compound in the inhibition of serotonin uptake, and was also a weak norepinephrine uptake inhibitor (Bertilsson et al. 1980). When marketed, zimelidine was the most serotonergically specific medication available for the treatment of depression.

The antidepressant activity of zimelidine was established in several double-blind clinical studies with placebo and/or standard tricyclic agents. These studies clearly established the antidepressant efficacy of zimelidine in comparison with standard tricyclic antidepressants and suggest its superiority in treating certain subgroups of depressed patients. This literature has been reviewed in detail by the Asberg group (1986a).

Additional research was designed to compare the efficacy of zimelidine, a serotonergic drug, with noradrenergic agents in the treatment of depression. Hiramatsu and associates (1983) compared zimelidine with imipramine in a double-blind protocol that enlisted depressive patients. This study included both inpatients and out-patients and evaluated efficacy based on the Hamilton Rating Scale for Depression. In general, zimelidine and imipramine were found to be of comparable efficacy. However, patients over 40 years of age were significantly more responsive to zimelidine than to imipramine, as were those with a history of at least three episodes of depression and those who had a poor history of response to other antidepressants.

Nystrom and Hallstrom (1985) compared zimelidine with maprotiline in the treatment of 75 depressive outpatients. Patients were randomly assigned to one of the two conditions, and, following treatment, were rated according to a selection of items from the Comprehensive Psychopathology Rating Scale (Asberg et al. 1978). Although each drug demonstrated a considerable antidepressant effect, zimelidine was found to be significantly more effective than maprotiline among patients with a previous history of depressive episodes.

Finally, Aberg-Wistedt (1982) compared zimelidine with desipramine in a two-phase study. The first phase consisted of a 4-week, double-blind trial involving 65 inpatients with entry Hamilton Depression scores at or above 15. These patients carried diagnoses of both unipolar and bipolar depression. Zimelidine and desipramine were found to be equally efficacious in the treatment of depression in the first phase of the study. Twenty patients did not respond to treatment, defined by at least a 30% reduction in Hamilton Depression scores, and were offered continued treatment with the alternative antidepressant.

The second phase of this study involved the 16 patients who chose to continue and to receive the crossover treatment. Of these patients, 11 crossed over to zimelidine and 5 to desipramine treatment. Eight of the patients who had failed to respond to desipramine subsequently responded to zimelidine, and three of the five who had not responded to zimelidine were responsive to subsequent treatment with desipramine. Clinical comparisons were made between the two groups of responders in this crossover phase of the study. Patients responding to zimelidine experienced significantly less psychomotor retardation than those responding to desipramine. Aberg-Wistedt (1982) also observed that two patients with bipolar depression developed mania during crossover treatment with desipramine, whereas two patients with bipolar depression who were treated with zimelidine during the second treatment period did not show symptoms of mania.

Aberg-Wistedt and associates (1984) also used biochemical measures to compare patients treated with zimelidine and with desipramine. Biochemical differences between the two groups were ascertained on the basis of a smaller subsample comprised of those 19 patients who had agreed to lumbar puncture prior to beginning treatment in the first phase of the study. Aberg-Wistedt grouped patients on the basis of CSF 5-HIAA levels. Sixteen patients had CSF 5-HIAA levels above 15 ng/ml, and three measured below this level. This distribution of CSF 5-HIAA was consistent with the bimodal distribution of CSF 5-HIAA observed by Asberg and colleagues (1976). In patients with levels of CSF 5-HIAA of greater than 15 ng/ml, zimelidine, a serotonergic agent, and desipramine, a noradrenergic tricyclic, were equally efficacious in the treatment of depression. The three patients with low CSF 5-HIAA responded better to zimelidine than those with higher levels (as evidenced by significantly lower posttreatment Hamilton Depression scores). Due to the limited number of patients in this study, conclusions regarding the efficacy of zimelidine in patients with low CSF 5-HIAA levels should be interpreted with caution.

The studies described in this section suggest that zimelidine, and possibly other serotonin uptake inhibitors, may be particularly useful in treating subgroups of patients who are less likely to respond to standard TCAs. Continued research is needed to define more clearly these patient populations, in terms of both clinical and biochemical differences. However, zimelidine was withdrawn from the market in 1983 (Nilsson 1983) because of reports of adverse drug reactions. Specifically, during the first weeks of treatment with zimelidine, a number of patients developed neurologic complications, including Guillain-Barre syndrome, which was associated with hypersensitivity reactions, including fevers and myalgias.

Fluvoxamine

Fluvoxamine is another of the new selective serotonin uptake inhibitors that has been marketed throughout Europe since 1984. One of the features that distinguishes this drug from other antidepressants is its relatively short half-life and its lack of an active metabolite. The half-life of fluvoxamine is approximately 15 hours (Claassen et al. 1977), appreciably less than the half-life of fluoxetine, which is 1 to 3 days for the parent compound and 7 to 15 days for norfluoxetine (the N-demethylated metabolite of fluoxetine) (Lemberger et al. 1985). Fluvoxamine's side-effect profile is similar to those observed among selective serotonin uptake inhibitors that remain on the market today. Reported side effects include headache, nausea, lack of weight gain, and agitation (Benfield and Ward 1986). Like fluoxetine, fluvoxamine is devoid of anticholinergic side effects, causes only a clinically insignificant slowing of the heart rate (Roos 1983), and is safe in overdose (Banerjee 1988).

Fluvoxamine's efficacy as an antidepressant treatment has been shown through studies comparing it with placebo and with standard

TCAs, including imipramine and clomipramine. These studies demonstrated that fluvoxamine was as efficacious as either comparison tricyclic. The literature reporting these findings has been reviewed in detail by Benfield and Ward (1986).

Fluvoxamine's efficacy in the treatment of refractory depression was suggested by the results of a single-blind study recently conducted by Delgado and colleagues (1988). Participants were drawn from a pool of 38 consecutively admitted, depressed inpatients who met the authors' criteria for refractory status. A patient was included if he or she had failed at least one trial of antidepressant of 4 weeks' duration with documentation of a therapeutic blood level and/or a dose of at least 300 mg/day of imipramine or its equivalent. In this sample, the number of previously failed treatments was much higher than admission criteria in the majority of patients. After fluvoxamine treatment, patients with clinical global improvement were classified as partial responders. Those who also demonstrated a 50% decrease in Hamilton Depression scores, with a final score of 15 or less, were classified as marked responders.

Of the 38 patients who originally met criteria for inclusion, 28 completed the study. These patients received a 2-week placebo trial, followed by a 4 to 6 week trial of fluvoxamine. Eight patients responded to fluvoxamine alone. An additional eight patients responded to lithium augmentation of fluvoxamine. Two patients responded when perphenazine was added to fluvoxamine and lithium treatment. Finally, 10 patients failed to respond to any course of treatment. The inability of fluvoxamine treatment to produce a response in the majority of the 28 patients who completed the study should not be taken out of context. It is noteworthy that six of the patients who responded to the addition of lithium to fluvoxamine had previously failed to respond when lithium was added to a TCA.

Fluoxetine

Since its pharmacologic effects were first described in 1974, fluoxetine has been studied for its efficacy and safety in the treatment of depression (Wong et al. 1974). The antidepressant effect of fluoxetine, a selective serotonin uptake inhibitor, has been assessed in controlled studies comparing its efficacy with placebo and with standard TCAs. In clinical trials comparing fluoxetine and placebo, patients receiving fluoxetine improved significantly on scores of the Hamilton Rating Scale for Depression in comparison to patients taking placebo. However, stringent criteria for a 50% reduction in Hamilton Depression scores or a final Hamilton Depression score of less than 8 were not met in a study of 47 patients by Fabre and

Crismon (1985) or in the following fluoxetine versus placebo studies. In studies by the Rickels group (1986) and Wernicke and co-workers (1987), patients on the average were still mildly depressed at the completion of the 6-week study period. In a study of 70 depressive outpatients with Hamilton Depression scores greater than 20, Fieve and associates (1986) reported significant improvement in response to fluoxetine treatment. However, the mean Hamilton Depression scores decreased only 5.6 points, which is consistent with the "residual depression" noted in trials comparing placebo with fluoxetine.

One possible explanation for the residual mild depression noted concerns the Hamilton Rating Scale for Depression itself. In this scale, sleep disturbances are weighted heavily (3 of the 17 items). Thus, the profile of a drug devoid of sedative properties or one like fluoxetine with side effects including insomnia and anxiety could account for the residual "mild depression" in fluoxetine-treated patients.

The results of studies comparing fluoxetine and other antidepressants, including imipramine (Bremner 1984; Cohn and Wilcox 1985; Reimherr et al. 1984), amitriptyline (Chouinard 1985; Feighner 1985), and doxepin (Feighner and Cohn 1985), show that fluoxetine and standard comparison TCAs are comparable in terms of efficacy. In the above studies, entry Hamilton Depression scores were above 20. Endpoint Hamilton Depression scores of patients who took standard TCAs were comparable to those treated with fluoxetine in that a residual mild depression was present in both groups. Thus, it is important to consider the efficacy of fluoxetine in comparison with standard tricyclic agents, in addition to placebo studies.

One of the more impressive differences between tricyclics and fluoxetine concerns their respective side effect profiles. Fluoxetine is slowly absorbed with peak plasma concentrations occurring in 6 to 8 hours. Elimination half-life of the parent drug is 1 to 3 days after ingestion. Elimination half-life for its major metabolite N-demethylfluoxetine, which retains its activity and serotonergic specificity, ranges from 7 to 15 days. The extended half-life of this drug and its active metabolite is extremely problematic for patients who experience clinically significant side effects. Predominant side effects include anorexia, nervousness, and insomnia. These side effects are reported more frequently with fluoxetine than with TCAs. However, TCAs are associated with different problems, including a less favorable anticholinergic profile and cardiovascular side effects. Cardiac effects of fluoxetine are minimal. ECG analysis of 312 patients placed on fluoxetine revealed a decrease in heart rate of only three beats per minute (Fisch 1985). Unlike TCAs, fluoxetine has been associated with modest weight loss or lack of weight gain (Chouinard

1985). In addition, the low therapeutic index of TCAs in comparison with fluoxetine, which is relatively safe in overdose, should be considered when treating patients at high risk for suicide (Wernicke 1985). There is a well-known association between the ingestion of TCAs and morbidity and mortality (Davis 1975). In contrast, only one death has been linked to the use of fluoxetine (Wernicke 1985). Wernicke's findings, although based on a limited amount of data, suggest that when taken in excessive amounts fluoxetine is safer than most other antidepressants, TCAs in particular. This is notable given the long half-life of fluoxetine and its metabolites.

Drug interactions with fluoxetine are significant. On the basis of animal models utilized by Marley and Wozniak (1983), 5-HT reuptake inhibitors were extremely hazardous when used in combination with MAOIs. Consistent with the animal model and with the long half-life of fluoxetine and its metabolite, three fatalities were reported when tranylcypromine was administered subsequent to the discontinuation of fluoxetine following an indeterminate length of time. Therefore, clinicians are advised to wait a minimum of 5 weeks after discontinuation of fluoxetine before prescribing an MAOI (Sternbach 1988). Steiner and Fontaine (1986) reported toxic reactions following the addition of L-tryptophan as an adjunct to fluoxetine in all five patients they attempted to treat with the combination treatment. Reported symptoms included agitation, poor concentration, gastrointestinal side effects, and restlessness.

Finally, there are reports that the addition of fluoxetine to TCAs increases their efficacy, although there is disagreement as to whether it is safe to do so. Rosenthal and others (in press) reported that fluoxetine enhanced the response of three patients who had histories of poor response to TCAs alone. Specifically, 20 mg to 40 mg of fluoxetine was administered to patients who had been previously treated with TCAs for a number of weeks. A robust clinical improvement was noted and sustained after the addition of fluoxetine. The only noted side effect of the combined treatment involved one patient who complained of motor restlessness and hand tremor that responded to low doses of alprazolam.

In contrast to the above case reports, Vaughan (1988) noted that the addition of 20 mg of fluoxetine per day to the regimen of two patients taking therapeutic doses of a TCA resulted in elevated tricyclic blood levels and symptoms of tricyclic toxicity, including decreased energy, sedation, psychomotor retardation, and increased dysphoria. The author warned that toxic side effects resulted even when tricyclic doses of nortriptyline, for example, were decreased from 175 mg to 100 mg/day prior to adding fluoxetine treatment.

Thus, it appears that combined treatment with fluoxetine and TCAs necessitates careful monitoring of tricyclic blood levels and a substantial reduction in the doses of the TCA.

The question as to whether fluoxetine may be more beneficial for certain types of depressed patients than standard TCAs has also received attention. In addition, Reimherr and colleagues (1984) compared the efficacy of fluoxetine versus imipramine (51% versus 44%) in a population in which 7% responded to placebo. However, when patients with a clear history of poor response to past antidepressant treatments were compared, more impressive differences emerged. Specifically, 17 (43%) of 40 patients receiving fluoxetine, and 8 (30%) of 27 patients receiving imipramine responded to treatment. Similarly, the efficacy of fluoxetine among patients with chronic histories of depression was superior to that of imipramine among chronic patients with duration of symptoms greater than 2 years. These differences were statistically significant.

The combination of fluoxetine and other antidepressant treatments has also received attention in the literature. Pope and colleagues (1988) reported that five treatment-refractory patients responded to lithium carbonate given in conjunction with fluoxetine. Clinical response was maintained for up to 8 months. Side effects due to combined use of lithium and fluoxetine were not mentioned, if present.

In conclusion, fluoxetine is the only serotonergic reuptake inhibitor that is currently marketed in the United States. This drug's efficacy and side-effect profile compares favorably with standard TCAs. Whether fluoxetine will occupy a prominent place in the treatment of specific populations of depressed patients, including those unresponsive to TCAs, is not yet clear.

CONCLUSION

Tryptophan and 5-HTP

In summary, there is evidence to suggest that serotonergic compounds may be efficacious in the treatment of refractory depression. However, studies involving serotonin precursors have not definitively supported a role for their use in refractory depression. There are a number of methodological issues with previous research, including dose and time course of treatment, that deserve consideration. These are reviewed by Gelenberg and colleagues (1982). In addition, the use of 5-HTP alone or in combination with a decarboxylase inhibitor is not an efficacious alternative for treatment-refractory patients. The combination of 5-HTP and MAOIs may be useful to patients who have failed to respond to previous antidepressant treatments.

The clinician should be aware of the toxicity of tryptophan when given concomitantly with MAOIs or selective serotonin reuptake inhibitors. Because tryptophan is readily available as an over-the-counter amino acid, patients who are not improving on prescribed regimens alone may be tempted to consider adding this compound to their treatment regimens.

Serotonin Reuptake Inhibitors

The unique biochemical characteristics of serotonin reuptake inhibitors may offer a different treatment profile than TCAs (Potter et al. 1988). Specifically, zimelidine, fluvoxamine, and fluoxetine have been found to be efficacious in the treatment of depressed patients who did not respond to TCAs and/or more efficacious than TCAs in patients who had a history of previous episodes of depression. Other researchers have described subtypes of depressive patients with weight gain and hypersomnia as more likely to respond to selective serotonin reuptake inhibitors. Finally, the side-effect profile of serotonin reuptake inhibitors is markedly different from that of TCAs. Unlike TCAs, serotonin reuptake inhibitors have a benign cardiac profile, are less sedating, have negligible anticholinergic activity, and are relatively safe in overdose.

In conclusion, serotonin reuptake inhibitors are a distinct class of antidepressants that may be of use in the treatment of refractory depression.

REFERENCES

Aberg-Wistedt A: Comparison between zimelidine and desipramine in endogenous depression. Acta Psychiatr Scand 66:129–138, 1982

Aberg-Wistedt A, Ross SB, Jostell KG, et al: A double-blind study of zimelidine, a serotonin uptake inhibitor, and desipramine, a norepinephrine uptake inhibitor, in endogenous depression: clinical and biochemical findings, in Frontiers in Biochemical and Pharmacological Research in Depression. Edited by Usdin E, Asberg M, Bertilsson L, et al. New York, Raven Press, 1984, pp 439–447

Agren H: Symptom parents in unipolar and bipolar depression correlating with monoamine metabolites in the cerebrospinal fluid, II: suicide. Psychiatry Res 3:225–236, 1980

Agren H: Life at risk: markers of suicidality in depression. Psychiatr Dev 1:87–103, 1983

Ananth J, Ruskin R: Treatment of intractable depression. International Pharmacopsychiatry 9:218–229, 1974

Angst J, Woggon B, Schoepf J: The treatment of depression with L-5-hydroxytryptophan versus imipramine. Arch Psychiatr Nervenkr 224:175–186, 1977

Asberg M, Thoren P, Traskman L, et al: Serotonin—a biochemical subgroup within the affective disorders. Science 191:478–480, 1976

Asberg M, Eriksson B, Martensson B, et al: Therapeutic effects of serotonin uptake inhibitors in depression. J Clin Psychiatry 46 (suppl 4): 23–35, 1986a

Asberg M, Montgomery SA, Perris C: A comprehensive psychopathological rating scale. Acta Psychiatr Scand Suppl 271:5–27, 1978

Asberg M, Nordstrom P, Traskman-Bendz L: Cerebrospinal fluid studies in suicide, in Psychobiology of Suicidal Behavior. Edited by Mann JJ, Stanley M. New York, New York Academy of Sciences, 1986b, pp 243–255

Ayd FJ: Treatment-resistant depression: therapeutic strategies, in Affective Disorders Reassessed: 1983. Edited by Ayd FJ, Taylor IJ, Taylor BT. Baltimore, MD, Ayd Medical Communications, 1983, pp 115–125

Ayuso-Gutierrez JL, Lopez-Ibor AJ: Tryptophan and an MAOI (nialamide) in the treatment of depression. International Pharmacopsychiatry 6:92–97, 1971

Baldessarini RJ: Biomedical Aspects of Depression and Its Treatment. Washington, DC, American Psychiatric Press, 1983

Banerjee AK: Recovery from prolonged cerebral depression after fluvoxamine overdose. Br Med J [Clin Res] 296:1774, 1988

Banki CM, Molnar G, Vojnik M: Cerebrospinal fluid amine metabolites, tryptophan and clinical parameters in depression: psychopathological symptoms. J Affective Disord 3:91–99, 1981

Barbeau A, McDowell FH: L-Dopa and Parkinsonism. Philadelphia, PA, FA Davis, 1970

Benfield P, Ward A: Fluvoxamine: a review of its pharmacodynamic and pharmacokinetic properties and therapeutic efficacy in depressive illness. Drugs 32:313–334, 1986

Bertilsson L, Tuck JR, Siwers B: Biochemical effects of zimelidine in man. Eur J Clin Pharmacol 18:483–487, 1980

Bremner JD: Fluoxetine in depressed patients: a comparison with imipramine. J Clin Psychiatry 45:414–419, 1984

Broadhurst AD: L-tryptophan versus ECT. Lancet 1392–1393, 1970

Brotman AW, Rosenbaum JF: MAOIs plus tryptophan: a cause of the serotonin syndrome? Biological Therapies in Psychiatry 7:45–46, 1984

Chouinard G: A double-blind controlled clinical trial of fluoxetine and amitriptyline in the treatment of outpatients with major depressive disorder. J Clin Psychiatry 46:32–37, 1985

Claassen V, Davies JE, Hertting G, et al: Fluvoxamine, a specific 5-hydroxytryptamine uptake inhibitor. Br J Pharmacol 60:505–516, 1977

Cohn JB, Wilcox C: A comparison of fluoxetine, imipramine, and placebo in patients with major depressive disorder. J Clin Psychiatry 46(3):26–31, 1985

Cole JO, Hartmann E, Brigham P: L-tryptophan: clinical studies. McLean Hosp J 5:37–71, 1980

Collins GH: The use of parenteral and oral chlorimipramine (Anafranil) in the treatment of depressive states. Br J Psychiatry 122:189–190, 1973

Coppen A: The biochemistry of affective disorders. Br J Psychiatry 113:1237–1264, 1967

Cronholm B, Ottosson JO: Experimental studies of the therapeutic action of electroconvulsive therapy in endogenous depression. Acta Psychiatrica et Neurologica Scandinavica, Supplement UM 145:69–101, 1960

Danish University Antidepressant Group: Citalopram: clinical effect profile in comparison with clomipramine: a controlled multicenter study. Psychopharmacology (Berlin) 90(I):131–138, 1986

Davis JM: Antidepressant drugs, in Comprehensive Textbook of Psychiatry. Edited by Kaplan HI, Freedman AM, Sadock BJ. Baltimore, MD, Waverly Press, 1975, pp 1941–1956

Delgado PL, Price LH, Charney DS, et al: Efficacy of fluvoxamine in treatment-refractory depression. J Affective Disord 15:55–60, 1988

Dudley DL, Volberding N, Loebel JP: Intravenous chlorimipramine and refractory depression. Gen Hosp Psychiatry 2:61–64, 1980

Fabre LF, Crismon ML: Efficacy of fluoxetine in outpatients with major depression. Curr Ther Res 37:115–123, 1985

Feighner JP: A comparative trial of fluoxetine and amitriptyline in patients with major depressive disorder. J Clin Psychiatry 46:369–372, 1985

Feighner JP, Cohn JB: Double-blind comparative trials of fluoxetine and doxepin in geriatric patients with major depressive disorder. J Clin Psychiatry 46(3):20–25, 1985

Fieve RR, Goodnick PJ, Peselow ED, et al: Pattern analysis of antidepressant response to fluoxetine. J Clin Psychiatry 47:560–562, 1986

Fisch C: Effect of fluoxetine on the electrocardiogram. J Clin Psychiatry 46(3):42–44, 1985

Gelenberg AJ, Gibson CJ, Wojcik JD: Neurotransmitter precursors for the treatment of depression. Psychopharmacol Bull 18:7–18, 1982

Glassman AH, Platman SR: Potentiation of a monoamine oxidase inhibitor by tryptophan. J Psychiatr Res 7:83–88, 1969

Goodwin FK, Post RM, Dunner DL, et al: Cerebrospinal fluid amine metabolites in affective illness: the probenecid technique. Am J Psychiatry 130:73–79, 1973

Gram LF: Receptors, pharmacokinetics and clinical effects, in Drugs and Psychiatry, Vol I: Antidepressants. Edited by Burrows GD, Norman T, Davis B. Amsterdam, Elsevier/North-Holland, 1983, pp 81–96

Hiramatsu K-I, Takahashi R, Mori A, et al: A multicentre double-blind comparative trial of zimelidine and imipramine in primary major depressive disorders. Acta Psychiatr Scand [Suppl] 308:41–54, 1983

Kahn RS, van Praag HM, Wetzler S, et al: Serotonin and anxiety revisited. Biol Psychiatry 23:189–208, 1988

Kielholz P, Terzani S, Gaspar M: Treatment for therapy resistant depressions. International Pharmacopsychiatry 14:94–100, 1979

Kiloh LG: Electroconvulsive therapy, in Handbook of Affective Disorders. Edited by Paykel ES. New York, Guilford, 1982, pp 262–275

Kline NS, Sacks W: Treatment of depression with an MAO-inhibitor followed by 5-HTP—an unfinished research project. Acta Psychiatr Scand [Suppl] 280:233–241, 1980

Lemberger L, Bergstrom RF, Wolen RL, et al: Fluoxetine: clinical pharmacology and physiologic disposition. J Clin Psychiatry 46(3):14–19, 1985

Links PS, Akiskal HS: Chronic and intractable depressions: terminology, classification, and description of subtypes, in Treating Resistant Depression. Edited by Zohar J, Belmaker RH. New York, PMA Publishing, 1987, pp 1–22

Lopez-Ibor JJ: Ensayo clinico de la monochlorimipramina. Abstract presented at Fourth World Congress of Psychiatry, Madrid, Spain, 1966

Lopez-Ibor JJ Jr, Saiz-Ruiz J, Perez de los Cobos JC: Biological correlations of suicide and aggressivity in major depressions (with melancholia): 5-hydroxyindoleacetic acid and cortisol in cerebral spinal fluid, dexamethasone suppression test and therapeutic response to 5-hydroxytryptophan. Neuropsychobiology 14:67–74, 1985

Marley E, Wozniak KM: Clinical and experimental aspects of interactions between amine oxidase inhibitors and amine re-uptake inhibitors. Psychol Med 13:735–749, 1983

Murphy DL, Siever LJ, Insel TR: Therapeutic responses to tricyclic antidepressants and related drugs in non-affective disorder patient populations. Prog Neuropsychopharmacol Biol Psychiatry 9:3–13, 1985

Nelson JC, Charney DS: The symptoms of major depressive illness. Am J Psychiatry 138:1–13, 1981

Nies A, Robinson DS: Monoamine oxidase inhibitors, in Handbook of Affective Disorders. Edited by Paykel FS. New York, Guilford, 1982, pp 246–261

Nilsson BS: Adverse reactions in connection with zimelidine treatment: a review. Acta Psychiatr Scand [Suppl] 308:115–119, 1983

Nolen WA, Van De Putte JJ, Dijken WA, et al: L-5HTP in depression resistant to re-uptake inhibitors: an open comparative study with tranylcypromine. Br J Psychiatry 147:16–22, 1985

Nystrom C, Hallstrom T: Double-blind comparison between a serotonin and a noradrenaline reuptake blocker in the treatment of depressed outpatients: clinical aspects. Acta Psychiatr Scand [Suppl] 308:6–15, 1985

Oreland L, Widberg A, Asberg M, et al: Platelet MAO activity and monoamine metabolites in cerebrospinal fluid in depressed and suicidal patients in healthy controls. Psychiatry Res 4:21–29, 1981

Palanappian V, Ramachandran V, Somasundaram O: Suicidal ideation and biogenic amines in depression. Indian Journal of Psychiatry 25:286–292, 1983

Pare CMB: Potentiation of monoamine oxidase inhibitors by tryptophan. Lancet 2:527–528, 1963

Pare CMB, Young DPH, Price K, et al: 5-Hydroxytryptamine and dopamine in brainstem, hypothalamus, and caudate nucleus of controls and of patients committing suicide by coal-gas poisoning. Lancet 2:133–135, 1969

Pope HG, McElroy SL, Nixon RA: Possible synergism between fluoxetine and lithium in refractory depression. Am J Psychiatry 145:1292–1294, 1988

Potter WZ, Rudorfer MV, Lesieur P, et al: Biochemical effects of selective serotonin-reuptake inhibitors in man. Advances in Biological Psychiatry 17:18–30, 1988

Rapport MM, Green AA, Page IH: Serum vasoconstrictor (serotonin), IV: isolation and characterization. J Biol Chem 176:1243–1251, 1948

Reimherr FW, Wood DR, Byerley B, et al: Characteristics of responders to fluoxetine. Psychopharmacol Bull 20:70–72, 1984

Rickels K, Amsterdam JD, Avallone MF: Fluoxetine in major depression: a controlled study. Current Therapeutic Research 39:559–563, 1986

Roos BE: Tryptophan, 5-hydroxytryptophan, and tricyclic antidepressants in the treatment of depression. Monogr Neural Sci 3:23–25, 1976

Roos JC: Cardiac effects of antidepressant drugs: a comparison of the tricyclic antidepressants and fluvoxamine. Br J Clin Pharmacol 15:439S–445S, 1983

Rosenthal JS, Kaswan M, Hemlock C, et al: Fluoxetine enhancement of tricyclic antidepressants: three case reports. Am J Psychiatry (in press)

Secunda SK, Cross CK, Koslow S, et al: Biochemistry and suicidal behavior in depressed patients. Biol Psychiatry 21:756–767, 1986

Shaw DM, Camps EF, Eccleston EG: 5-Hydroxytryptamine in the hindbrain of depressive suicides. Br J Psychiatry 113:1407–1411, 1967

Shaw DM, Johnson LJ, MacSweeney DA: Tricyclic antidepressants and tryptophan in unipolar affective disorder. Lancet 2:1245, 1972

Sourkes TL: Toxicology of serotonin precursors. Advances in Biological Psychiatry 10:169–175, 1983

Squires RF: Monoamine oxidase inhibitors: animal pharmacology, in Handbook of Psychopharmacology, Vol 14. Edited by Iversen LL, Iversen SD, Snyder SH. New York, Plenum Press, 1978, pp 1–58

Stanley M, Stanley B: Reconceptualizing suicide: a biological approach. Psychiatric Annals 18:646–651, 1988

Steiner W, Fontaine R: Toxic reaction following the combined administration of fluoxetine and L-tryptophan: five case reports. Biol Psychiatry 21:1067–1071, 1986

Sternbach H: Danger of MAOI therapy after fluoxetine withdrawal. Lancet 2:850–851, 1988

Takahashi S, Kondo H, Kato N: Effect of L-5-hydroxytryptophan on brain monoamine metabolism and evaluation of its clinical effect in depressed patients. J Psychiatr Res 12:177–187, 1975

Thomas JM, Rubin EH: Case report of a toxic reaction from a combination of tryptophan and phenelzine. Am J Psychiatry 14:281–282, 1982

Twarog BM, Page IH: Serotonin content of some mammalian tissues and urine and a method for its determination. Am J Psychiatry 175:157–161, 1953

Van Hiele LJ: L-5-hydroxytryptophan in depression: the first substitution therapy in psychiatry? The treatment of 99 outpatients with "therapy-resistant" depression. Neuropsychobiology 6:230–240, 1980

van Praag HM: Central monoamine metabolism in depressions, I: serotonin and related compounds: Compr Psychiatry 21:30–43, 1980

van Praag HM: Depression, suicide and the metabolism of serotonin in the brain. J Affective Disord 4:275-290, 1982a

van Praag HM: Monoamine precursors in Depression: Present State and Prospects, in Treating Resistant Depression. Edited by Zohar J, Belmaker RH. New York PMA Publishing Corp., 1987

van Praag HM, van den Burg W, Bos ERH, et al: 5-Hydroxytryptophan in combination with clomipramine in "therapy-resistant" depression. Psychopharmacologia 38:267–269, 1974

Vaughan DA: Interaction of fluoxetine with tricyclic antidepressants. Am J Psychiatry 145:1478, 1988

Vestergaard P, Sorensen T, Hoppe E, et al: Biogenic amine metabolites in cerebrospinal fluid of patients with affective disorders. Acta Psychiatr Scand 58:88–96, 1978

Walinder J, Skott A, Carlsson A, et al: Potentiation of the antidepressant action of clomipramine by tryptophan. Arch Gen Psychiatry 33:1384–1389, 1976

Walinder J. Carlsson A, Persson R: 5-HT reuptake inhibitors plus tryptophan in endogenous depression. Acta Psychiatr Scand [Suppl] 290:179–190, 1981

Wernicke JF: The side effect profile and safety of fluoxetine. J Clin Psychiatry 46(3):59–67, 1985

Wernicke JF, Dunlop SR, Dornseif BE, et al: Fixed-dose fluoxetine therapy for depression. Psychopharmacol Bull 23:164–168, 1987

Wong DT, Horng JS, Bymaster FP, et al: AS selective inhibitor of serotonin uptake: Lilly 110140, 3-p-(trifluoromethylphenoxy)-N-methyl-3-phenylpropylamine. Life Sci 14:471–479, 1974

Zarifian E, Rigal F: New antidepressants and trends in the pharmacotherapy of depressive disorders. Psychiatr Clin North Am 6:129–139, 1983

Chapter 9

Thyroid Function in Refractory Depression

Julie A. Hatterer, M.D.
Jack M. Gorman, M.D.

Chapter 9

Thyroid Function in Refractory Depression

O ver the past 20 years, the study of the interface between psychiatry and endocrinology has grown exponentially. The development of new, highly sensitive radioimmunoassays for thyroid hormones as well as the characterization of thyrotropin-releasing hormone (TRH) as a tripeptide (Boler et al. 1969; Burgus et al. 1969) have allowed researchers to examine relationships between the hypothalamic-pituitary-thyroid (HPT) axis and a variety of psychiatric syndromes. From the start, the focus has been primarily on affective disorders.

It has long been known that changes in mood are common symptoms of thyroid disease (e.g., depression in hypothyroidism, tense dysphoria in hyperthyroidism), so logically investigators have looked for disturbances in thyroid function in patients presenting with mood disorders. The fact that lithium and, more recently, carbamazepine have been shown to have both antimanic and antithyroid effects (Roy-Byrne et al. 1984) provides additional indirect evidence for a connection. However, the nature of this connection has proven to be quite complex.

This complexity is readily apparent in the finding of a blunted thyrotropin-stimulating hormone (TSH) response to TRH in 25% of depressed patients (Loosen and Prange 1982), whereas 10% of anergic depressed patients show an exaggerated TSH response to TRH (Gold et al. 1982). Patients with depression are thus heterogeneous in terms of thyroid testing. In addition, as other psychiatric disorders have been examined, the abnormalities seen in depression are found to be less specific than once thought. Studies have revealed blunted TSH response to TRH in patients with alcoholism (Loosen et al. 1979) and panic disorder (Roy-Byrne et al. 1986), whereas exaggerated responses and subclinical hypothyroidism have also been seen in bipolar patients (Wilson and Jefferson 1985).

The use of thyroid hormone as an adjuvant to antidepressant

medications grew out of the aforementioned findings as well as the observation of enhanced imipramine effect and toxicity in hyperthyroid mice (Prange and Lipton 1962). A number of studies have shown L-triiodothyronine (T3) to accelerate clinical response to tricyclics (Prange et al. 1969; Wilson et al. 1970) and even turn tricyclic nonresponders into responders (Goodwin et al. 1982; Schwarcz et al. 1984). Unfortunately, very few of these have looked at the relationships between preexisting thyroid function tests and response to treatment with thyroid hormone. Therefore, it is difficult to determine the mechanism by which thyroid hormone exerts its effects, that is, via changes in thyroid status versus pharmacologic effects.

Few would argue that alterations in thyroid function can be found and presumably play a role in depressive symptomatology. The difficulty lies in deciphering what these changes mean: Are they causative or merely correlative, and what if anything will righting the system do? These questions are further confounded by the fact that changes in thyroid function tests (TFTs) occur along a continuum with varying definitions of abnormal used. Studies have shown that up to 75% of depressed patients will have a blunted TSH response to TRH stimulation depending on the definition of blunting used (Loosen 1985). Also, depression is not a single entity, and abnormalities in thyroid function have been found to differ among subtypes of depression; for example, patients with atypical depression do not show TSH blunting when compared to endogenous depressive patients and normal controls (McGrath et al. 1984).

To discuss thyroid function in refractory depression, one must add a third axis, "refractoriness" or "response to treatment," to the two mentioned above. Any given patient in this three-dimensional space will show a certain subtype/severity of depression with his or her own thyroid profile and response to treatment. Ideally, studies of response to treatment should specify the other coordinates and how thyroid status changes with treatment. Although some have written about thyroid function in refractory or resistant depression, no uniform definition has been used. This, therefore must be the starting point.

A WORKING DEFINITION OF REFRACTORY DEPRESSION

Despite the fact that no mutually agreed-upon definition of refractory depression exists, most authors conclude that up to 20% of patients with depression are refractory to treatment (Zis and Goodwin 1979). Definitions of refractory range from "failure to respond to treatment" to elaborate multidimensional systems (Fawcett and Kravitz 1985). To our knowledge, no one has systematically studied thyroid function in patients who have failed at least two adequate antidepressant trials (generally used as minimum criterion for refractory depression). However, substantial literature exists on thyroid function and response to pharmacotherapy or electroconvulsive therapy (ECT). Thus, the definition of refractory used here will be broad. This chapter will explore thyroid function in patients who fail to respond to antidepressant treatment and in those who relapse after treatment. The use of thyroid function tests as predictors of response and relapse and of thyroid hormones to enhance or produce recovery will be examined. A theoretical framework will be discussed upon which future studies can be designed.

THYROID ILLNESS AND ANTIDEPRESSANT RESPONSE

Before concluding that a depressed patient is indeed refractory or resistant to antidepressant treatment, one must be certain that in fact the patient suffers from major depression. In their study of 60 outpatients with treatment-resistant depression defined as "an ongoing and unremitting depressed state in a patient who has been treated with at least two different antidepressants or an antidepressant and a course of electroconvulsive therapy (ECT)," Remick and colleagues found that one sixth of the group had been misdiagnosed (Remick et al. 1982). Fawcett and Kravitz (1985) have cautioned that hidden psychotic symptoms may contribute to the conclusion that a patient is refractory to standard treatment for nonpsychotic depression.

Similarly, a missed diagnosis of hypothyroidism or even hyperthyroidism presenting with depression can lead to repeated failed trials of antidepressants or even ECT. Up to 40% of patients with hypothyroidism will show a diagnosable depression with complaints of lethargy, fatigue, cognitive impairment, and constipation (Sachar 1975). Patients with clinical or grade I hypothyroidism (i.e., low thyroxine (T_4, free T_4 [FT_4], elevated TSH, and exaggerated TSH response to TRH stimulation) require treatment with thyroid hormone replacement. L-Thyroxine (Synthroid) is the treatment of choice. In the majority of cases, the symptoms of depression improve once the patient regains a euthyroid state. However, very little has been written about hypothyroid patients who continue to be depressed despite adequate thyroid replacement. Our clinical investigation of thyroid and metabolic function in a sample of 27 depressed in- and outpatients at various points in their treatment included patients in this category (Hatterer and Gorman, unpublished data). At the time of study, five patients were receiving thyroxine for diagnosed hypothyroidism; all were adequately replaced on the basis of clinical presentation and thyroid indices. Only one of the five showed full response to antidepressant treatment, and one was found to be refractory, defined in this sample as having failed a trial of both a tricyclic antidepressant (TCA) and a monoamine oxidase inhibitor (MAOI) (minimum of 6 weeks of phenelzine at 60 mg/d, imipramine at 200 mg/d or equivalent). MAOIs had produced partial recovery in the remaining three patients. Interestingly, two of these three had been unable to tolerate tricyclics while on thyroxine, leading one to speculate whether their troubling side effects may have been caused by overreplacement.

Russ and Ackerman (personal communication, March 1989) performed a 5-year retrospective chart review of 11 psychiatric admissions carrying a diagnosis of both depression and hypothyroidism. Two had grade I and nine had grade II hypothyroidism (elevated TSH with normal T_4, FT_4, and T_3). Two independent raters, blind to thyroid status, rated antidepressant response using the Global Assessment of Functioning (GAF) Scale (DSM-III-R) (American Psychiatric Association 1987). The five patients with untreated hypothyroidism at the start of antidepressant treatment (with tricyclic or ECT) showed no or only partial antidepressant response even with concurrent thyroid replacement. Five patients showed complete or near complete recovery from depression. Four of the five had received thyroid replacement prior to antidepressant treatment; three were euthyroid, and one had received 23 days of L-thyroxine but was still chemically hypothyroid. The fifth patient responded to L-thyroxine alone. Taken together, these findings suggest that correction of a hypothyroid state prior to antidepressant treatment is necessary, but not necessarily sufficient, for full antidepressant response.

Hypothyroidism should be considered in the differential of a newly diagnosed, depressed patient, and many clinicians routinely obtain T_4 and T_3 levels on such patients. Much has been written on subclinical hypothyroidism in depression; however, the importance of this diagnosis and its potential treatment remain unclear. Subclinical hypothyroidism refers to cases who are clinically euthyroid with normal T_4, FT_4, and T_3, but who show an elevated TSH and exaggerated TSH response to TRH (grade II or mild hypothyroidism) or a normal TSH and exaggerated TSH response (grade III hypothyroidism).

Subclinical hypothyroidism is a common disorder with an overall prevalence of 2% to 7% (Tunbridge et al. 1977). Researchers have noted a relatively high prevalence of subclinical hypothyroidism and symptomless autoimmune thyroiditis (subclinical hypothyroidism with the presence of antithyroid antibodies) in patients with major depression. Dackis and co-workers (1986) found 12.2% of 270 depressed patients to suffer from grade I–III hypothyroidism, with 11.5% receiving a diagnosis of subclinical hypothyroidism. Sixty percent of patients with hypothyroidism were found to have measurable titers of antimicrosomal antibodies. Gold and colleagues' 1982 study of 100 consecutive admissions to a psychiatric hospital with complaints of depression and lack of energy found 15% to have previously undiagnosed subclinical hypothyroidism. Nemeroff and associates (1985) reported 20% of 45 psychiatric inpatients with "prominent depressive symptoms" to have detectable antithyroid antibody titers versus 5% to 10% in the general population.

These studies fall short in that no control groups, either of normals or psychiatric patients, are offered for comparison. Nevertheless, they raise the question as to whether depressed patients with subclinical hypothyroidism (with or without the presence of antithyroid antibodies) suffer from an organic affective disorder that may respond to thyroid hormone alone. The endocrine literature suggests that replacement therapy for subclinical hypothyroidism may be indicated, particularly in the presence of antithyroid antibodies, given the likelihood of progression to clinical hypothyroidism (Tunbridge et al. 1981). The Cooper group's 1984 double-blind study of thyroxine or placebo treatment in 33 subjects with subclinical hypothyroidism found that 14 (42%) complained of poor energy and easy fatigability versus 25% of normal controls who complained of poor energy and 20% with easy fatigability (statistically significant). Following a year of treatment, the group that received L-thyroxine at .05 mg daily showed a statistically significant reduction of symptoms compared to the placebo group; 8 of 17 patients receiving thyroxine versus 3 of 16 who received placebo were improved overall. Although the authors do not specifically address changes in energy or fatigability, they do recommend that a trial of thyroxine be given to patients with symptoms compatible with mild hypothyroidism.

Could the small percentage of patients with grade III hypothyroidism, only diagnosable with a TRH stimulation test, comprise a group of patients resistant to standard antidepressant treatment? Prange and Loosen (1980) have argued that 5% of depressed women are marginally hypothyroid and that these patients respond poorly to TCA unless their thyroid state is corrected. Few systematic studies have addressed this issue. Baruch and colleagues (1985) performed a complete baseline thyroid evaluation including TRH stimulation test in 30 women hospitalized for major depression. After 5 weeks of treatment with at least 150 mg clomipramine or imipramine, 9 women showed no improvement, whereas 21 responded favorably. No differences were found in baseline thyroid function tests between the two groups; however, the nine patients with refractory depression had a higher mean baseline Δ max TSH response to TRH than did the responders. Although the increment in TSH values did not meet the standard cut-off ($30\,\mu U/ml$) used for subclinical hypothyroidism, values were at the upper limits of normal. The authors speculated that a subtle hypothyroid state may contribute to poor antidepressant response.

In our clinical investigation described above, four patients were found to have grade III hypothyroidism. Two with atypical depression were considered refractory, and neither benefited from the addition of thyroid hormones to their antidepressant regimens. One depressed patient with symptomless autoimmune thyroiditis failed to respond to imipramine, but showed complete resolution of her depression on thyroxine at 0.025 mg per day alone. The fourth patient showed a good response to amitriptyline alone. In a separate study of 16 women with refractory depression, the discovery of grade II or III hypothyroidism in six led to the addition of thyroxine to the regimens of two patients and an increase in dosage of the remaining four patients, all of whom then showed recovery (Gewirtz et al. 1988). These findings support Prange's conclusion that correction of even mild hypothyroid states may be necessary for full antidepressant response. On the other hand, a percentage of patients will remain refractory to treatment even with thyroid hormone treatment.

Hyperthyroidism rarely presents with a typical depressive syndrome; however, case reports have described patients with "apathetic hyperthyroidism" who show depression and withdrawal (Brenner 1978). Taylor (1975) describes a 56-year-old man presenting with a 12-month history of a progressive, agitated depression. After a week of treatment with amitriptyline, he developed an acute confusional state, tachycardia, and a febrile illness. Thyroid function tests revealed the patient to be thyrotoxic, and treatment with propranolol and carbimazole led to rapid resolution of his depressive as well as physical symptoms. This case illustrates the need to be alert to the rare presentation of hyperthyroidism with depression.

THYROID FUNCTION AND PREDICTION OF TREATMENT OUTCOME

Having noted alterations in thyroid function in depressed patients, investigators naturally turned to studying their predictive value in terms of treatment response and relapse. The TSH response to TRH stimulation has been a focus of predictor studies. In their 1986 study of 114 patients with a variety of diagnoses, the Schonbeck group found that patients with an initially blunted TSH response recovered more frequently than those with a normal response regardless of diagnosis. Of the 83 depressed patients, 90% with a blunted response versus 76% with a normal baseline response recovered when treated with intravenous clomipramine, a statistically significant difference. Prange (1986) has reported findings that pretreatment measures of FT4 Index (FT4I) *within the normal range* correlated with treatment response using ECT or chemotherapy in hospitalized, depressed patients.

Kirkegaard (1981), Langer and colleagues (1980), and Targum (1983) looked at the correlation between response to antidepressants or ECT and changes in the TRH stimulation test performed during depression and upon recovery. Using the difference in Δ max TSH between the first and second testing (i.e., $\Delta\Delta$ max TSH), Langer and Kirkegaard have shown that an increased Δ max TSH correlates well with a favorable clinical response and that normalization of an initially blunted TSH response to TRH is consistent with clinical recovery. On the other hand, Targum (1983) did not find normalization of TSH blunting (defined as $\Delta\Delta$ max of TSH > 2.0 μU/ml) to be significantly associated with the timing of improvement. Similarly, Targum and colleagues' 1982 study of 47 depressed patients found that in the 8 women with an initially exaggerated TSH response to TRH stimulation, persistence or diminution of TSH response did not appear to be related to clinical response.

The recent finding of elevated cerebrospinal fluid (CSF) TRH in depressed patients compared to controls with neurological disease (Kirkegaard et al. 1979) and with somatization disorder (Banki et al. 1988) suggests a possible explanation for TSH blunting. It is hypothesized that in depressed patients, chronic hypersecretion of TRH may lead to downregulation of TRH receptors on thyrotrophs in the anterior pituitary. Such patients would thus show a blunted TSH response to TRH challenge. However, these investigators found no association between elevated CSF TRH and blunted TSH response, and Kirkegaard reported no change in CSF TRH levels with successful treatment with ECT. The Banki group (1988) states this discordance is not surprising, because only one third of TRH in the brain is located in the hypothalamus, so measures of CSF TRH derive largely from nonhypothalamic sources.

Relapse following recovery has also been shown to be associated with results on the TRH stimulation test. Schonbeck and associates

(1986) followed 60 patients on clomipramine maintenance therapy for 1 year. Of those patients with a blunted TSH response upon recovery, 52% relapsed as compared to 36% with a normal response. The difference in risk of relapse was found to be greatest within the first 2 months. Similarly, the Kirkegaard group (1979) has shown that patients whose $\Delta\Delta$ max TSH is less than 2.0 μU/ml following successful treatment with ECT are more likely to relapse within 6 months if prophylactic treatment is not instituted. Those who show an increased Δ max TSH upon recovery remain well without treatment.

THYROID HORMONE POTENTIATION OF ANTIDEPRESSANT RESPONSE

The use of T3 to accelerate TCA response has been widely documented and recently reviewed (Prange et al. 1984). At least eight double-blind, placebo-controlled studies with 200 patients have been conducted, and all but two have found T3 in low doses to be effective in accelerating response. Women appear to benefit more than men. The addition of T3 does not confer any long-term advantage because response rates to TCA are generally found to be similar for both treated and untreated groups.

More germane to the subject of this chapter is the handful of systematic studies on the use of thyroid hormones to enhance tricyclic response or convert nonresponders into responders. Overall, the findings summarized in Table 9-1 have shown that adjuvant treatment with T3 may lead to significant improvement in anywhere from 56% to 90% of tricyclic nonresponders. However, a few controlled studies have shown no antidepressant effect of T3 compared to placebo or historical controls (Gitlin et al. 1987; Thase et al. 1985). Methodological shortcomings and differences between studies bear closer examination.

The first difference noted is in the identification of the sample. As mentioned above, diagnostic accuracy is crucial, making early studies that did not specify diagnostic criteria difficult to interpret. Equally confounding is the inclusion of diagnoses other than major depression, such as in Earle's 1970 study. Although treatment studies of depression often include bipolar patients, they may differ from unipolar patients in terms of tricyclic response. The inclusion of bipolar depressed patients in studies of thyroid hormone enhancement poses additional problems, because these patients may have unrecognized thyroid disturbance. Investigators have speculated that rapid cyclers suffer from an underlying HPT axis disturbance that becomes clinically manifest during lithium treatment (Cho et al.

Table 9-1. Adjunctive T$_3$ treatment in depressed patients with poor response to tricyclics

Reference	Patients	N	History of anti-depressant response	Dose	Results	Comments
Earle (1970)	M,F, outpt, UPD, BPD, schizoaffective	25	17 Pts who had "become resistant" to TCA, 8 with "inadequate response"	IMI, AMI, 150 mg QD, Pro 40 mg QD, 25 μg T$_3$	56% Improved on T$_3$, 50% relapsed on T$_3$ during follow up	Multiple diagnoses; Lack of standarized TCA Rx; No standardized rating antidep response
Ogura et al. (1974)	M,F, UPD, BPD, inpt, outpt	44	Insufficient "therapeutic effect" of TCA ± major and minor tranquilizers	IMI, AMI. DMI, NT at doses around 75 mg QD, 20–30 μg T$_3$	66% With good to excellent T$_3$ response, usually within 4 days	No specification of previous TCA Rx; Pt population mixed, but authors note no difference in T$_3$ effectiveness across dx; No report of follow up with T$_3$ taper
Banki (1975)	M,F, Primary Dep, inpt	96	Poor response to AMI, TRIMI at day 10 defined as Hamilton Score <20%	AMI 75–200 mg QD, TRIMI 100–300 mg, 20–40 μg T$_3$	T$_3$ Effective 39/52 pts, 10/44 responded to increased TCA dose alone	Standardized rating TCA response; Short duration of trial may select slow responders vs. resistant pts; Control group of TCA alone
Banki (1977)	M,F, UPD, BPD, inpt	49	Poor response to AMI at day 14 as above	AMI 75–200 mg QD, T$_3$ 20–40 μg, control with increased AMI to 300–350 mg QD	23/33 Marked improvement with T$_3$, 4/16 controls improved with increased TCA alone	As above; No difference noted between UPD, BPD in T$_3$ effectiveness; ? random assignment to control; Raters not blind

Table 9-1.   Adjunctive T_3 treatment in depressed patients with poor response to tricyclics (continued)

Reference	Patients	N	History of anti-depressant response	Dose	Results	Comments
Tsutsui et al. (1972)	10M, 1F, protracted dep with blunted TSH response to TRH	11	TCAs in varying doses, duration not specified	Various doses TCAs, 5–25 µg T_3	10/11 Pts rated improved by T_3 particularly in initiative, dep. mood	Lack of standardized TCA Rx, rating of response; Normalization of TSH blunting in 4 pts tested upon recovery
Goodwin et al. (1982)	M,F, UPD, BPD, inpt	12	Minimal or no response to IMI, AMI for at least 26 days by global clinical ratings	IMI/AMI 150–300 mg QD, T_3 25–50 µg	8/12 Pts with marked improvement with T_3 beginning within 1–3 days	Double blind Rx; Plasma TCA levels pre and post T_3; T_3 suppressed T_4, but no change in TCA levels
Targum et al. (1984)	M,F, MD, inpt	21	Minimum 4 weeks TCA Rx without improvement by Hamilton Rating Scale for Depression	Varying TCA doses not specified 25 µg T_3 or 100 µg T_4	7/21 Showed rapid improvement within 1 week of T_3	TCA regimen not specified; Lack of standardized thyroid Rx; 5 of 6 with exaggerated baseline TSH response to TRH vs. 2/15 with normal or blunted response showed full recovery with thyroid hormone
Schwarcz et al. (1984)	M,F, UPD	8	DMI up to 6 weeks without response by Hamilton Rating Scale for Depression	DMI 200–300 mg QD, T_3 25–50 µg	50% Converted to responders with T_3 by week 4	Small sample size; No association between baseline thyroid testing, TRH stimulation test, and T_3 response

Study	Subjects	n	Treatment criteria	Dose/regimen	Results	Comments
Gitlin et al. (1987)	M,F, UPD, outpt	16	IMI × 4 weeks without improvement by clinical ratings, Hamilton Rating Scale for Depression	IMI up to 300 mg 25 µg T_3 placebo-controlled crossover after 2 weeks	No difference between T_3 and placebo, significant time effect with all pts improving over time	Double-blind, placebo-controlled study; Plasma TCA levels measured; Thyroid function test before and after T_3; 5 pts with exaggerated TRH test results at baseline showed no differential response of T_3 vs. placebo
Joffe and Singer (1987)	M,F, MD	26	Failure to respond to TCA by Hamilton Rating Scale for Depression	T_3 37.5 µg QD, T_4 150 µg given double-blind with TCA	Significantly more pts responded to T_3 than T_4 at week 3	Preliminary findings; Double-blind control; T_4 has ½ life 5–7 days vs. short T_3 ½ life; Duration of trial only 3 weeks
Thase et al. (1985)	M,F, recurrent UPD, outpt	20	Poor response to IMI and psychotherapy for at least 12 weeks	IMI (mean dose = 245 mg QD) T_3 25 µg	25% T_3 with clinical improvement, 25% remission vs. 20% and 15% of historical comparison group on IMI and therapy	Use of control historical comparison group; 13 pts with baseline TRH stimulation tests (all WNL) did not correlate with T_3 response

Note. UPD = unipolar depression. BPD = bipolar depression. IMI = imipramine. AMI = amitriptyline. PRO = protriptyline. DMI = desipramine. NT = nortriptyline. TRIMI = trimipramine. MD = major depression.

1979; Cowdry et al. 1983). Given lithium's antithyroid effects, bipolar (or unipolar) patients treated with lithium may also confound results if they are not lithium free for at least 1 month.

The determination of tricyclic nonresponse varies from study to study, as can be seen in Table 9-1. Studies that recruited previously treated patients lack standardization in terms of medication, dose, and duration. Similarly, they suffer from a lack of standardized rating criteria to determine previous nonresponse as well as response to adjuvant T3. More recent work used standardized treatment and used either ratings of global clinical impression (CGI) or changes in Hamilton Depression Rating Scale (Hamilton 1964) scores to define response. When specified, the TCA dose is generally sufficient (i.e., 150 mg to 300 mg qd of imipramine, desipramine, etc.) as is the duration of treatment (4 to 6 weeks), and some studies have provided tricyclic blood levels to confirm adequate dosage.

Nevertheless, the question arises as to whether patients deemed responders to T3 enhancement would have responded to tricyclic alone had it been given longer or in higher doses. The use of a placebo control in a double-blind fashion is helpful in determining whether duration of antidepressant trial is the critical element. Both the Goodwin group (1982) and the Gitlin group (1987) studied patients under double-blind conditions. Goodwin's population consisted of 12 hospitalized patients (6 women, 6 men) with major depression (unipolar or bipolar) who had shown minimal or no clinical response to amitriptyline or imipramine at 150 mg to 300 mg for at least 26 days. Ten patients received 25 µg T3, and two patients received 50 µg T3 in a double-blind fashion. Eight of the 12 patients showed marked improvement in their depressive syndrome, usually beginning within 1 to 3 days. T3 was found to suppress serum thyroxine but did not alter imipramine or desipramine plasma levels. Although well designed in terms of standardized rating of history of nonresponse to TCA and of response to T3 potentiation, Goodwin's study can be faulted for the heterogeneity of the sample (four unipolar, four bipolar II, four bipolar I) as well as the variability of previous tricyclic treatment. The authors state doses were adjusted by a "non-blind physician to the maximum consistent with acceptable side effects" (p. 35). Four patients had combined imipramine/desipramine plasma levels under 200 ng/ml (i. e., below what is generally considered a therapeutic level), three of whom had been treated for under 30 days. Following the addition of T3, all four converted to full responders. Because no placebo was used, one could argue that these patients may simply have responded to a longer imipramine trial.

Gitlin and associates (1987) are the sole investigators to have used a placebo-controlled, double-blind design. Unlike other reports that involved only inpatients, their sample consisted of 16 outpatients drawn from a larger sample of 42 who met RDC criteria for major depression. Following a week of single-blind placebo treatment, nonresponding patients were treated with imipramine up to 300 mg a day for 4 weeks. Those 16 who showed no improvement defined on the basis of a failure to achieve a 50% drop in Hamilton score and a CGI of 1 or 2 were entered into the T3 study. Subjects were randomized to either placebo or T3 at 25 µg given for 2 weeks. At the end of this period, patients were crossed over to the other regimen for another 2 weeks. Imipramine dose was maintained throughout the 4-week period. Thyroid testing, including TSH, T3, T4, FT4, and TRH stimulation test, was performed at baseline, after 4 weeks of imipramine, and after the placebo-T3 period. Imipramine and desipramine plasma levels were drawn prior to randomization, and patients achieved a mean of 220 ± 132 ng/ml. The results of this very well-designed study found no difference in the efficacy of T3 versus placebo in enhancing antidepressant response. However, a strong time effect was noted; patients showed significant improvement over the 4 weeks independent of the drug or order of administration. The authors note that their study is limited by small sample size and that depressed outpatients may differ from inpatients in treatment response. Gitlin's finding of a significant time effect is consistent with the work of the Quitkin group (1984), who reported that a proportion of depressed patients will show a marked response to antidepressant treatment at 6 weeks, but not after 4 weeks. Gitlin suggests that a study of T3 potentiation in patients who have failed 8 weeks of a TCA perhaps would yield a more T3 responsive group.

Banki (1977, 1975) used a somewhat different control group, one that helps address the question of dosage. After a short trial of an antidepressant, patients were treated either with adjunctive T3 or else with an increase in dose. Banki's first study consisted of 96 patients with primary depression who, after 10 days of treatment with amitriptyline (75 mg to 200 mg/d) or trimipramine (100 mg to 300 mg/d), had failed to show a decrease of Hamilton score of >20%. T3 (20 µg to 40 µg/d) was effective in 39 of 52 patients, whereas only 10 of 44 responded to increased daily dosage alone. This statistically significant difference was replicated in a second study of 49 women with bipolar or unipolar depression treated initially for 14 days with amitriptyline (100 mg to 200 mg/d). T3 (20 µg to 40 µg) produced marked clinical improvement in 23 of 33 patients, whereas only 4 of 16 of those who had their antidepressant dosage raised to 300 mg to 350 mg a day improved. Banki's work, although innovative, falls short in that the sample was heterogeneous in terms of diagnosis, patients were not blind to their treatment condition, nor is it stated whether they were randomly assigned. His results may also be biased by a time effect, as subjects were on antidepressant alone for a very brief period, and the total duration of treatment was 4 to 5 weeks.

The mechanism by which T3 enhances antidepressant response is unknown, although several theories have been put forth. Pharmacologic hypotheses include the demonstrated ability of T3 to alter the effects of TCAs on postsynaptic generation of cyclic AMP (Frazer et al. 1974), and the possibility that thyroid hormones alter tricyclic blood levels has been found not to be the case by Garbutt and associates (1979).

The leading hypothesis derives from the evidence that depressed patients show changes in the HPT axis, and that T3 potentiation is effective because it corrects an underlying dysfunction in the axis' adaptive capacity. One way to explore this theory is to study the relationship of pretreatment thyroid status to response to thyroid enhancement of tricyclic treatment. The few reports in the literature reveal conflicting results. In Gitlin's previously mentioned 1987 study, five patients showed an exaggerated TSH response to TRH at baseline. These subjects showed no differential antidepressant effect of T3 compared to placebo. Thase et al. 1985 also found no correlation between baseline TRH stimulation tests and response to T3 potentiation of imipramine. He studied 20 outpatients with unipolar major depression who were unresponsive to imipramine (mean dose 245 mg/d) for 12 weeks. Patients then received 4 weeks of open treatment with T3 at 25 μg a day. Controls were a historical comparison group continuing to receive imipramine. After 4 weeks of T3 treatment, the two groups showed no statistically significant differences in antidepressant response, and TRH stimulation tests (all within the normal range) were not found to be correlated to response to thyroid hormone.

On the other hand, Targum and colleagues' 1984 study of 21 depressed inpatients, all of whom had failed "conventional antidepressant treatment" for a minimum of 4 weeks, did find a relationship between TRH stimulation tests and thyroid hormone potentiation. Seven out of 21 responded to either 25 μg T3 or 100 μg T4 added to their regimen. Full response (Hamilton score < 12) was seen in 5 of 6 patients with an exaggerated TSH response versus 2 of 15 patients who had a normal or blunted response prior to thyroid treatment. This report suffers from lack of standardized treatments, both TCA and thyroid, as well as from a lack of a double-blind placebo control. The raters may have known the patients' thyroid status, thereby biasing their evaluation. A single case report comprises the literature on T3 potentiation of MAOIs. Interestingly, the patient described showed an initially blunted TSH response to TRH stimulation with normal thyroid indices. This 68-year-old woman with psychotic major depression was unresponsive to combined treatment with desipramine and neuroleptic, and showed poor response to a year-long trial of neuroleptic-phenelzine. Nevertheless, she showed rapid resolution of her depression when T3 at 30 µg a day was added to her regimen of phenelzine and thiothixene (Hullett and Bidder 1983). The authors speculate that the blunted TSH response reflected a subtle thyroid dysfunction and "that it was necessary to correct both etiological components in order to achieve a significant clinical response" (p. 320).

A THEORETICAL FRAMEWORK

It is clear that patients with depression show a variety of disturbances in the HPT axis and that thyroid hormone can accelerate the action of antidepressant response and even convert nonresponders into responders in a certain percentage of patients. To date, Whybrow and Prange (1981) have offered the most comprehensive hypothesis to explain these observations. In their view, thyroid hormones are important for their modulating effects on catecholamines in the central nervous system. During times of adaptive demand, such as in depression (or mania), adequate mobilization of these hormones fosters recovery. Indirect evidence suggests that increased availability of thyroid hormones promotes central noradrenergic transmission via enhancement of β-adrenergic receptor function (Fregley et al. 1975; Nakashima et al. 1971). Assuming that depression is in part caused by decreased availability of norepinephrine centrally, persons with a normal thyroid axis will respond with an increase of circulating thyroid hormones and thereby compensate for declining catecholamine levels. On the other hand, persons whose thyroid axis is disturbed, such as those with low normal levels of T3 and T4, subclinical hypothyroidism, or blunted TSH response to TRH (not associated with increased thyroid hormone levels), will not fare as well. Such a theory is bolstered by observations that depression is 2 to 3 times more prevalent in women than men and that women are more likely to suffer from thyroid disease and to show clinical indications of mildly depressed thyroid function (e.g., slower ankle reflex time). The benefits of thyroid hormones in accelerating tricyclic response in women and converting nonresponders to responders are also used as indirect evidence for this hypothesis.

We have recently speculated that depressed patients may suffer from reduced peripheral sensitivity to thyroid hormones in addition to HPT axis dysfunction (Gewirtz et al. 1988). Studies have found depressed patients to have blunted tissue response to a variety of hormones, including insulin (Winokur et al. 1988; Wright et al. 1978). In our work on thyroid and metabolic function in refractory depressive patients receiving antidepressants, we found a small percentage of patients who had a low resting metabolic rate. This group included patients who were chemically euthyroid as well as some on thyroid hormone for diagnosed hypothyroidism. The addition of L-thyroxine or L-triiodothyronine, or an increase in preexisting thyroid dose produced recovery in these patients (Gewirtz et al. 1988). Measurement of metabolic rate may be a useful tool in assessment of refractory patients, particularly those on thyroid hormones who have failed standard antidepressant treatment. Correction of a blunted tissue response with sufficient thyroid hormone may be necessary for full antidepressant response.

Ideally, to test the model, one should examine the association of both pretreatment thyroid function tests and the results of TRH stimulation testing to the response to antidepressant treatment and subsequent thyroid potentiation. There is evidence that normal-range TFTs correlate with response to ECT (Prange 1986) and to relapse on lithium (Hatterer et al. 1989). Patients in the low normal range may show greater early improvement with thyroid hormone. On the other hand, patients with subclinical hypothyroidism whose defect is more severe may require longer treatment before one sees the effects. Obtaining serial TFTs during antidepressant treatment and upon recovery would also help to explore the possibility of a threshold of thyroid hormone levels required for antidepressant response.

If in fact thyroid enhancement of TCAs works via its effects on a deficient thyroid axis, then L-thyroxine should work equally well if not better than L-triiodothyronine. Thyroxine is preferable to T_3 for the treatment of hypothyroidism because it mimics normal physiology by producing adequate levels of both T_4 and T_3 (DeGroot et al. 1984). Only Joffe and Singer (1987) have compared T_4 to T_3 in depressed patients who have failed antidepressants, and they found T_3 to be superior at 3 weeks. However, given T_4's longer half-life, a period greater than 3 weeks may be required to see its full benefits. Clearly further study of this question is needed.

We have employed a broad definition of "refractory" in order to discuss the literature. In fact, no one has examined thyroid function in a rigidly defined refractory population. Some have speculated that such a group would show a greater prevalence of subclinical hypothyroidism with a better response to thyroid potentiation (Targum et al. 1984). Research is needed to explore differences in thyroid status in refractory patients and whether such patients would preferentially respond to thyroid potentiation. Ideally, one would wish to recruit a homogeneous population of patients with a history of refractory depression, then document this by serial medication trials. At a set point, for instance, following failed TCA and MAOI trials, one could perform a double-blind, placebo-controlled trial of adjuvant T3 or T4. Thyroid function tests, TRH stimulation tests, and measurements of resting metabolic rate would be performed after a drug-free washout period, prior to each medication trial and upon recovery. Response to thyroid could be assessed and correlated to pretreatment thyroid status as well as to change in thyroid function resulting from potentiation. We are currently conducting such a project and hope that our findings will shed light on this complex relationship.

REFERENCES

American Psychiatric Association: Diagnostic and Statistical Manual of Mental Disorders, 3rd Edition, Revised. Washington, DC, American Psychiatric Association, 1987

Banki CM: Triiodothyronine in the treatment of depression. Orv Hetil 116:2543–2547, 1975

Banki CM: Cerebrospinal fluid amine metabolites after combined amitriptyline-triiodothyronine treatment of depressed women. Eur J Clin Psychopharmacol 11:311–315, 1977

Banki CM, Bissette G, Arato M, et al: Elevation of immunoreactive CSF TRH in depressed patients. Am J Psychiatry 145:1526–1531, 1988

Baruch P, Jouvent R, Widlocher D: Increased TSH response to TRH in refractory depressed women (letter). Am J Psychiatry 142:145–146, 1985

Boler J, Enzmann F, Folkers K, et al: The identity of chemical and hormone properties of thyrotropin-releasing hormone and pyroglutamyl-histidyl-prolineamide. Biochem Biophys Res Commun 37:705–710, 1969

Brenner I: Apathetic hyperthyroidism. J Clin Psychiatry 39:479–480, 1978

Burgus R, Dunn TF, Desiderio D, et al: Structure moleculaire du facteur hypothalamique hypophysiotrope TRF d'origine ovine: mise en evidence par spectrometrie de masse de la PCA-HIS-PRO-NH2. Comptes Rendus Hebdomadaires des Seances de l'Academic des Sciences; D: Sciences Naturelles Paris 269:1870–1873, 1969

Cho JT, Bone S, Dunner DL: The effect of lithium treatment on thyroid function in patients with primary affective disorder. Am J Psychiatry 136:115–116, 1979

Cooper DS, Halpern R, Wood L: L-thyroxine therapy in subclinical hypothyroidism—a double-blind, placebo-controlled trial. Ann Intern Med 101:18–24, 1984

Cowdry RW, Wehr TA, Zis AP, et al: Thyroid abnormalities associated with rapid-cycling bipolar illness. Arch Gen Psychiatry 40:414–420, 1983

Dackis CA, Goggans FG, Bloodworth R: The prevalence of hypothyroidism in psychiatric populations. Fair Oaks Hospital Psychiatry Letter 4:49–54, 1986

Degroot LJ, Larsen PR, Reketoff S (eds): The Thyroid and Its Diseases. New York, John Wiley, 1984

Earle BV: Thyroid hormone and tricyclic antidepressants in resistant depressions. Am J Psychiatry 126:143–145, 1970

Fawcett J, Kravitz HM: Treatment refractory depression, in Common Treatment Problems in Depression. Edited by Schatzberg AF. Washington, DC, American Psychiatric Press, 1985

Frazer A, Pandey G, Mendels J, et al: The effect of triiodothyronine in combination with imipramine on [^{3}H]-cyclic AMP production in slices of rat cerebral cortex. Neuropharmacology 13:1131–1140, 1974

Fregley MF, Nelson EL, Resch GE, et al: Reduced beta adrenergic responsiveness in hypothyroid rats. Am J Physiol 229:916–924, 1975

Garbutt J, Malekpour B, Brunswick D, et al: Effects of triiodothyronine on drug levels and cardiac function in depressed patients treated with imipramine. Am J Psychiatry 136:980–982, 1979

Gewirtz GR, Malaspina D, Hatterer JA, et al: Occult thyroid dysfunction in patients with refractory depression. Am J Psychiatry 145:1012–1014, 1988

Gitlin MJ, Weiner H, Fairbanks L: Failure of T3 to potentiate tricyclic antidepressant response. J Affective Disord 13:267–272, 1987

Gold MS, Pottash ALC, Extein IL: "Symptomless" autoimmune thyroiditis in depression. Psychiatry Res 6:261–269, 1982

Goodwin FK, Prange AJ, Post RM, et al: Potentiation of antidepressant effects by l-triiodothyronine in tricyclic nonresponders. Am J Psychiatry 139:34–48, 1982

Hatterer JA, Kocsis JH, Stokes PE: Thyroid function in patients maintained on lithium. Psychiatry Res 26:249–257, 1989

Hullet FJ, Bidder TG: Phenelzine plus triiodothyronine in a case of refractory depression. J Nerv Ment Dis 171:318–320, 1983

Joffe RT, Singer W: Thyroid hormone potentiation of antidepressants. Paper presented at the 18th International Congress of the International Society of Psychoneuroendocrinology. North Carolina, June 1987

Kirkegaard C: The thyrotropin response to thyrotropin-releasing hormone in endogenous depression. Psychoneuroendocrinology 6:189–212, 1981

Kirkegaard C, Faber J, Hummer L, et al: Increased levels of TRH in cerebrospinal fluid in patients with endogenous depression. Psychoneuroendocrinology 4:227–235, 1979

Langer G, Schonbeck G, Koinig G, et al: Evidence for neuroendocrine involvement in the therapeutic effects of antidepressant drugs, in Progress in Psychoneuroendocrinology. Edited by Brambilla F, Racagni G, de Wild D. Amsterdam, Elsevier/North Holland Biomedical Press, 1980

Loosen PT: The TRH induced TSH response in psychiatric patients: a possible neuroendocrine marker. Psychoneuroendocrinology 10:237–259, 1985

Loosen PT, Prange AJ: Serum thyrotropin response to thyrotropin-releasing hormone in psychiatric patients: a review. Am J Psychiatry 139:405–416, 1982

Loosen PT, Prange AJ, Wilson IC, et al: TRH (Protirelin) in depressed alcoholic men: behavioral changes and endocrine responses. Arch Gen Psychiatry 36:540–547, 1979

McGrath PJ, Quitkin FM, Stewart JM, et al: A comparative study of the pituitary TSH response to thyrotropin in outpatient depressives. Psychiatry Res 12:185–193, 1984

Nakashima M, Maeda K, Sekiya A, et al: Effect of hypothyroid status on myocardial responses to sympathomimetic drugs. Jpn J Pharmacol 21:875–881, 1971

Nemeroff CB, Simon JS, Haggerty JJ, et al: Antithyroid antibodies in depressed patients. Am J Psychiatry 142:840–843, 1985

Ogura C, Okuma T, Uchida Y, et al: Combined thyroid (triiodothyronine) tricyclic antidepressant treatment in depressive states. Folia Psychiatr Neurol Jpn 28:179–186, 1974

Prange AJ: Thyroid function in depressive illness. Paper presented at the 25th Anniversary of the American College of Neuropsychopharmacology. Puerto Rico, December 1986

Prange AJ, Lipton MA: Enhancement of imipramine mortality in hyperthyroid mice. Nature 4584:588–589, 1962

Prange AJ, Loosen PT: Some endocrine aspects of affective disorders. J Clin Psychiatry 41:29–34, 1980

Prange AJ, Wilson IC, Rabon AM, et al: Enhancement of imipramine antidepressant activity by thyroid hormone. Am J Psychiatry 126:457–469, 1969

Prange AJ, Loosen PT, Wilson IC, et al: The therapeutic use of hormones of the thyroid axis in depression, in The Neurobiology of Mood Disorders, Vol I. Edited by Post R, Ballenger J. Baltimore, MD, Williams & Wilkins, 1984

Quitkin FM, Rabkin JG, Ross D, et al: Duration of antidepressant drug treatment: what is an adequate trial? Arch Gen Psychiatry 41:238–245, 1984

Remick RA, Barton JS, Patterson B, et al: On so-called treatment resistant depression. Paper presented at the 51st Annual Meeting of the Royal College of Physicians and Surgeons of Canada. Quebec City, September 1982

Roy-Byrne PP, Joffe RT, Uhde TW, et al: Carbamazepine and thyroid function in affectively ill patients—clinical and theoretical implications. Arch Gen Psychiatry 41:1150–1153, 1984

Roy-Byrne PP, Udhe TW, Rubinow DR, et al: Reduced TSH and prolactin responses to TRH in patients with panic disorder. Am J Psychiatry 143:503–507, 1986

Sachar EJ (ed): Handbook of Psychiatry. New York, Basic Books, 1975

Schonbeck G, Langer G, Koinig G, et al: The TSH response to TRH as predictor of outcome to antidepressant and neuroleptic drug treatment, in Biological Psychiatry 1985—Developments in Psychiatry, Vol 7. Edited by Shagass C, Josiassen RC, Bridger WH. New York, Elsevier Science Publishing, 1986

Schwarcz G, Halaris A, Baxter L, et al: Normal thyroid function in desipramine nonresponders converted to responders by the addition of l-triiodothyronine. Am J Psychiatry 141:1614–1616, 1984

Targum SD: The application of serial neuroendocrine challenge studies in the management of depressive disorder. Biol Psychiatry 18:3–19, 1983

Targum SD, Sullivan AL, Byrnes SM: Compensatory pituitary-thyroid mechanism in the major depressive disorder. Psychiatry Res 6:85–96, 1982

Targum SD, Greenberg RD, Harmon RL, et al: Thyroid hormone and the TRH stimulation test in refractory depression. J Clin Psychiatry 45:345–346, 1984

Taylor JW: Depression in thyrotoxicosis. Am J Psychiatry 132:552–553, 1975

Thase ME, Kupfer DJ, Janett DB: Active L-triiodothyronine (T3) in imipramine-resistant recurrent unipolar depression. Paper presented at the Fourth World Congress of Biological Psychiatry, Philadelphia, PA, September 1985

Tsutsui S, Yamazaki Y, Namba T, et al: Combined therapy of T3 and antidepressants in depression. J Int Med Res 7:138–146, 1972

Tunbridge WMG, Evered DC, Hall R, et al: The spectrum of thyroid disease in a community: the Wickham survey. Clin Endocrinol (Oxf) 7:481–493, 1977

Tunbridge WMG, Brewis M, French JM. et al: Natural history of autoimmune thyroiditis. Br Med J 282:258–262, 1981

Whybrow PC, Prange AJ: A hypothesis of thyroid-catecholamine interaction. Arch Gen Psychiatry 38:106–113, 1981

Wilson IC, Prange AJ, McKlane TK, et al: Thyroid enhancement of imipramine in nonretarded depression. N Engl J Med 282:1063–1067, 1970

Wilson WH, Jefferson JW: Thyroid disease, behavior and psychopharmacology. Psychosomatics 26:481–492, 1985

Winokur A, Maislin G, Phillips JC, et al: Insulin resistance after oral glucose tolerance testing in patients with major depression. Am J Psychiatry 145:325–330, 1988

Wright JH, Jacisin JJ, Radin NS, et al: Glucose metabolism in unipolar depression. Br J Psychiatry 132:386–393, 1978

Zis AP, Goodwin FK: Major affective disorder as a recurrent illness. Arch Gen Psychiatry 35:835–839, 1979

Chapter 10

Chronic Depression Versus Treatment-Refractory Depression: Evaluation and Treatment

James H. Kocsis, M.D.

Chapter 10

Chronic Depression Versus Treatment-Refractory Depression: Evaluation and Treatment

Not all chronic depressions are treatment refractory and not all refractory depressions are chronic. The clinical evaluation of a chronically depressed patient should include a careful assessment of prior treatments. Inquiry about the type of treatment given, the adequacy of dosage, and the degree of compliance can help to distinguish treatment-refractory depression from inadequately treated chronic depression.

Most discussions of the issue of treatment resistance in depression have focused on acute and episodic recurrent forms, and on the reasons treatments might fail and lead to the development of chronicity. A definition of "chronic" depression must be arbitrary, yet recent nosological systems, such as the Research Diagnostic Criteria (RDC) (Spitzer et al. 1978) and the DSM-III (American Psychiatric Association 1980), have agreed in defining chronicity as a persistent duration of symptoms for 2 years or longer. However, it is possible for a depression to fulfill the usual definition of "refractory" in under 2 years if adequate treatment has already been given. Thus, not all refractory depressions fulfill the 2-year criterion usually employed for defining chronic depression.

Other chapters in this book are devoted to the evaluation and treatment of refractory depressions that develop in the context of an acute or recurrent episodic course of illness. This chapter focuses primarily on diagnosis and treatment of chronic forms of depression. A particular emphasis is given to factors associated with the development of treatment resistance in the setting of a preexisting chronic depression.

DIAGNOSIS AND CLASSIFICATION OF CHRONIC DEPRESSION

Recent renewed interest in states of chronic depression has been stimulated by suggestions that they are responsive to thymoleptic medications (Akiskal et al. 1980; Kocsis et al. 1988). Investigations of the epidemiology, clinical features, and treatment response have been facilitated by the development of diagnostic criteria for chronic depression (i.e., Intermittent Depression (RDC), Dysthymic Disorder (DSM-III), and Dysthymia (DSM-III-R) (American Psychiatric Association 1987). Several structured clinical interviews have also recently been developed to guide researchers in selection of cases fulfilling the above diagnostic criteria for use in epidemiologic and treatment studies.

Historically, chronic depressions having an onset at an early age have been regarded either as characterologic with a psychosocial etiology, or alternately, as variants or prodromes of affective illness. Frances (1980) pointed out that an important conceptual shift occurred in the classification of chronic depression by the American Psychiatric Association between DSM-II (1968) and DSM-III (1980). In DSM-II, chronic depressions were classified as subtypes of personality disorders and neuroses. In DSM-III, chronic depression was designated as Dysthymic Disorder and was placed in the Affective Disorders section.

The essential characteristics of DSM-III Dysthymic Disorder were a persistent depressed mood or marked hypohedonia for at least 2 years, the presence of at least 3 of a list of 13 associated depressive symptoms, and the absence of psychosis or a preexisting severe mental disorder.

Subsequent to the publication of DSM-III, Akiskal (1983) suggested a more elaborate classification of the chronic depressions. He proposed subcategories based on the age of onset (early vs. late), the primacy of the depressive syndromes (primary vs. secondary), and the responsiveness to thymoleptic medication (character spectrum vs. subaffective dysthymia). These suggestions were considered, and some were adopted in the development of the criteria for Dysthymia in DSM-III-R. The revised criteria continued to call for persistent depressed mood for at least 2 years. However, the required threshold for the associated depressive symptoms was reduced to at least two from a list of six. The onset of the depressive syndrome was required to be insidious (no clear evidence of a Major Depression in the first 2 years). In addition, criteria were given for subclassifying a primary and a secondary type of dysthymia and for dividing an early onset from a late onset.

Another suggestion for a subcategory of chronic depressions came from Keller and Shapiro (1982). Based on data gathered during a naturalistic follow-up study done in a large group of depressed patients, the authors coined the term "double-depression" to refer to the superimposition of acute major depressive episodes on long-standing chronic depressive symptoms. Long-term outcome was found to be worse in patients with double-depression than in a comparison group that had a major depression. Kocsis and Frances (1987) have criticized the concept of double-depression. They have pointed out that the severity criteria for defining Intermittent Depression in the RDC or Dysthymic Disorder in the DSM-III were very close to the thresholds required for Major Depression. Thus, minor variations in symptom levels could have caused patients to just make or just miss the criteria for major depression and create an artifactual prevalence of "double-depression."

Our own recent study (Kocsis et al. 1989) investigated variations in the course of chronic depression. Subjects were assessed for fluctuations in the number of depressive symptoms over the previous 2 years. Outpatients who fulfilled DSM-III criteria for both Dysthymic Disorder and Major Depressive Disorder were categorized into three groups. Thirty-eight percent had experienced a chronic, stable number of symptoms for at least 2 years; 31% had experienced a mild recent symptom exacerbation; and the remainder reported a major recent symptom increase, namely, double-depression.

The results suggest that chronic depressives who currently fulfill DSM-III or DSM-III-R criteria for major depression cannot all be assumed to have experienced recent symptom exacerbation, as implied by the term "double-depression." Many chronic depressive patients have experienced a moderate level of symptom severity and have continually fulfilled DSM-III or DSM-III-R criteria for Major Depressive Disorder for longer than 2 years. In summary, the question of whether a Major Depression superimposed on a Dysthymic Disorder represents a qualitative change in diagnosis or a fluctuation in severity of an underlying chronic depression remains controversial.

Whereas the clinical concepts embodied in the terms "dysthymia" and "depressive personality" usually have pertained to depressions with an insidious onset at an early age, another subgroup of chronic depressions has been described that has an age of onset in middle or later life. Akiskal (1983) reported that such patients experienced the onset of a major affective episode in mid-life followed by the development of chronicity, and did not give previous histories of low-grade chronic depression. Development of chronicity in that sample was also associated with shortening of the latency to rapid-eye-movement

sleep on electroencephalographic recordings, familial affective loading, high levels of psychosocial stress, use of depressive antihyperten-
sive agents, and dependence on alcohol or sedative hypnotic drugs
(Akiskal et al. 1981).

Our own recently reported study of imipramine treatment of
chronic depression (Kocsis et al. 1988) found that one third of the
sample reported an onset of depression above the age of 25 years.
However, in contrast to the findings of Akiskal, the older age onset
group in this sample reported an insidious onset of symptomatology,
which was not followed immediately by a period of major depression,
that is, they had a course similar to that reported by the early age onset
cases. The implications of the age of onset and course of the disorder
for purpose of classification and for selection of treatment remain
matters for further investigation.

Little data have been gathered to validate the proposed subtypes of
chronic depression discussed above or to justify their use for the
selection of effective treatments. A review of the existing studies
reveals that several investigators have now compared patients having
chronic depression to those having acute major depression. For
example, Akiskal and colleagues (1980) divided dysthymic outpatients based upon response to thymoleptic medications and compared these subgroups to a sample of episodic unipolar controls.
Thymoleptic-responsive chronic depression occurred more often in
males and was associated with hypersomnia, psychomotor retardation, and pharmacologic hypomania. Nonresponders had an excess
of unstable personality traits and of substance abuse. Other research
groups have also reported on comparisons of the clinical characteristics of outpatients having chronic depression versus those having
acute depressive episodes. Rounsaville and associates (1980) and
Kocsis and colleagues (1986) have found very similar demographics,
clinical features, and drug treatment responses in the two groups. The
Keller group (1983), working with a mixed sample of outpatients and
inpatients, reported that the chronic depressives scored somewhat
higher on measures of severity of illness, but were otherwise quite
similar in clinical characteristics to the patients having Major Depressive Disorder only. Although treatments were not controlled and were
often judged to be inadequate, double-depressive patients were found
to experience more relapses during a 2-year follow-up period.
Another recent report by Klein and associates (1988) comparing
outpatients with episodic major depression to a group with chronic
depression found the latter to be more impaired and to have more
severe depressive symptoms. Also characterizing the chronic group
were greater comorbidity, more personality disturbance, lower levels

of social support, more chronic stressors, and less likelihood of recovery after 6 months.

In summary, these five comparisons of acute versus chronic depressive syndromes in psychiatric clinics suggest that the chronic depressions are often somewhat more severe at the time of presentation, that they may be associated with more personality pathology and social impairment, and that they have a worse long-term prognosis. Chronicity of depression thus appears to have important diagnostic and prognostic implications.

COMORBIDITY AND SECONDARY CHRONIC DEPRESSION

Chronic depression has been found to be associated with a high prevalence of comorbid conditions in both community (Weissman et al. 1988) and clinical (Klein et al. 1988; Kocsis et al. 1990) samples. The National Institute of Mental Health (NIMH)-Epidemiologic Catchment Area Study (Weissman et al. 1988) found that affective, anxiety, and substance abuse disorders were highly prevalent in persons with dysthymia. Klein and associates (1988) conducted a study in psychiatric outpatients with chronic depression. High comorbidity was found with anxiety, eating, substance abuse/dependence, and severe personality disorders (borderline, antisocial, and schizotypal). The Kocsis group (1990) reported high rates of comorbid "cluster C" (avoidant, dependent, obsessive-compulsive) personality disorders in a dysthymic outpatient sample.

These data on comorbidity do not address issues of primacy of diagnosis or causal relationships. Dysthymia may be viewed as either a cause of or a complication of the comorbid disorders. Alternatively, dysthymia and comorbid conditions may represent different aspects of an underlying trait or disorder. One strategy that could begin to unravel the nature of relationships between dysthymia and comorbid disorders would be prospective longitudinal study. Friedman and co-workers (1983) have made an interesting attempt to explore the chronological development of affective disorders and comorbid conditions. Psychiatric inpatients with a history of having the onset of a primary affective disorder in adolescence were evaluated at a mean age of 20 years. The average onset of affective illness for the group had been 7 years earlier. Of those cases reporting a history of insidious chronic depression, about one-third maintained a simple course of depression, and two-thirds developed comorbid conditions, most commonly drug/alcohol abuse. The implications of this simple versus complicated course of dysthymia remain untested, but are likely to be enormous. In general, the presence of comorbid psychiatric or medical disorders is likely to have great importance in the clinical management of a chronic depression.

Thus far we have considered various possible subtypes of primary chronic depression, including those that may have an early or a late age of onset, and those that might become complicated by secondary or comorbid diagnoses. Another separate group of chronic depressive states can be viewed as secondary, that is, as complications of other primary psychiatric or medical disorders that have antedated the development of the depression. In a sample of outpatients with chronic depression described by Akiskal and co-workers (1981), for example, 36% were classified as secondary depressions. Two-thirds of the secondary cases had another psychiatric diagnosis that was considered to be the primary disorder. Somatization disorder, obsessive-compulsive disorder, and agoraphobia were the most common primary diagnoses. The other one-third of the secondary cases had a chronic, severe medical illness that was thought to be a primary diagnosis. Secondary depressions were not associated with shortening of the latency to onset of rapid-eye-movement sleep or with family histories of depression, characteristics found in the primary dysthymics. Some secondary depressions were said to have responded to monoamine oxidase inhibitors (MAOIs), but little information was given about their treatment.

In another sample of outpatients with dysthymia identified by Markowitz and associates (unpublished), one-third had significant medical illnesses as a primary diagnosis. A study by Klein and colleagues (1988) reported that one third of chronic depressive patients were diagnosed as secondary, although the primary disorders were not specified.

In a clinical investigation of alcoholism, Schuckit (1985) documented the importance of a primary diagnosis for the treatment and prognosis of the alcoholic patient. It is likely that the primary diagnosis carries similar implications for the treatment and prognosis of secondary chronic depression. However, this issue has not been systematically investigated, and very little information is available about treatment. What is certain at present is that a very substantial percentage of chronic depressions identified in clinical settings can reasonably be classified as having a secondary dysthymia.

CHRONIC DEPRESSION VERSUS REFRACTORY DEPRESSION AND TREATMENT PLANNING

The introduction to this chapter stated that not all chronic depressions are necessarily treatment refractory. The formulation of a plan for treatment will be highly dependent on the evaluation of the adequacy of any prior psychotherapy or medication trials. Operational definitions of adequate treatment are somewhat arbitrary and vary for the different therapies. In general, for the tricyclic antidepressants, a daily dosage of at least 150 mg of imipramine or its equivalent must be given over a period of several weeks before a trial can be considered adequate. Additional evidence can be derived from the measurement of steady-state plasma drug concentrations when the therapeutic range is known. For MAOIs, there is good evidence that a dosage of at least 60 mg per day of phenelzine or its equivalent is required for adequate treatment of depression. The clinical evaluation must also assess compliance with prior treatments as a part of the assessment of adequacy. The above guidelines for adequacy of drug treatment have been developed in studies of acute and episodic recurrent depression. However, Kocsis and associates (1988) reported that doses and plasma drug concentrations of imipramine similar to those usually employed for acute major depression were required for the treatment of chronic depression.

Many chronic depressives have traditionally been treated with long-term, dynamically oriented psychotherapy; however, there has been no systematic reporting of outcome for this form of treatment. Anecdotal clinical experience has suggested that some patients do improve and may recover while receiving treatment with psychotherapy alone. Evaluation of the adequacy of psychotherapy trials is fraught with difficulty. We have used a criterion of at least 6 months of once-a-week psychotherapy to define minimal treatment adequacy. However, this definition obviously does not address many important issues such as the type of psychotherapy, the skill and training of the therapist, and the therapist-patient fit. Thus, it is only possible to make very crude estimates about adequacy of psychotherapy.

The first clinical decision about the treatment of a chronic depression should then be based in part on an assessment of prior psychotherapy and drug treatment. If a patient has never received treatment or has only received inadequate trials, either psychotherapy or antidepressant medication can be prescribed initially. To some extent, this decision will be based on cultural background and on personal belief systems about depression. Some patients are loath to take drugs, and others cannot tolerate the idea of talk therapy. If no marked improvement occurs after several weeks of medication at adequate dosages or after several months of psychotherapy, then a switch to another medication or the addition of either psychotherapy or medication should be considered. Sequential trials of a tricyclic antidepressant, an MAOI, and psychotherapy in combination with medication should probably be completed before a chronically depressed patient is considered treatment refractory.

The subsequent management of a refractory chronic depression, which has not responded to adequate trials of antidepressant medication and psychotherapy, is completely unknown. Until more research has been undertaken in this area, it would seem reasonable to treat such individuals in a fashion similar to other treatment-refractory depressions. Thus, one might undertake sequential adequate trials of treatments using various classes of antidepressant medications, pharmacologic enhancing agents, and psychotherapies alone and in combination with drugs. It is probably wise to educate a chronic depressive patient about the numerous treatment possibilities that do exist as a way of maintaining hope. Hopelessness, which may become a precursor of suicide, can be an unfortunate complication of these conditions. Every effort should be made to avoid it.

REFERENCES

Akiskal HS: Dysthymic disorder: psychopathology of proposed chronic depressive subtypes. Am J Psychiatry 140:11–20, 1983

Akiskal HS, Rosenthal TL, Haykal RF, et al: Characterologic depressions: clinical and sleep EEG findings separating "subaffective dysthymias" from "character spectrum disorders." Arch Gen Psychiatry 37:777–783, 1980

Akiskal HS, King D, Rosenthal TL, et al: Chronic depressions, part 1: clinical and familial characteristics in 137 probands. J Affective Disord 3:297–315, 1981

American Psychiatric Association: Diagnostic and Statistical Manual of Mental Disorders, 2nd Edition. Washington, DC, American Psychiatric Association, 1968

American Psychiatric Association: Diagnostic and Statistical Manual of Mental Disorders, 3rd Edition. Washington, DC, American Psychiatric Association, 1980

American Psychiatric Association: Diagnostic and Statistical Manual of Mental Disorders, 3rd Edition, Revised. Washington, DC, American Psychiatric Association, 1987

Frances AJ: The DSM-III personality disorders section: a commentary. Am J Psychiatry 137:1050–1054, 1980

Friedman RC, Hurt SW, Clarkin JF, et al: Primary and secondary affective disorders in adolescents and young adults. Acta Psychiatr Scand 67:226–235, 1983

Keller MB, Shapiro RW: "Double depression": superimposition of acute depressive episodes on chronic depressive disorders. Am J Psychiatry 139:438–442, 1982

Keller MB, Lavori PW, Endicott J, et al: "Double depression": two-year follow-up. Am J Psychiatry 140:689–694, 1983

Klein DN, Taylor EB, Harding K, et al: Double depression and episodic major depression: demographic, clinical, familial, personality, and socioenvironmental characteristics and short-term outcome. Am J Psychiatry 145:1226–1231, 1988

Kocsis JH, Frances AJ: A critical discussion of DSM-III dysthymic disorder. Am J Psychiatry 144:1534–1542, 1987

Kocsis JH, Voss C, Mann JJ, et al: Chronic depression: demographic and clinical characteristics. Psychopharmacol Bull 22:192–195, 1986

Kocsis JH, Frances AJ, Voss C, et al: Imipramine treatment for chronic depression. Arch Gen Psychiatry 45:253–257, 1988

Kocsis JH, Mason BJ, Frances AJ, et al: Prediction of response of chronic depression to imipramine. J Affective Disord 17:255–260, 1989

Kocsis JH, Markowitz JC, Prien RF: Comorbidity of dysthymic disorder, in Comorbidity of Mood and Anxiety Disorders. Edited by Maser JD, Cloninger CR. Washington, DC, American Psychiatric Press, 1990, pp 317–328

Rounsaville BJ, Sholomskas D, Prusoff BA: Chronic mood disorders in depressed outpatients. J Affective Disord 2:73–88, 1980

Schuckit MA: The clinical implications of primary diagnostic groups among alcoholics. Arch Gen Psychiatry 42:1043–1049, 1985

Spitzer RL, Endicott J, Robins E: Research Diagnostic Criteria (RDC) for a Selected Group of Functional Disorders, 3rd Edition. New York, NY, New York State Psychiatric Institute, Biometrics Research, 1978

Weissman MM, Leaf PJ, Bruce ML, et al: The epidemiology of dysthymia in five communities: rates, risks, comorbidity, and treatment. Am J Psychiatry 145:815–819, 1988

Chapter 11

Axis II Personality Disorders and Personality Features in Treatment-Resistant and Refractory Depression

Ellen Frank, Ph.D.
David J. Kupfer, M.D.

Chapter 11

Axis II Personality Disorders and Personality Features in Treatment-Resistant and Refractory Depression

INTRODUCTION

Among the many patient characteristics that appear to contribute to difficulty in achieving a rapid and sustained recovery in the treatment of nonbipolar, nonpsychotic depression is the presence of personality pathology or personality disorder. Clinicians and researchers have often observed the co-occurrence of affective disorder and personality pathology. What has been difficult to elucidate, however, are the mechanisms that underlie this association.

Akiskal and co-workers (1983) proposed four general hypotheses regarding the relationship of personality to affective illness: 1) certain personality features *predispose* an individual to affective illness, 2) personality *modifies* affective illness, 3) personality disturbance represents a *complication* of affective illness, and 4) personality pathology represents an *attenuated expression* of affective disorder. The *predisposing factors hypothesis* (Abraham 1960; Chodoff 1972; Freud 1959) regards personality features as etiologic with respect to depression, particularly obsessional and dependent traits. Those who view personality variables as *modifiers* of affective illness make no etiologic speculation; however, a number of these investigators commented on the way in which personality may affect the clinical presentation, course, treatment, and outcome of a depressive episode. Lazare and Klerman (1968), Akiskal and associates (1978), and Vaz Serra and Pollitt (1975) have suggested that presenting symptoms of depressive illness are strongly related to personality features. Other investigators have pointed to the prognostic value of personality features.

Supported in part by NIMH grants MH-29618 and MH-30915, and a grant from the John D. and Catherine T. MacArthur Foundation Research Network on the Psychobiology of Depression.

Weissman and colleagues (1978) found that high neuroticism scores were predictive of poor outcome in depressed patients.

Personality disturbance has also been seen as a *complication* of affective illness. In some cases, the complication is characterized as state dependent, that is, present only during the acute phase of depressive illness. Neuroticism (Hirschfeld and Klerman 1979), orality, and dependency (Hirschfeld et al., 1983) are the features most often associated with the depressed state. Weissman and Paykel (1974) noted short-term sequelae of depression in the form of disturbed marital adjustment and other areas of social functioning that persisted for several months after symptomatic recovery but ultimately resolved. These sequelae may represent a complication of depressive illness caused by personality disturbance, or they may represent more slowly resolving aspects of the depressive episode itself as Weissman has implied (Weissman et al. 1974). Cassano and colleagues (1983), Klein (1974), and others have described long-term sequelae, primarily in the form of demoralization, which do not resolve and, indeed, appear to worsen with each successive episode in those patients experiencing recurrent illness.

The idea that personality represents an *attenuated expression* of affective illness can be traced to Kraepelin (1921). Kraepelin's longitudinal observations suggested a course in which long-standing personality defects occasionally gave rise to full-blown episodes of illness. Much more recently, the work of Akiskal and colleagues (Akiskal 1981; Akiskal et al. 1977) has provided support for the Kraepelinian view through a prospective study of patients with long-standing interpersonal difficulties. Indirect support for the attenuated expression hypothesis has also been found in some genetic investigations (Angst et al. 1980), but not in others (Gershon et al. 1975).

The focus of this chapter is on the extent to which personality disturbance may modify the course of depressive illness and, in particular, the course of treatment. For the last 8 years, we have been engaged in a long-term maintenance trial, the Maintenance Therapies in Recurrent Depression Protocol, which we believe has shed considerable light on the question of how personality modifies acute treatment response.

Early in the Maintenance Therapies in Recurrent Depression Protocol, we noted that personality disturbance appeared to operate as a barrier to treatment response among recurrent unipolar patients being treated with combined pharmacotherapy and psychotherapy. We had already observed that patients who showed a relatively rapid (within 4 to 6 weeks) and sustained response to an acute treatment consisting of tricyclic antidepressant medication and interpersonal psychotherapy (Klerman et al. 1984) differed from those patients who showed a slower and more erratic recovery in terms of baseline biological characteristics (Frank et al. 1984). We decided next to explore what, if any, personality features were associated with these treatment response patterns.

We have now completed recruitment of patients for this protocol and can report on the relationship between acute treatment response and personality disturbance in a cohort consisting of 151 recurrent unipolar patients.

METHODS

Study Design

In order to enter the Maintenance Therapies in Recurrent Depression Protocol, subjects between the ages of 21 and 65 years were required to present in their third or greater episode of unipolar depression, with the immediately preceding episode being no more than 2 1/2 years prior to the onset of the present episode. A minimum Hamilton Rating Scale for Depression (Hamilton 1960) score of 15 and a minimum Raskin (Raskin et al. 1969) of 7 were also required.

Following a 2-week, drug-free washout period, subjects were reevaluated with respect to severity of depression and then given a complete initial evaluation including biological (all-night sleep EEG and neuroendocrine studies) and psychosocial (social adjustment, social support, and so forth) measures. However, because of the probable influence of acute illness on personality measures, *personality was not evaluated at this time*. All subjects then received the same acute treatment regimen consisting of imipramine (150 mg to 300 mg) and interpersonal psychotherapy (IPT) offered weekly for 12 weeks, then biweekly for 8 weeks, and then monthly. At whatever point in this acute treatment regimen the patient had maintained a Hamilton score ≤ 7 and a Raskin score ≤ 5 for 3 weeks, a second biological and psychosocial evaluation was completed. At this evaluation, personality was assessed for the first time using both self-report and interview measures. In order to continue in the study, patients were then required to remain in continuation treatment for an additional 17 weeks, during which both Hamilton and Raskin scores and imipramine dose were to remain stable. A third evaluation was then conducted, following which patients were randomly assigned to one of five maintenance treatments for a period of 3 years or until they experienced a recurrence of illness.

Measures

This section focuses on results from both the self-report and interview measures of personality. The Hirschfeld-Klerman Personality Battery (Hirschfeld et al. 1983) is a 436-item self-report inventory that encompasses 17 scales drawn from 5 preexisting personality inventories (see Table 11-1). Subjects were asked to complete the battery over the course of the 3 nights they spend in the sleep laboratory for each evaluation.

The Personality Assessment Form (PAF) was constructed for use in the National Institute of Mental Health (NIMH) Treatment of Depression Collaborative Research Program (Elkin et al. 1985) and was further refined for use in the Maintenance Therapies protocol (Jacob and Turner, 1983, personal communication). It is a structured interview designed to assess personality using the DSM-III (American Psychiatric Association 1980) personality disorder characteristics (see Table 11-2). In the Maintenance Therapies study, the PAF was

Table 11-1.   Components of the Hirschfeld-Klerman Personality Battery

Inventory	Scales
Guilford-Zimmerman Temperament Survey (GZTS)	General activity Restraint Ascendance Sociability Emotional stability Objectivity Thoughtfulness
Interpersonal Dependency Inventory (IDI)	Emotional reliance on another person Social self-confidence Assertion of autonomy
Lazare-Klerman Armor Personality Inventory (short version) (LKA)	Obsessionality Hysterical pattern Orality
Maudsley Personality Inventory (MPI)	Neuroticism factor Extraversion factor
Minnesota Multiphasic Personality Inventory (MMPI)	Ego control (EC-5) Ego resiliency (ER-S)

administered by the subject's primary clinician (a psychiatric social worker or clinical psychologist) who asked a series of 15 to 25 probe questions for each DSM-III category and then, using the information obtained in the interview as well as their own impressions of the patient gathered over the course of several months of therapy sessions, rated the extent to which the patient conformed to the descriptions of each of the DSM-III personality disorders. This permitted dimensional (scale = 0 to 6) as opposed to categorical (disorder present vs. absent) ratings.

Subjects

Subjects for our investigation were the 150 of the 230 patients entered into the acute treatment protocol who were able to complete 16 weeks of acute treatment, and on whom personality data were collected. Clinical characteristics of the 151 patients are presented in Table 11-3.

The 150 patients represent almost two thirds of the 230 patients to be accepted into the Maintenance Therapies protocol. Of this original group of 230, only 128 patients completed both the acute and continuation treatment phases. Thirty-one patients failed to show even modest response to the combined treatment regimen of imipramine and IPT and were offered alternative treatment. Twenty-two patients developed intolerable side-effects, 4 developed previously undetected medical problems, and 19 were discontinued for a variety of other reasons. Only 27 patients actually dropped out or were terminated for noncompliance.

Table 11-2. Dimensions of the Personality Assessment Form

Cluster	Personality category
Odd/eccentric	Paranoid Schizoid Schizotypal
Dramatic	Antisocial Histrionic Borderline
Anxious/fearful	Avoidant Dependent Compulsive Passive-aggressive

Table 11-3. Baseline demographic characteristics of normal, slow, and partial responders

	Normal N = 65	Slow N = 53	Partial N = 32	Total group N = 150
Sex				
Male	21 (32%)	10 (19%)	8 (25%)	39 (26%)
Female	44 (68%)	43 (81%)	24 (75%)	111 (74%)
Age at screening	41.11 (±11.42)	39.50 (±10.63)	38.91 (±10.62)	40.07 (±10.94)
Age at onset of illness	26.67 (±11.72)	27.33 (±9.44)	26.59 (±11.19)	27.31 (±10.78)
Baseline HRSD	21.21 (±4.52)	21.96 (±4.67)	22.56 (±4.96)	21.77 (±4.67)
Number previous episodes[a]	8.46 (±9.64)	4.90 (±2.75)	4.81 (±2.10)	6.43 (±6.85)
RDC endogenous	59 (91%)	49 (92%)	26 (84%)	134 (90%)

Note. HRSD = Hamilton Rating Scale for Depression. RDC = Research Diagnostic Criteria. NR = normal responder. SR = slow responder. PR = partial responder.
[a] $P \leq .005$, NR > PR, NR > SR.

Although only 128 were entered into the maintenance phase, 150 achieved a sufficient level of remission to be evaluated with respect to personality features and disorders. The group of 150 patients was further divided by acute treatment response types, with 65 of the subjects showing a clear-cut remission of symptoms within 8 weeks and remaining well for the subsequent 8 weeks ("normal responders"), 53 of the subjects showing a more variable response but nonetheless achieving remission by 16 weeks of acute treatment ("slow responders"), and 32 subjects failing to show a complete response at 16 weeks ("partial and nonresponders"). The algorithm for classification of response types is presented in Table 11-4. There were no significant differences among the response groups on any demographic or clinical characteristic.

Data Analysis

Data on the Hirschfeld-Klerman Battery were first examined in an analysis of variance. However, because depressed state is known to have an impact on measures of personality and because the three responder types were thought to differ on severity of depression at the time that personality was assessed, an analysis of variance was run on Hamilton scores at the time of the personality assessment. This analysis yielded a highly significant ($P < .0001$) difference among the three groups with the normal responders showing a mean of 3.36 compared to 6.14 for the slow responders and 7.84 for the partial responders. Each of these means is significantly different from the other. Therefore, the analysis of Hirschfeld-Klerman data was repeated with the Hamilton scores as a covariate.

With respect to the PAF data, we began with a simple 3×2 chi-square test in which we dichotomized PAF ratings such that a 0–3 was thought to represent disorder absent and a 4–6 was used to represent disorder present. However, because of the concern regard-

Table 11-4. Algorithm for determining treatment response type

HRSD			% Change in HRSD from baseline to 16 weeks	Type of responder
8 Weeks	12 Weeks	16 Weeks		
≤7	<10	≤7	≥50	Normal
≤7	≥10	≤7	≥50	Slow
>7	≥0	8–10	≥60	Slow
Any patient who does not fit into above categories				Partial

Note. HRSD = Hamilton Rating Scale for Depression.

ing the influence of Hamilton scores, these data were reexamined in a log-linear analysis in which three sets of variables were entered: 1) the Hamilton score at the time the PAF was administered (dichotomized into two categories, ≤ 7 and > 7), 2) the patient's response type (normal, slow, or partial), and 3) the PAF scores (dichotomized into < 4 and ≥ 4).

RESULTS

Mean Hirschfeld-Klerman Battery scores for all three response groups are displayed in Table 11-5. Analysis of covariance on the 17 Hirschfeld-Klerman scales with the 17-item Hamilton Rating Scale for Depression used as a covariate yielded significant differences among the groups on objectivity, ($P = .03$), orality ($P = .02$), and neuroticism ($P = .003$). There was also a trend for emotional stability to be significantly different in the three groups ($P = .07$). When post-hoc tests were run on the adjusted group means for these four scales using the Student Neuman-Keuls comparison with alpha levels set at $P < .05$, normal responders were found to be more "objective" than slow and partial responders, although the slow and partial responders did not differ. Normal responders were found to be less "oral" than slow responders, but neither group differed from the partial responders. Finally, the normal responder group was significantly less neurotic than either the slow or partial responders, but, again, slow and partial responders did not differ. There were no significant differences between pairs of groups with respect to emotional stability.

As Table 11-6 reveals, frequency of positive evaluation on several of the PAF scales was extremely low. This is because patients meeting criteria for the most severe personality disorders were screened out of the protocol prior to entry. Log-linear analysis of these data revealed three personality variables to be significantly associated with either Hamilton type (≤ 7 vs. > 7) or response type (normal, slow, or partial responder). The Hamilton by dependent personality interaction was found to be significant ($P = .002$), with more than the expected number of patients with a dependent score of 4 or greater (probable or definite dependent personality disorder) also being in the group with higher Hamilton scores. Not surprisingly, a similar effect was found for dysthymia ($P = .004$). The only personality variable related to response type was compulsive personality, with significantly fewer normal responders being categorized as having probable or definite compulsive personality disorder ($P = .016$). No three-way interactions were observed. It should be noted that the failure to find other significant interactions, especially for those personality attributes with

Table 11-5. Mean Hirschfeld-Klerman Battery scores for normal, slow, and partial responders

	Normal	Slow	Partial
General activity	15.97 ± 5.67	14.77 ± 7.66	14.38 ± 6.04
Restraint	19.47 ± 4.46	19.48 ± 4.67	19.74 ± 3.71
Ascendance	14.61 ± 5.90	12.47 ± 6.49	13.06 ± 5.90
Sociability	17.86 ± 7.25	15.75 ± 7.52	14.68 ± 6.70
Emotional stability	16.55 ± 6.62	12.36 ± 6.71	11.56 ± 6.25
Objectivity	18.66 ± 4.23	15.79 ± 5.83	14.58 ± 5.11
Thoughtfulness	17.55 ± 4.94	18.12 ± 5.05	19.00 ± 4.97
Emotional reliance	41.92 ± 9.32	44.32 ± 9.26	48.29 ± 10.39
Lack of social self-confidence	31.97 ± 8.59	35.06 ± 9.35	36.10 ± 7.73
Assertion of autonomy	26.49 ± 7.67	27.10 ± 6.75	27.84 ± 7.43
Obsessionality	11.72 ± 4.18	11.13 ± 3.73	11.22 ± 2.74
Hysterical pattern	7.86 ± 3.68	8.81 ± 3.27	9.72 ± 3.98
Orality	4.89 ± 3.64	7.55 ± 4.41	7.38 ± 4.04
Neuroticism	20.36 ± 11.03	28.83 ± 11.80	31.84 ± 10.80
Extraversion	23.69 ± 10.05	21.94 ± 11.40	18.03 ± 10.74
Ego control	17.83 ± 5.19	17.69 ± 4.21	17.68 ± 4.94
Ego resiliency	22.95 ± 5.53	21.15 ± 5.71	19.45 ± 5.54

small numbers of members, may indicate a lack of power associated with the small numbers rather than a true lack of association. Because the PAF evaluation was not initiated until several months after the protocol was started, PAF data were available on only 122 of the 150 patients.

DISCUSSION

The data reported here serve to confirm our clinical observations regarding this cohort of recurrent unipolar patients. First, those patients who showed a relatively rapid and sustained response to combined pharmacotherapy and psychotherapy evidenced significantly less personality pathology once they were well than those who showed a more prolonged and erratic pattern of recovery, although both groups were clinically remitted at the time the personality assessments were made. Second, those patients who failed to achieve remission even after more than 4 months of combined treatment were more like the slow than the normal responders in terms of their personality profiles.

Deciding when in the course of recurrent depressive illness it is most appropriate to assess personality presents the clinical researchers with a peculiar dilemma. By waiting until the patient has recovered, one diminishes the influence of the "state" effect of acute illness; however,

Table 11-6. Proportion of normal, slow, and partial responders categorized as positive[a] on PAF attributes

PAF Category	Normal	Slow	Partial
Paranoid	1 (2%)	3 (7%)	3 (12%)
Schizoid	2 (4%)	3 (7%)	5 (20%)
Schizotypal	1 (2%)	2 (5%)	0 (0%)
Histrionic	5 (9%)	5 (11%)	6 (24%)
Narcissistic	3 (5%)	4 (9%)	3 (12%)
Antisocial	4 (7%)	4 (9%)	1 (4%)
Borderline	5 (9%)	6 (14%)	4 (16%)
Avoidant	13 (24%)	13 (30%)	7 (28%)
Dependent	10 (18%)	11 (25%)	8 (32%)
Compulsive	6 (11%)	13 (30%)	9 (36%)
Passive-aggressive	5 (9%)	4 (9%)	3 (12%)
Dysthymic	3 (5%)	6 (14%)	4 (16%)

Note. PAF = Personality Assessment Form.
[a]Patients were categorized as positive if they were rated 4 or greater on an attribute.

assessment following treatment may be confounded by treatment outcome, or, in the case of this investigation, by the failure of treatment to bring about a full remission of depressive symptoms. Whereas both the normal and slow responders could be considered free of depressive symptoms at the time the personality evaluation was completed, the partial responders were significantly more symptomatic at the time their personality evaluations were carried out. This problem would be of greater concern had significant differences been observed between the slow and the partial responders; however, it was the normal responders who appeared to differ from the partial and slow responders. In no case were the slow and partial responders found to differ in terms of personality.

Three self-rated personality features were found to be important discriminators: 1) the Objectivity Scale of the Guilford-Zimmerman Temperament Survey (Guilford 1975); 2) the Orality Scale from the Lazare-Klerman-Armor Personality Inventory (Lazare et al. 1966); and, not surprisingly, 3) the Neuroticism (N) Scale of the Maudsley Personality Inventory (Eysenck 1962). Any number of investigations of patients with depressive illness have found the Neuroticism (N) Scale to be an important predictor and/or discriminator; however, as Vaz Serra and Pollitt (1975) point out, there is some question as to just what the scale measures. Garside and colleagues (1970) argued that the N Scale measures depression as well as neuroticism, and, indeed, a simple inspection of the scale items would suggest that this might be the case. Twenty-five years ago Coppen and Metcalfe (1965) reported that N scores tended to go down significantly with recovery from depressive illness, and that this change was most pronounced among endogenous depressive patients.

The finding that the slow and partial responders are characterized by low objectivity and high orality is consistent with clinicians' evaluation of them on the PAF as being significantly more dependent and compulsive. These are among the personality traits one would anticipate would emerge most strongly in a cohort of depressed patients such as this one in which borderline personality disorder was an exclusion criterion.

In this context, it should be pointed out that the patient population being examined provides an especially stringent test of the hypothesis that personality variables might influence treatment response because the population consists entirely of recurrent depressive patients, almost all of whom meet criteria for endogenous illness and none of whom meets criteria for borderline personality disorder or antisocial personality.

The results that point to relatively large and unidirectional personality differences between those patients who responded almost immediately to the combined treatment regimen and those who either responded more slowly or failed to remit fully suggest that, whatever other relationships may exist between personality and affective illness, the presence of personality pathology alters the rate of treatment response. Because two treatments, imipramine and IPT, were being offered at the same time, at least two alternative explanations for our findings are possible. The simplest explanation is that all three groups are responding to both components of treatment; however, one group is responding more rapidly than the other two. Why this would be so is not altogether clear. A more logical explanation is that the normal responders, who appear to have more biologically based disorders (see Frank et al. 1987), are responding primarily to the tricyclic medication, which has a relatively rapid onset of action, whereas the slow responders, who appear to have more interpersonally based depressions, are responding primarily to the weekly interpersonal psychotherapy, which would be expected to have a much slower onset of action. Furthermore, it should be noted that about one third of those categorized as only partial responders at 16 weeks ultimately achieved remission, were entered into the continuation phase of the study, and had a sufficiently long remission (20 weeks) to be considered eligible for the maintenance phase of the protocol.

What, if any, message can the clinician working with recurrent patients take from the data presented here? The most obvious message appears to be that we should perhaps alter our notion of when a patient should be considered treatment resistant or refractory. Although 8 weeks appears to have become a clinical standard for exploring alternate treatments, with seriously ill recurrent outpatients, this may be premature. Because our protocol required that all patients entering the experimental maintenance phase have previously responded to the combination of imipramine and IPT, we were strongly motivated to adhere to our original treatment intervention, rather than try alternatives. Almost half of those patients who ultimately responded to combined treatment and *remained well for the subsequent 5 months* would otherwise have been called treatment resistant or refractory at 8 weeks.

The second message to be taken from these results is that those patients who present for treatment with more Axis II features are likely to be the patients who will respond more slowly to treatment. We can say with some confidence that this is true for combined treatment; whether it is also true for either pharmacotherapy alone or psychotherapy alone will have to be explored in other treatment designs.

Finally, we can perhaps conclude that there may be some advantage to combined pharmacotherapy/psychotherapy for those patients whose so-called refractoriness has its origins in personality disturbance. By persisting with the combined treatment regimen, we were ultimately able to achieve remission in almost double the number of patients who would have been considered treatment successes at 8 weeks of treatment.

REFERENCES

Abraham K: Notes on the psychoanalytic investigation and treatment of manic-depressive insanity and allied conditions, in Selected Papers on Psychoanalysis. New York, Basic Books, 1960, pp 137–156

Akiskal HS: Subaffective disorders: dysthymic, cyclothymic, and bipolar II disorders in the "borderline" realm. Psychiatr Clin North Am 4:25–46, 1981

Akiskal HS, Djenderedjian AH, Rosenthal RH, et al: Cyclothymic disorder: validating criteria for inclusion in the bipolar affective group. Am J Psychiatry 134:1227–1233, 1977

Akiskal HS, Bitar AH, Puzantian VR, et al: The nosological status of neurotic depression: a prospective three- to four-year follow-up examination in the light of the primary-secondary and the unipolar bipolar dichotomies. Arch Gen Psychiatry 35:756–766, 1978

Akiskal HS, Hirschfeld RMA, Yerevanian BI: The relationship of personality to affective disorders: a critical review. Arch Gen Psychiatry 40:801–809, 1983

American Psychiatric Association: Diagnostic and Statistical Manual of Mental Disorders, 3rd Edition. Washington, DC, American Psychiatric Association, 1980

Angst J, Frey R, Lohmeyer B, et al: Bipolar manic-depressive psychoses: results of a genetic investigation. Hum Genet 55:237–254, 1980

Cassano GB, Maggini C, Akiskal HS: Short-term, subchronic and chronic sequelae of affective disorders. Psychiatr Clin North Am 6:55–68, 1983

Chodoff P: The depressive personality: a critical review. Arch Gen Psychiatry 27:666–673, 1972

Coppen A, Metcalfe M: Effect of a depressive illness on the M.P.I. Br J Psychiatry 111:236–239, 1965

Elkin I, Parloff MB, Hadley SW, et al: NIMH Treatment of Depression Collaborative Research Program: background and research plan. Arch Gen Psychiatry 42:305–316, 1985

Eysenck HJ: Manual of Maudsley Personality Inventory. San Diego, CA, Educational and Industrial Testing Service, 1962

Frank E, Jarrett DB, Kupfer DJ, et al: Biological and clinical predictors of response in recurrent depression: a preliminary report. Psychiatry Res 13:315–324, 1984

Frank E, Kupfer DJ, Jacob M, et al: Personality features and response to acute treatment in recurrent depression. J Personality Disord 1:14–26, 1987

Freud S: Heredity and the aetiology of the neuroses, in Collected Papers. New York, Basic Books, 1959, pp 138–154

Garside RF, Kay DWK, Roy JR, et al: MPI scores and symptoms of depression. Br J Psychiatry 116:429–432, 1970

Gershon ES, Mark A, Cohen N, et al: Transmitted factors in the morbid risk of affective disorders: a controlled study. J Affective Disord 12:283–299, 1975

Guilford JP: Factors and factors of personality. Psychological Bulletin 82:802–814, 1975

Hamilton M: A rating scale for depression. J Neurol Neurosurg Psychiatry 23:56–62, 1960

Hirschfeld RM, Klerman GL: Personality attributes and affective disorders. Am J Psychiatry 136:67–70, 1979

Hirschfeld RM, Klerman GL, Clayton PJ, et al: Personality and depression: empirical findings. Arch Gen Psychiatry 40:993–998, 1983

Klein D: Endogenomorphic depressions: toward a terminologic revision. Arch Gen Psychiatry 31:447–454, 1974

Klerman GL, Weissman MM, Rounsaville BJ, et al: Interpersonal Psychotherapy of Depression. New York, Basic Books, 1984

Kraepelin E: Manic-Depressive Illness and Paranoia. Edinburgh, E&S Livingstone, 1921

Lazare A, Klerman G: Hysteria and depression: the frequency and significance of hysterical personality features in hospitalized depressed women. Am J Psychiatry 124:48–56, 1968

Lazare A, Klerman GL, Armor DJ: Oral, obsessive, and hysterical personality patterns. Arch Gen Psychiatry 14:624–630, 1966

Raskin A, Schulterbrandt J, Reatig N, et al: Replication of factors of psychopathology in interview, word behavior and self-report ratings of hospitalized depressives. J Nerv Ment Dis 148:87–98, 1969

Vaz Serra A, Pollitt J: The relationship between personality and the symptoms of depressive illness. Br J Psychiatry 127:211–218, 1975

Weissman M, Paykel ES: The Depressed Woman: A Study of Social Relationships. Chicago, IL, University of Chicago Press, 1974

Weissman MM, Klerman GL, Paykel ES, et al: Treatment effects on the social adjustment of depressed patients. Arch Gen Psychiatry 30:771–778, 1974

Weissman MM, Prusoff BA, Klerman GL: Personality and the prediction of long-term outcome of depression. Am J Psychiatry 135:797–800, 1978

Index